THE
Power
OF
Face
Reading

Rose Rosetree

Women's Intuition Worldwide

The Power of Face Reading

Copyright © 2001 by Rose Rosetree
Illustrations © 1998 by Robin Ludt
Face Reading Secrets® is a term used by Rose Rosetree for her unique method of facial anaylsis. First Edition published 1998. Second Edition 2001. Reprint 2003.
Printed in Canada 10 9 8 7 6 5 4 3 2 * Acid-free paper.
Library of Congress Control Number: 2001088456

Publisher's Cataloging-in-Publication
(Provided by Quality Books, Inc.)

Rosetree, Rose
    The power of face reading – 2nd ed.
    p. cm.
    Includes bibliographical references and indexes.
    ISBN: 0-9651145-1-1

    1. Physiognomy. I. Title.
BF851.R67 2001   138
          QBI01-200063

QUANTITY DISCOUNTS are available on bulk purchases to **corporations, schools,** and **professional organizations** using this book for training, fundraising or other volume needs.

Women's Intuition Worldwide

P.O. Box 1605, Sterling, VA 20167-1605
Tollfree Order Line: 800-345-6665
E-mail: Rosetree@Starpower.net

**Visit our website:
www.Rose-Rosetree.com**

Ten ways
To use this book

10. *For a quick, impersonal browse,* turn to **Index I: Famous Faces**. It lists nearly 500 celebrities. Choose one who interests you, be it Martha Washington or the Marquis de Sade. When you look up that person's face, you'll discover one way face reading is fun.

9. *For a quick browse that's more personal,* turn to **Index II: Face Data**. The premise of face reading is that all your physical features are meaningful. Go ahead and investigate your face, one part at a time.

8. *For first aid with a relationship,* pinpoint whatever the person does that bugs you most. Is it procrastination, deception, a bad temper? Look it up in **Index III: Behavior**. When you read about a problem, you'll find it linked to a strength. This is how face reading gives you a breath of fresh air—if not directly *through* another person's nostrils, at least *about* them.

7. *For deeper insights about a relationship,* read this book along with a close friend. Discuss the similarities and differences that show in your faces. Go through the book systematically, start to end, and you'll discover how delightful it can be to "face" the truth about each other.

6. *For sales, if you're in a hurry,* read the chapter on **Ears** first, then the chapter on **Noses**. By then you'll see the value in face reading.

5. *For better communication, in sales or simply in life,* check out the chapters on **Cheeks**, **Eyebrows**, and **Mouths**. Learn about your strengths so you can emphasize them when dealing with others.

4. *For do-it-yourself diversity training,* pay special attention to your VERY traits (as explained in Chapter Four) and the traits described as their exact opposites, such as full lips versus thin lips. Until you gain this perspective, it's common to underestimate or even dislike people who are extremely different from you. Our goal is to demolish the expectation that good people will be "just like me." Face reading can shake you out of unconscious habits that limit your relationships. (*Ethnic* diversity isn't the stumbling block for most people anyway, so much as *human* diversity.)

3. *For higher self-esteem,* hire yourself as your own face reader. Read this book cover-to-cover along with a mirror big enough to show your whole face. Systematically you'll unfold layer after layer of talent. You'll laugh. You'll also probably do a fair amount of emotional healing. I can guarantee that by the time you reach the last page your face will never look the same again. You'll open up to a kind of perfection you've never dared to see before.

2. *If you're an identical twin and at least 18 years of age,* this book is must reading. Grab a mirror. Then grab your twin, or at least a clear photo of your twin's face. Read about ways you are similar and also ways you are different. By your age you will definitely have developed facial differences related to who you are inside. And contrary to what you've been told your whole life, each adult develops a unique face, twins included. Twins have been among my most appreciative clients.

1. *If you are David Letterman, or another lover of lists,* I dare you to start listing faces. Bird watchers keep lifetime lists of their sightings. Why not begin your own **face reader's list**? Even if you've been a people watcher since childhood, face reading will add a new dimension. *Every face is perfect*—as a reflection of the inner person.

■■■

Praise
for face reading

"It's like she's known you forever... but that's crazy, because you just met. Still, she has described you perfectly, and not just your surface traits."

—The Washington Post

"She doesn't immediately seek feedback on her accuracy. She sits back, confident that she's at least partly on target. When she does ask, it's with a flat sense of curiosity, like someone peering out of a rain-splattered window to check on a storm's progress."

—The Washington Times

"[Governor John Engler and Mayor Terry McKane] were highly skeptical... [but] both men said they found Rosetree's readings uncannily true"

—Lansing State Journal

"I decided to send her a picture of myself... with the caveat that my wife would 'check' her report for accuracy. 'She's got your number,' was my wife's simple response."

—The Catholic Standard

"All over America, singles are finding that face reading is far more reliable than computer dating. Rose Rosetree is the acknowledged expert and has evolved her own system from the ancient Chinese system of physiognomy."

—Daily Mail (United Kingdom)

"As Rose Rosetree says, 'The truth of what we are shows in our faces and each face, in its distinctive way, is perfectly beautiful.'
—*Style* (Hong Kong)

"HOW we communicate is just as important as WHAT we communicate. We need to fine tune what we say according to how the listener hears. Face Reading Secrets come in handy because you are made aware of personal style."
—*The Topeka Capital-Journal*

"Face reading performs a real deep service to people in terms of self-acceptance. When you learn how to look at your face and you understand what it means, you end up with a real appreciation of how you look."
—*The Indianapolis Star*

"Rosetree's goal is to demolish societal standards which separate so-called good looks from bad. All facial features have meaning and value, she declares, regardless of their popularity or apparent lack of appeal."
—*Aloha Magazine*

"The *Chronicle* has examined many aspects of the major candidates for mayor of San Francisco during the past few months. Today... Rosetree turned her expertise on candidates in the S.F. mayoral race, emphasizing that she knew nothing about them in advance."
—*The San Francisco Chronicle*
(This editorial-page article resulted in 100 requests for books and readings from San Franciscans.)

"[County Supervisor] Moore said [Rosetree's] assessment—especially the part about saving money—was accurate.... "I shop at Frugal Fannie's. Does that tell you anything?"
—*The Fairfax Journal*

Acknowledgments

I'm thankful there is such a thing as face reading, which has helped so many people over thousands of years (one of them being me). Besides bringing meaning to an aspect of life that otherwise seems to lack fairness and meaning, face reading has a way of creating community. Since 1971 I've taught personal development and, thus, have had plenty of time to encounter what Carl Jung would call the *shadow* side of the teaching world: competitiveness, jealousy, and the rest. But my fellow face professionals have eased my way with their generosity and supportive friendship.

I'll never forget the kindness extended to me by these colleagues: R. Neville Johnston, Carl Wagner, Sr. June Canoles, Joanna Brandt and, of course, Narayan-Singh. Someone else, when asked to write a foreword to the book of a "competing" teacher might have bristled. But Narayan, like all these superb teachers, knows we are working together. He said, simply, "Tell me how I can be of service to you."

Another influence on this book is the thousands of people who have lent me their ears, and other face parts, for the purpose of face reading. This appreciation goes double for those who have studied with me in order to become face readers. (You'll encounter some of my students' questions later, in the virtual classroom sections of this book.) I thank you all, knowing from personal experience how vulnerable one can feel at first, exposing one's face to the stare of someone whose job is to open up your physical features as if each one represents a door to your soul. I remember gulping before the professional gaze of Timothy Mar the first time my face was read. It was as if I was about to plunge into a swimming pool. And much as I love to swim, or gain deeper insight into life's mysteries, how can you predict if the waters will sting you with coldness?

A different kind of risk has been taken by those who have professionally gambled by hiring me as a teacher or trainer or party entertainer. Space doesn't permit my thanking you all here. So I'll single out those whose help has been especially important for my career: Deb Weitz, of FIRST CLASS Adult Education Center; Maureen McCracken, of Healing Touch of the Greater Washington Area; Audrie Smilie, of Oxford Management; Sam and Martha Ashelman, who have made me a "longtime friend" of the Coofont Spa in West Virginia; Sheila Weiner, whose enterprising talents brought me my first major out-of-town engagements; and Juli Verrier, of Long & Foster, the first to design a lavish convention booth around my face reading services.

For the creation of this, my fifth how-to on face reading, special thanks go to illustrator Robin Ludt, editors Amy Patton, Sue and Alex Kramer.

As for my husband, Mitch Weber, and our son Matt, it would take pages, entire books full of them, to thank them fully for their inspiration, their support, and all the ways they remind me to laugh.

■■■

Contents

FACE READING SECRETS®
at a glance

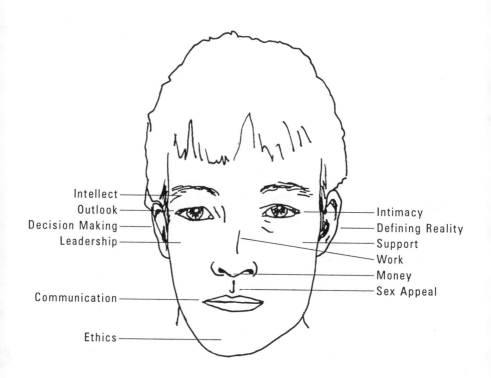

Intellect

Outlook

Decision Making

Leadership

Communication

Ethics

Intimacy

Defining Reality

Support

Work

Money

Sex Appeal

Foreword

From the earliest times, human beings have had to read each other's faces to survive. Our brains evolved via face reading. As a result, we are all natural-born face readers.

Systematic study of faces started with the shamans. Generally it has remained an esoteric understanding for the rare specialist. For instance, the Chinese system involves an apprenticeship training process sometimes lasting 40 years. Therefore, systematic forms of face reading have not been readily available.

In the West, during the Middle Ages, this began to change. A man by the name of Lavater began seriously studying and drawing faces, starting an unusual tradition of seeking to make face reading public domain. Historically, however, we humans have been effectively paranoid (that is, intensely judgmental). Due to this pattern, face reading literature has been harsh in the extreme. Once I read this: "A concave nose is one step away from animality and bestiality." Now who has concave noses? Most children, for starters.

No wonder only the most dedicated students of physiognomy attempt to survey the full range of literature in this field, 60 titles since Lavater that I, personally, have encountered. As I was reviewing this literature for my first book on the meaning of facial features, I ran across a little gem of a book called, *I Can Read Your Face*. It was Rose Rosetree's first work in this field, unlike anything I had seen before. It was the first face reading book that came from the heart—and the real truth of the matter.

Now, nine years later, Rose has written what I consider to be another breakthrough book, applying face reading to everyday situations with lots of examples of events and people to concretize what she is talking about. She makes face reading understandable, easy to learn, and memorable.

Her communication style is refreshingly upbeat, zestful, enthusiastic, and passionately involved (like her lifestyle, to judge from her anecdotes and my personal experience of her). Beneath the surface you'll find a depth of understanding about people and the meaning of faces that doesn't exist elsewhere in the literature.

Rose works from the realization that every human characteristic involves both a set of talents and a set of challenges. Then she proceeds to show us how to more deeply appreciate every person we encounter. Her general approach is that we are all in this together, and that we need to love ourselves and each other to make the whole thing work.

In effect, she is picking up and transmitting a collective soul change that is happening now. What it all comes down to is that if we don't move to coming from the heart, we human beings won't enjoy being human much longer. I believe a massive transformation is taking place and Rose is part of it, teaching us how to put it into action in our relationships with ourselves, with each other, with the community and with the human race.

Her loving wisdom-sharing will stick to your soul. This book is a delight to read, a revelation that leads to transformation. I heartily encourage you to join Rose Rosetree in this great evolutionary adventure.

Narayan Singh Khalsa, Ph.D.
Boulder, Colorado
November 1997

1. Power, anyone?

Like you, perhaps, my fascination with faces didn't start off as a lust for power. That came later.

Oh, I'm kidding. But it *is* true that face reading makes a person more powerful. Knowledge is power. And since most people don't have a clue about the kind of in-depth knowledge available from faces, you're going to have an advantage over them if you can look and learn, rather than overlook.

Here's a hint about what you'll be seeing: Face reading does NOT mean looking at expression, which most folks assume is the ultimate insider's view. At this point, let's simply make a distinction between **expression reading** and face reading; in the next chapter we'll explore the difference more fully.

Does it shock you to think of reading the physical face itself? **Face reading** has been practiced for thousands of years. Its formal name is **physiognomy** (fizzy-OG-nuh-me), which means interpreting the face to learn about the inner person.

When you do this, a side benefit is that you discover new things about your own face you never noticed before, like ear position and the degree of overlip definition. Since 1986, I've done thousands of face readings for people like you. And most have made surprising discoveries about their physical faces. How could this be? Before they didn't pay close attention. Why should they? Most face parts weren't meaningful.

But they will be now. So I recommend you keep a mirror by your side while you read this book. Discoveries about your face are part of the fun of face reading.

You're going to learn more than that, though. This how-to will teach you how to do face reading, why to do it, everything except when to do it. (That part you'll have to figure out for yourself.)

Face reading knowledge is power. In the coming pages, we'll emphasize three practical ways it can increase *your* personal power.

1. Sales

Developing better skills for **sales** excites many of my face reading students, and not only the sales professionals who want to earn more money. All of us find ourselves in situations where we need to sell ourselves and negotiate with others. Most of us would like to do it better. For instance, Mickey Kantor, former U.S. trade representative, is no slouch in the persuasion department. But he has reportedly found himself at a loss when dealing with his 10-year-old daughter. "I have to negotiate with her every day and I usually lose," he has complained.

Maybe you don't have to psych out a crafty kid or a foreign government, but better communication skills still could come in handy. On a job interview—for any kind of job—wouldn't it help if you could get inside information about your prospective boss? Once hired, couldn't you serve your clients better if you knew more about them? And if your company should downsize, might your ability to read people help you to survive as one of the fittest?

A great *Peanuts* comic strip delivered this punch line: "I love humanity. It's just people I can't stand." Face reading helps you to deal with people. You learn about one person at a time, one cheek at a time, one sale at a time.

Personal admission here: Some people's eyes light up at the thought of how their insights could bring sales. Other people (myself included) are more likely to cringe: "What, use my insights to manipulate people? Heaven forbid." The best sales people, though, will tell you they don't coerce their customers. They communicate. They educate. Only after this do they ask to redecorate.

Even if you don't stand to gain a nickel from reading faces, you'll profit inwardly when you explore this deeper human knowledge. Which is *your* priority for now, the material side of life or the spiritual side? Either way, face reading will enrich you.

2. Relationships

The power of face reading shows in **relationships**, especially those situations where people normally feel the opposite of powerful—like singles events, meeting your prospective mother-in-law, wondering about your grumpy new next-door neighbor with the rottweiler.

What do all these situations have in common? Lacking an abracadabra wand, you're stuck with people. They are stuck with you. How can both of you make the best of it? Without power, you're left wishing these strangers would be nice. You hope they'll see the real you (which is, of course, magnificent). You wish. You smile. And, mentally, you cross your fingers.

But your mind doesn't have fingers! That's just the most obvious reason why this sort of stance won't ever make a person feel, or be, powerful. Knowledge is power. If you're wise, you'll wish you could see *the best* in all the strangers who enter your life. And I don't mean reminding yourself of a cheery slogan, like "God is in this person; so as long as I can ignore the rest, we'll get along fine."

Nor does seeing the best in a person mean slapping on a quick label. Some folks assume face reading means you decide in 30 seconds whether a person is "good" or "bad." Aw, come on. We're mixtures. If you want to learn about problems as well as the pretty stuff, don't worry. When you read faces, that can be arranged.

Face reading informs you of practical things, like how a person makes decisions, spends money, works most productively, handles details. Who has a goofy sense of humor? Who won't laugh unless the humor is wry and dry? Who is a deep-down nonconformist? Who uses body language to convey the exact *opposite* of what she is really feeling?

Maybe I should mention right now that your ability to use my system of Face Reading Secrets does NOT require that you be observant about how people look. You don't have to remember people's faces or otherwise be visually oriented. (I'm not.) To read the Secrets, all you need is curiosity, plus a willingness to look at human face parts when they are right in front of you. It's simple. You've heard of doing things on a case-by-case basis? Well, you're going to gain your new level of knowledge on a face-by-face basis.

The face parts you'll investigate are richly varied. And the Secrets they'll tell you go far beyond the stereotypes you're probably expecting. In fact, face reading is guaranteed to smash all the stereotypes that keep you from seeing people as individuals. That is part of what brings you more power in relationships.

Another part of relationship empowerment is that face reading gives you license to climb out of ruts. Bored with someone you see on a daily basis? Let face reading help you to appreciate that person in an entirely new context.

And why not claim your power by letting face reading help you to avoid burnout? Do you come into contact with so many people that their faces are starting to blur together? Sure, a vacation might help. But the cheapest and best vacation could be a few hours with this book. Give yourself a deluxe vacation—from limited ways of looking at people.

3. Self-Esteem

It's the dirty little secret of my face reading classes: We don't respect our own faces enough. And we expect the lack of respect. Not one of my thousands of clients has come to me pleading: "Help, I've fallen out of love with my face. When I see my face in the mirror, it no longer thrills me with its magnificence. What's wrong?" My clients, you see, are grownups. By contrast, my son at age three loved his looks so much that he'd make little kiss marks on the mirror. When was the last time you or I did that?

Enthusiasm over your looks should not be confused with **vanity**, excessive pride in one's appearance. No, it's a matter of **self-esteem.** We have the right to thoroughly like what we see. But now that you're no longer three years old, much of what you see in life—in the mirror or elsewhere—is covered with layer upon layer of interpretation. Symbols, memories, fears, and habits of criticism all distort that image in the mirror. Not the least important of these associations is how your view of your face links up to your opinion of the rest of you. Bad face equals bad self. And alas, nearly nobody likes his or her face enough. American society in the new millennium has seen to that.

Daily we're bombarded by innumerable images of celebrities and models who have been cosmetically enhanced, possibly surgically altered, and definitely wearing identifiable hairstyles; next, photographers have placed flattering lights around them and then(the final indignity for the rest of us) these unnaturally beautiful people have been airbrushed. Even *they* don't look as good as their photos.

All this is mighty discouraging. And we take this discouragement so deep, we take it for granted.

Face reading helps self-esteem even if you don't come right out and admit you could like your face more. How come? You'll discover that every detail about your face means something wonderful—the angle of your lips, the chunkiness of your cheeks. Face Reading Secrets is based on this premise: *God don't make no junk.*

Find out how this applies to your face, the faces of your loved ones, and the faces of those you think might be loved-one material. Chapter by chapter, I'll show you what to look for and suggest what it means.

Power, anyone? Won't you have more of it as a face reader? And won't you be able to use it for good? Then join my **virtual classroom**, where I've assembled a group of people like you (well, a few, perhaps, are a bit stranger). It's my attempt to turn this how-to book into a typical face reading class. Your fellow students will ask questions that may be bouncing around in your mind right now:

Q. Just how accurate is face reading?

A. Since I began to teach Face Reading Secrets, I've read thousands of faces. At the end of each reading, I ask for feedback about my accuracy. About 99 percent of the time the response is positive. And this system is so easy to learn, my students have a high level of accuracy, too.

Q. Is it ethical to snoop into people's lives by reading faces?

A. The short answer is yes. For the long answer, let's use an example. Say you're looking for a job. Don't you find out all you can about a new boss?* Job interviews don't tell all you need to know, either.

What a charade, actually! On the surface, those who play the game discuss formal business matters with unnatural politeness. Below the surface, however, a frantic search is going on: everyone's checking out personality, listening for clues about character, trying hard to get at the truth... because on weekdays, you'll probably spend more hours with this work partner than with your spouse. What it will be like when you are cooped up together?

Considering that valid need to know, how would you react if your friend George offered you first-hand information about this mystery person? Would you hesitate to listen? Then why hesitate to get first-hand information for yourself by reading faces?

* Likewise, if you're the one who's hiring, don't you have more than a passing curiosity about your job applicants?

The inside scoop on personality might show you the difference between a choice that really is as great as it looks and a potential disaster. We can make an analogy to **graphoanalysis**, the study of character based on handwriting samples. Did you know that 80% of businesses in France today rely on graphoanalysis? According to Carol Moore, a professional Handwriting Examiner from Virginia whose testimony is used in court, graphoanalysis is even more respected in Israel, to such an extent that you can't get a job or even rent an apartment without having your handwriting done. Wherever you live, it pays to learn about the inner person. Face Reading Secrets can provide similar information—and it's easier to learn.

Managers have studied with me to help them make better hiring decisions or to bring out the best in personnel they've already hired. Human resource staff find the results comparable to more complicated personality tests but much easier to administer: all they have to do is look at the job applicant.

One manager put it best: "The face is a walking résumé."

Perhaps you've heard a story about President Lincoln, who was asked to appoint a certain man to his cabinet. When Lincoln declined, the reason he gave was, "I don't like the man's face."

"But the poor man is not responsible for his face," protested his trusted adviser.

Lincoln disagreed. He said, "Every man over forty is responsible for his face." He was right.

Q. Don't you think it could ever be wrong to read someone's face?

A. Yes. Avoid reading the face of anyone under the age of 18. Kids haven't had enough time to form a face of their own. If you're a parent, you've seen how fast they change: One day they look more like Mom, another they look more like Dad; one year the nose threatens to take over the rest of the face; next year, other face parts catch up. So it's better to let those unpredictable faces develop at their own pace before slapping labels onto them. Sure, you'll probably read kids' faces anyway (my husband and I started reading our son the day he was born), but just don't confuse impressionable young people by reading their faces out loud.

Q. What if you're under 18 yourself? Shouldn't you read faces?

A. Are you kidding? You can never start reading faces too early. By the time you're ready to vote, you could be a master physiognomist, which will come in handing with voting, among other things. Just take with a generous grain of salt whatever you see in *your* face until it turns 18. And don't read your friends. Instead focus on adults, especially teachers and other authority figures. Considering how much power they have over you, you deserve to use this way of empowering yourself by learning their Secrets.

Q. Could I use face reading the way I use tarot cards?

A. I don't expect to come out with a deck of face parts any time soon. Even if what we're dealt in life changes over time, it's not going to change as fast as you can shuffle a deck of cards.

Fortune-telling is what you're asking about, really. Face reading helps you to create a brighter future but not by predicting it. Instead, face reading can help you acknowledge your greatest talents, enabling you to lead with them. That's a powerful way to move into your future.

Face reading also appeals to people who wouldn't be caught dead with a fortune-teller. I think of Eddie Dean, a reporter from the hip *City Paper* in Washington, D.C. To give you an idea of his irreverence, he called our interview "A visit to the realm of Dorian Gray and Mr. Potato Head." But Eddie loved my readings of local celebrities, and when it came to my reading of *his* face, he called it a "dead-on analysis" and concluded, "At this point, I'm feeling not only validated but truly vindicated for taking up space on the planet: Face reading is a damn sight better way of getting to know yourself than babbling to some

high-priced shrink." No doubt Eddie also would have preferred it to
tarot reading.

**Q. What if, after you learn face reading, you can't stop your-
self? Could face reading turn me into some kind of a weirdo,
where I drive myself and other people crazy?**
   A. Look, when you learn to read faces you're not heading for The
Twilight Zone. You won't obsessively go for the deep stuff every time
you see a couple of ears or a chin. This is a skill. You can turn it off or
on at will.
   Q. But how will I know when to use it?
   A. Think of face reading knowledge like a TV set. When you choose
to know more about people, zap!, you can turn it on. When you're
more interested in something else, say sex, your brain can be otherwise
occupied. Automatically the part of you that does face reading will turn
off.

**Q. If face reading doesn't drive people crazy, I'm curious
about what effect it does have. Has anyone told you what you
do is scary?**
   A. Some people whose faces I've read have called it scary at first.
They don't expect it to be so accurate. But since I do this with love,
people warm up. Once I was hired to read faces at a party where
people warmed up to such an degree, they extended my booking until
it lasted 11 hours. In general, face reading can help people to like you
more. No guarantees, but it could happen. When you have the intent to
connect with people more deeply, this changes the level of the relationship—even if you don't breathe a word about what you've discovered
by reading a face. Your intent to connect with a deeper knowing automatically invites that other person to do the same with you. Can't *you*
feel when people reach out to you, versus going through the motions of
conversation, being deep down not interested, or silently judging you?

Don't you respond differently when someone shows genuine interest in you as a person?

Q. Do you seriously mean that you can go up to a stranger, make comments about his nose, and he's going to love you forever?

A. Ethics, as well as good manners, dictate that you only read faces out loud when people ask you to. And they only ask if they're willing to hear what you say. Of course, that doesn't mean they're necessarily true believers. Sometimes people test you.

Recently I was hired by a personnel company to give face readings for a convention of office managers who run law firms. One fellow who came to our booth, at the D.C. Convention Center, had a loud, obnoxious voice and manners to match. But I went ahead anyway, telling him about talents and challenges that showed in his face. Five hours later, he came back. Quietly he said, "I just have to tell you, until today I've always hated my nose. What you said made a bigger difference to me than you can ever know."

Q. What's the most embarrassing thing that has happened to you in your career as a face reader?

A. "In next year's election for D.C. mayor, you can study the records of the candidates, or you can study their faces." That's how an article in *The Washingtonian Magazine* introduced me to readers, only I never said that. My face readings of politicians were quoted accurately. But I was mortified that the magazine made it sound as though I would recommend voting for people based just on looks.

The same goes for hiring someone or marrying someone. Golly, I wouldn't even recommend kissing someone based just on looks.

What I do suggest is that you use face reading to supplement other information. Face reading tells a great deal, not as a substitute for common sense but as an extension of it.

2. Where does face reading come from?

Timothy Mar, the world's greatest face reader, stood before me. I felt very scared. He had been asked to read my face—not by me, but by a man who was trying to impress me, Bartholomew Rachmaninoff III.

Here's what had led to this pivotal point in my life. It was 1975. I had gone to my first meeting of Mensa, a club I had joined in the hope of making some friends, and I had just been treated to what, with all respect to the late Mr. Mar, was the most boring lecture of my life.

Mr. Mar had stood in a room crammed with people like me, certified smart and totally ignorant about physiognomy. The former diplomat and renowned exponent of Chinese face reading held up his latest face reading book and announced: "I want all of you to buy this book. So I won't tell you anything that's in it."

Salespeople, take note: This is not a highly effective way to sell books.

Mar had to talk about something for the next hour since he was our featured speaker, so he told us how nice it was for him that he could read faces. The audience fidgeted and would have fiddled with their virtual pets if they had been invented yet. Not realizing that I was attending the birth of my future career, I yawned.

Bartholomew Rachmaninoff III, seated next to me and likewise hoping to make some friends that night, apparently found my yawning attractive. So he followed me to the front of the room, along with about .04 percent of the listeners in the auditorium. We, the curious, the survivors, plied Mar with questions about face reading.

Finally he gave us specifics, commenting on noses and foreheads and cheeks. Eavesdropping from the sidelines, I was having a great time. Then Bartholomew decided to impress me.

"Please read her face," he asked Timothy Mar.

I flinched in advance, sure I was about to be humiliated. (Is it a coincidence that I would go on to write a book about face reading for self-esteem? Maybe not.)

After a brief professional stare, he said, "Beautiful."

My head swiveled around to see whom he was talking about.

Then he said, "Teacher."

I gulped. For the past four years I had done little else but teach classes in personal development. Teaching was my life. Shy or not, I finally dared to make contact with his eyes. Unfortunately, he was looking worried, extremely worried.

After a polite pause, he looked at me with an expression of great horror. "But you shouldn't pluck your eyebrows."

I looked back at him with an equally intense expression. It wasn't horror. It was shame. "But I don't pluck my eyebrows."

I waited to find out more, but Mar had slammed his mouth shut.

How I developed the system of Face Reading Secrets

In the months and years that followed, I read all the books on face reading in the English language. For a while, I virtually lived at the Library of Congress. Yes, I was hooked. It made such intuitive sense to me that a physical face could be meaningful. If your expression could count, if your body language could tell another layer of truth about you, what was your long-term face supposed to be, something thrown together like potato salad?

But my research took a great deal of intestinal fortitude—perhaps not unlike what it would have taken to study all the systems in the English language for making potato salad. I found out, for instance, what was allegedly so horrible about my eyebrows.

The ancient Chinese system of *Siang Mien,* * which is as old as acupuncture, has come down to us today as fascinating but pretty judgmental. It is organized around the concept that there is such a thing as "The best mouth" and "The best eyebrows." If you don't have these particular items, *Siang Mien* will tell you cheerfully, and sometimes in great detail, how come you're a loser.

My notorious eyebrow trait, for instance, involves the distribution of hair. Technically, my eyebrows are extreme "starters." (You'll read more about this trait in the Eyebrow chapter, coming up soon.)

According to *Siang Mien*, the interpretation is simple: "A person with eyebrows like this will never accomplish much in life."

Another bit of information I came across, once I worked my way over to ears, was equally effective at wrecking my day. *Siang Mien* taught me about ear position, a fascinating discovery. And there was good news: I had something relatively unusual, ears in a high position. Then came the bad news:

"He will have his greatest success early in life."

What was so terrible about that, aside from the obvious gender problem? When I read this pronouncement, I was well into my thirties. Apparently (unbeknownst to myself) I had already peaked.

I studied other systems of face reading, too. I'd heard about *You Are All Sampaku*, which used an eye trait to predict early death. This didn't appeal to me, hunting for death not being one of my hobbies.

---

* Pronounced SEE-ahng MEE-un.

I'd heard raves about macrobiotic face reading, but was turned off by interpretations of face traits along the lines of, "Your mouth shows your mother ate too many dairy products." Even if true, what could I do about it?

Gradually the desire built within me to take what I'd learned about physiognomy and develop a different system, one without dire predictions, a loving system that would be helpful to people. It would be based on the premise that "God don't make no junk."

Using my intuition, which had been developed by years of meditation, I asked inwardly about the meaning of face traits. If starter eyebrows didn't mean failure at life, what did they mean? How about ear position? When answers came, I tested them on myself, then on friends, and eventually paying clients.

"Yes! It's so true." they said, and not only to the cheerful parts.

Personal style, not just lifestyle

Clients often ask how I developed my system. Apart from intuition, my undergraduate degree from Brandeis helped, as did some graduate study towards a Master's Degree in Social Work. Among other things, academic study taught me about **lifestyle**.

You recognize that word, right? It means a way of life, as in choosing a healthy lifestyle to prevent heart disease or dressing up for dates to show the lifestyle to which you'd like to become accustomed. During the sixties, when I first learned this concept, lifestyle seemed to be a matter of *fate* (or, at least, sociology): college professors in Boston have one kind of lifestyle versus the lifestyle of social deviants. Today, however, the emphasis in considering lifestyle is *choice*. If your lifestyle has consequences you don't like, such as a heart attack, you can change that lifestyle—and probably should do so unless you're keen on racking up extra reincarnations.

Equally important as lifestyle, but so far a lesser known concept, is **personal style**. That means a person's comfort zone with behaving in a particular way, or being sensitive to a particular aspect of life.

For instance, some people care deeply about belonging. Their manners are great, and when they break the rules, they know it. By contrast, other people are geared more toward independence. They do things "my way" first. Later, as needed, they get around to the damage control.

These examples show different personal style around social conformity. It was a breakthrough for me to realize that face reading could give information about personal style. For the social conformity aspect, you find what you need to know by studying ear angles. That's right, the degree to which a person's ears stick out from the head relates to the need to belong to the crowd.

Why conformity? Why ear angles? That's the symbology of the face, a spiritual alphabet. It is what it is. When anatomists analyze the structure of the human heart, they study how it works, they don't invent it. Similarly, physiognomists study. We don't invent. Our job is to do our honest best to explore what is there. Because it's a spiritual level of truth, the research is carried out in consciousness rather than a physical laboratory.

Some folks believe this is possible, I've found, while others scoff. In the words of Henry Ford, "If you think you can do something, or you can't, in either case you're right." Personally, I think the scoffers miss out.

Since you are willing to consider the possibility that studying face traits like in-angled ears can show you a helpful level of truth about life, keep in mind two things—quite apart from the actual ears:

■ Reading personal style is different from assigning a fixed destiny. Your personal style can change, just as your lifestyle can. It's up to you.

- Personal style is neither good nor bad. Whether ears angle out like flying buttresses, or stick close to the head, more like window shutters fastened with extra-strength Velcro, either trait gives its owner at least one advantage in life.

Talent, not just personal style

A useful way to interpret personal style, I came to realize, is to relate it to **talent**. Talent happens when you become conscious of something you're naturally good at and start to use it on purpose.

For example, Andrea, with her ears close to the head, is a social chameleon, acting differently depending on whichever group she is with. For years she has beat herself up about this: "Where is my personality? Why am I so wishy washy?"

When a face reader like me suggests that her personal style with manners is to be uncommonly responsive to people's expectations, the feedback could be useful. Andrea may find it easier to accept herself.

But why stop short at self-acceptance? When Andrea consciously recognizes her personal style, right at that very moment, she can turn her personal style into a *talent*. Let's say that Andrea works in corporate sales and make visits on site. "Aha!" she thinks. "Not everybody can fit in everywhere, regardless of the client's corporate culture. I do this so effortlessly, I used to take it for granted." Acknowledging that she has talent can boost her confidence, even her job performance.

Aware of her finesse at matching each client's expectations, Andrea can become more effective than ever at asking for sales. She can also remind her boss of her talent. Say that she applies for a promotion as Regional Sales Manager. Andrea can stand out from other applicants by emphasizing her skills as Corporate Culture Consultant. Get the difference between feeling validated (personal style) and being empowered (using what you're good at—your talent—on purpose)?

Here are a few other examples of how face reading can empower you:

- Whenever you read about a trait of yours, you will learn about an aspect of your own personal style that you can use as a talent, for sales or any other kind of work.
- Talent is a reason for justifiable self-esteem.
- When you read about traits belonging to others, you will learn about styles different from yours. Explore them. Learn from them. You'll add zing to your relationships.
- If you're a manager or a parent, you can actively help to recognize and develop somebody else's talent—yet another way face reading can help you to shine in relationships.

Reframing

Another feature of Face Reading Secrets, not present in other face reading systems, is **reframing**. This means taking something that has bothered you in the past and putting it in a different context. It's like taking a family portrait out of an ugly old frame that emphasizes the "warts and all" aspect of how people look, then changing the frame to something shiny and new. Suddenly instead of seeing warts, you notice the sparkle in each person's eyes.

Face Reading Secrets can help you to reframe things you can't stand about yourself. Turns out, problems are often related to things you really like. It works like the flip side of a coin. When it comes to character, most of us don't associate the head of a coin with the tail, the upside with the downside. Nevertheless, many foibles and frailties are deeply connected to a person's most distinctive strengths.

Let's return to the example of Andrea, with her in-angled ears. Although she's highly sensitive to good manners, she may be easily annoyed by people whose manners are, frankly, lousy.

For years it has bothered Andrea that, try though she does to be a nice person, sometimes she acts like such a snob. "Where did he grow up, in a barn?" she'll catch herself muttering at elegant dinner parties.

It's helpful for Andrea to realize her snobbishness about manners reflects her high standards. It's the flip side of being so darned mannerly. Even if she keeps on noticing lousy manners in the future, now Andrea can do some reframing: "Why expect everyone to have manners as good as mine? Hey, I have a talent with manners. Maybe I can afford to be more patient with folks who don't."

With enough reframing, Andrea will stop being a snob in the first place. And then she will have mastered one of her life lessons.

Life lessons

Have you noticed? The place where you live is **The Learning Planet**. It's a one-room schoolhouse, where kindergartners sit cheek-by-jowl with graduate students. Like it or not, all of us are receiving a spiritual education. And, like it or not, it's an extremely public school.

Funnily enough, externals like social status, wealth, and fame don't necessarily reveal how well your classmates are doing at their spiritual lessons. People in high places can be highly evolved, or clods, or anything in-between. The meek who inherit the earth, spiritually, may have any corporate job title... or none.

Where face reading comes in is that it informs you about the **life lessons** a person is studying. Half of a life lesson involves learning to recognize and use your talents. The other half demands that you learn how to handle the flip side of your talent. Thus, each talent comes with a corresponding potential challenge—as you'll read later in juicy detail.

Does the face show you whether someone has learned a particular life lesson? Interestingly, it doesn't. (Auras can tell you, however; so can empathy, as presented in my other books.)

Until you have learned a life lesson, you'll suffer from its corresponding challenge. Face reading can help to reframe it. After you have gone on to learn a life lesson, the potential challenge won't apply to you any more. So when you read about a challenge you no longer have, go ahead: Give yourself a well-deserved pat on the back.

Controversy

To summarize, Face Reading Secrets offers you insights into life lessons, both talents and the challenges that potentially go with them. Such a perspective enables you to reframe your own shortcomings and those of others. This is a loving system, based on the premise that "God don't make no junk." Rather than assuming a person's face traits are a meaningless collection of genes, everything about a physical face becomes informative. You can only appreciate people more by reading their Secrets.

Nonetheless, face reading is controversial. It contradicts some common assumptions people make about reality. See if you can spot them in the following Q&A session.

Q. Although I'm willing to find out if there really is something to face reading, I'll tell you right off that I have doubts. Is it fair to read faces considering that our looks are based on heredity?

A. Genetics is part of the truth about life. It's not the entire truth and it may not even be a particularly *useful* kind of truth in the context of face parts.

Truth has many levels, you know. After all, a cell from your hand, when seen under a microscope, seems entirely different from the hand you hold out to greet a friend. Yet both these perspectives of your hand are true because of life's many interlocking levels. One of our privileges as human beings is the freedom to put our attention, at any one time, on whichever level of life we choose. We can make a mountain out of a molehill or a molehill out of a mountain.

Here's how I recommend handling heredity: When you're being a scientist, sure, consider face traits pure genetics. But even the greatest scientist has to come out of the lab sometimes and just be a person. As a person, your life will be enriched by the more holistic level of face reading. It combines something physical with something metaphysical* about the inner person.

Q. So you're claiming that genes have nothing whatsoever to do with how we look? It's not mere chance or coincidence?

A. No, I believe your soul chooses from what's available in the gene pool. And sometimes it's a pretty long reach in that pool to find the trait that's needed. For instance, one face reader pointed out that, in his family, there are four brothers. All of them look alike except "the rebel," whose face looks completely different from all the others. Coincidence? Not to a face reader.

Here's another example. Think of any couple you know who have been happily married for at least ten years. Haven't their faces started to look alike? Well, who did they inherit that from, their kids?

Another possible explanation is that, as face readers have said for thousands of years (long before modern-day genetics), there is a deep relationship between the inner person and the outer face.

* Or at least psychological. Depending on how much New Age "woo woo" you can stand, you can read this book as psychology or metaphysics. Thank life's interlocking levels for the choice.

Beliefs have consequences. If you believe that your life is determined by heredity, you limit your free will. Face Reading Secrets offers you the opportunity to take responsibility for your looks, like other aspects of your life. As you look deeply into faces, you'll be amazed at how much they change over time... and in ways that validate the spiritual growth of each person's life journey.

Q. My whole life I've suffered because of prejudice against my African-American features. Am I the only one to think that your so-called "physiognomy" is just a fancy word for prejudice?

A. No, unfortunately. But let's consider what face reading actually is, in contrast to your fears about it. Face reading is NOT a pretext for judging people as good or bad. It is an opportunity to learn, not judge. Face reading is NOT deterministic, because your face changes during your lifetime, and your face comes to reflect these changes.

Also face reading is NOT about putting people into racial categories. It's about the shapes and angles and proportions within a face. It is not about color or texture of hair, color of eyes, or color of skin.

Q. Surely you can't deny that certain features go with particular ethnic groups, can you?

A. Stereotyping does set us up to expect certain features to go with particular groups. But when you look, really look, you see individuals. That's the fascinating part.

Once, when I was interviewed on national television, the host asked this question: "How can you read faces of black people when they all look alike?"

Shock waves ran through the studio audience.

Interestingly, this talk show host had coffee-colored skin and blue eyes. Probably she, herself, was a mixture of black and white. So she really knew better than to ask such an insulting question. But she wanted to stir things up.

Publicly few people today would come out and say "All black people look alike" or "All people from East Asia look alike." We don't say it but frequently we think it. However, this is true in only the most superficial sense.

Laura, a friend of mine born in Taiwan but raised in America, told me before she made a trip to China: "It's going to be such fun to walk down the street and have everyone look just like me!" Oddly enough, though, no matter how large the crowd, Laura never had trouble recognizing her husband or son. The look-alike aspect was mainly a matter of coloring. It usually is.

What Laura prized, I suspect, was her cultural roots. Ethnic categories are wonderful as a means to value your heritage. And there's a wonderful level of ethnic pride that celebrates history, ancestors, culture. Nonetheless, there's another level of ethnic pride that has brought places like Bosnia the horrors of "ethnic cleansing." Face reading is a different subject altogether.

Q. But what if you've been conditioned to see the ethnic part first and foremost whenever you see people?

A. Then see it and move on. As a face reader, you have the freedom to write people off as ethnic stereotypes or you can look for individuals. Is it going to be time for molehills or mountains? When we see a new person, we're free to pick any category we want. For instance, you can scan a man's face for blemishes, like a dermatologist trolling for patients. You can visually weigh a woman's physique (and her character) in terms of fat—with practice, you might be able to estimate perfectly to the quarter ounce—which could be useful for something, though I'm not sure what.

When you're ready to learn more about how people tick, and value them as individuals, read faces.

Q. If we want to see the real person, instead of a stereotype, how can face reading help us?

A. You look at one face part at a time, and within that face part you keep on looking. Each face part has plenty of traits to choose from. So if you've been raised to believe that certain face parts, like noses, always go with one ethnic group, you're going to be in for a big shock.

Take the example of the nose trait I call the nose bonus. Some people have an extra chunk of nose that hangs down below the nose tip, between the nostrils. See it illustrated on the next page. You'll also see a real-life example in my photo at the end of this book. Ethnically, I'm of Jewish extraction, via Germany and Russia. My parents, sister, and cousins don't have this trait—nor did I, until well into my thirties. (Remember what I said before about how our faces aren't genetically determined, and how our faces change throughout a lifetime?) When you turn the page, you'll see more examples of people who have a nose bonus.

Q. So what does this nose trait mean, anyway?

A. If you have a *nose bonus*, your work must include service. When you don't believe, deep down, that you are helping people through your work, you can't stick with it, whatever else your job offers in terms of money or status.

And what does this meaning have to do with race? Nothing. If you're worried about any other trait being linked with a message of inferiority or other stereotyping, look it up in Index II, Face Data. Read what it means and quit worrying.

Q. Could you use face reading to actually overcome racial stereotypes?

A. By the time you've looked at a person long enough to spot three or more face traits, you'll be seeing a real person rather than a stereotype. Even the idea of looking at actual face parts can be freeing.

Just look at the drawing on Page 38 of Tiger Woods, America's most talented golfer. Because it's a line drawing, you're not pulled into the

NOSE BONUS

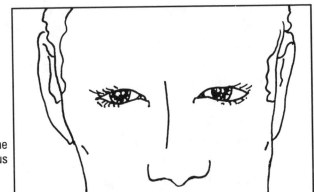

With the
bonus

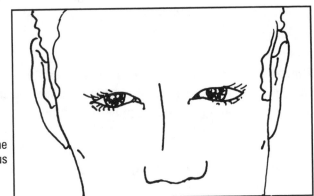

Without the
bonus

People with the Nose Bonus

Martin Luther King, Jr.	African-American civil rights leader
Albert Schweitzer	German medical missionary
Anwar Sadat	Egyptian political leader
Leo Esaki	Japanese physicist
Henri Bergson	French philosopher
Jacinto Benavente Martinez	Spanish playwright
Odysseus Elytis	Greek poet
Yuan T. Lee	Chinese-American chemist
Aung San Suu Kyi	Burmese human rights activist
Maireadé Corrigan	Irish pacifist
Har Gobind Khorana	Indian-American biochemist
Camillo Golgi	Italian pathologist
Dag Hammarskjöld	Swedish leader, U.N. Secretary General
Ivan Pavlov	Russian psychologist
Tiger Woods	American golfer

usual way of looking at a person in terms of color. Examine his face, bit by bit. He calls himself a **Cablinasian** because his heritage is:

- 1/4 Chinese
- 1/4 Black
- 1/4 Thai
- 1/8 Native American
- 1/8 White

What is Tiger Woods mostly? He's Everyman, a mixture, his own person. Today that's the way of our world. An elderly woman told a friend of mine, "Thank God, I'll never live to see the day your son marries someone who isn't Italian." It's sad. The days of intermarriage are

TIGER WOODS

Cablinasian

here, yet depending on your family background you've probably heard someone make a statement like this (just substitute the last word that fits with *your* heritage, anything from "Armenian" to "Zulu"). Many people can't accept intermarriage but that's not going to stop it. And I, for one, am glad. Tiger Woods' parents and grandparents may have shocked some of the relatives but the kid has turned out okay.

Another example of human diversity is Betty Crocker, one of America's most commercially successful (if physically nonexistent) home bakers. Her image was first created 15 years after the company began selling cake mixes. According to Pam Becker, a spokesperson for General Mills, Betty's face has been updated many times over the company's history to reflect "today's American woman."

Hairstyles have evolved, as has makeup. Eventually Betty's perennial housedress had to go, reflecting that a "today's woman" who identifies with Betty may no longer think of herself primarily as a housewife.

What hasn't changed over the years is that Betty has remained a blue-eyed Caucasian brunette. Finally that, too, was reconsidered. Betty received Makeover #9. This look was created for her official 75-year portrait. Seeking an image that consumers could identify with, the company ran an essay contest. The winners demonstrated that they enjoyed cooking and baking; that they were committed to family, friends, and community. The winning essayists also showed they were resourceful, finding creative ways to handle household tasks. Family of origin wasn't considered, Ms. Becker told me, but the 75 contest winners did wind up coming from diverse ethnic backgrounds.

Computer morphing combined all their faces to create one new Betty Crocker, whose image was then painted in the company's traditional manner. The 75-woman, new Betty look shines out from the cover of *Betty Crocker's New Cookbook*, published in 1996.

Betty's eyes are brown now, her complexion a tad darker. Ethnic stereotypers will have a hard time pinning her down. Otherwise results have been most satisfactory, as far as Pam Becker's concerned. "Some people will say, "She looks Hispanic." Others say "She looks a little

Islamic," and so on. When we hear 'She looks just like my neighbor or cousin or friend,' we know we've succeeded. Betty Crocker is supposed to be the human side of this company."

I asked one of the original parts of Betty how she felt about having her image morphed into a multi-ethnic face. Julie Leviner, from Wilmington, North Carolina, is a typical citizen of our melting pot nation: her parentage is Welsh, German, French, and Native American. Here's how Julie first reacted when she saw the new, improved Betty:

"Compared to the earlier versions of Betty Crocker, she had more of an ethnic look. But as I looked closer, I thought I saw a crooked tooth in her smile, a tooth that belonged to me. Sure enough, I checked with the man responsible for the image. He told me that when Betty was all put together the first time, she looked too perfect. 'So I pulled out your mouth,' he told me.

"When I could find a little bit of myself in her face, it didn't seem so ethnic any more."

Julie explained, "You always think of yourself as kind of normal."

And that's just the point. Don't you see yourself as "kind of normal"? Whatever your color of skin, you're a standard issue human being. As you look for specific details, like your teeth or the shape of your nostrils, that's where your individuality comes through. So it does for everyone. And face reading helps you to see that individuality in depth and detail.

■■■

3. How to see like a face reader

Gone are the days when you ate like a kid—at least I, and your mother, hope so. But remember your old ways for a few moments and they can teach you something useful about how to see like a face reader.

Kids are purposeful in the way they eat. They discriminate with the zeal (if not the sophistication) of a Zen master. During a childhood phase when all you wanted to eat was chicken, you'd pick it out of any casserole with unerring aim. Flinging sauce to the right and carrot cubes to the left, you would dive straight for the morsels you wanted. However otherwise limited your coordination, once you put your mind to it, you could lift off every single flake of parsley, no matter how minuscule. Chicken, only chicken, is what you would stuff into your mouth.

Kids are great at paying attention. In fact, a friend of mine who works as a magician has told me how tough it is to do sleight-of-hand for an audience of five-year-olds.

"You can't fool them," Ken complained. "The way tricks work is that you distract the audience while you do the business end of the illusion, but young children won't be distracted. They see all that you're doing, including what you are trying to hide. Typically, at the end, when I say, 'Ta da!,' their response is, 'Now what?' Those smart little kids are still waiting for the magical part."

The magic of childhood doesn't lie in someone else's illusions. Likewise, the magic in faces lies elsewhere than where we've been schooled to look. When we remember to see with the discriminating eyes of face readers, we can bypass layers of training that otherwise come automatically.

Old habits

Although the U.S. Bureau of the Census may not keep you on its official payroll, you've probably been collecting data since the age of five.

Within seconds of seeing a face you notice:

- Male or female.
- Old or young.
- Skin color (which is then used to cram a person into a category about race).
- Alive or dead (you may not see many of the latter walking down the street but, believe me, if you did, you'd notice).

How fast the **demographics** whiz by! A different set of information relates to **attractiveness**. Say you're single and cruising the Net, hoping to find a photo that belongs to your soulmate. Attractiveness can count so much, in some instances, it's all the date-seeker consciously registers. (Though, for safety's sake, anyone considering an Internet romance should first run, not walk, through the pages of this book. Then learn to do the three lie detector tests in its sequel, *Aura Reading Through ALL Your Senses.*)

Psychological research documents that most people select mates with a similar beauty quotient—if you're a 10, you probably won't date a three. Dare I say it? Much of what passes for face reading, profound psychological inquiry, or soulmate recognition among the hormone-driven really comes down to **cuteness screening**.

Often we're mesmerized by a **look**, more than an actual face. Physical features pass the test if they're framed by the right hairstyle, makeup, and aura (yes, aura, even if we don't register it consciously). "Yes" or "no," we decide, and as far as that face is concerned, we're finished. Doing this can be fun. Being on the receiving end, however, isn't nearly so delightful. In either case, a quick facial once over should not be confused with face reading.

Sometimes we can afford to indulge pure **social curiosity**. Does *wealth* show in a face? Often it does, through the teeth, the grooming, the angle of a head, the earrings (however many).

How about *social affiliations*? What tee-shirts won't tell you, face adornments may. Do you see a cross dangling anywhere, a tilak, or a nose ring?

Another option is to use more developed skills to gather **lifestyle data**. Maybe you've trained yourself to read body language, auras, or micro-expressions. They can help you to spot the subtle markings of a particular group. For example, I've found that one test to distinguish a cult from a more loosely formed religion is how alike the facial expressions of different members *appear* to be.

And on the secular side, have you ever sat at a restaurant next to a corporate lunch meeting, amazed that each and every face wears the company look? How did they manage to hire such similar looking people? Or how were they manufactured?

All of us are, or could become, familiar with one social affiliation that shows in faces. Open a magazine like *Vogue* and behold the deadpans of professional models in the fashion photos. Not everyone can look like that. At a minimum, it takes practice.

Sometimes **health** is what we try to read in faces. Physical or psychological wounding can show in the way a face is held. Depending on your experience, you may be familiar with subtle cues that show you a certain kind of alcoholic, or someone who lives with chronic arthritis or other physical pain.

Depression, sexual impotence, cruelty, shame—depending on what we've been through, each of us has learned to recognize a special collection of nuances. It shows to us as clear as day, even when other people don't suspect a thing.

That's admirable knowledge, hard won and useful. Still, let's not confuse it with face reading. Thank God, face reading can help a person to lighten up! Even if your lifestyle requires that you routinely deal with the suffering on faces, you owe it to yourself to look at faces in ways that can show you something more. Shadows of tragedy can teach us, but so does the light of talent.

Expression

Hands down, eyelashes up, the biggest habit Americans have about looking at faces is our fascination with **expression**. Mainstream American culture has taught us the habit of staring at each other's faces, not a universal custom by any means.

And *television* trains us to become expression watchers. When you learn how to watch TV, you find out that expression is the key to all important scenes: The plot thickens and bubbles. Just then, the camera moves in close for a tight shot of the emotional soup. Background music throbs. You learn that the main ingredient of the story, any story, is what shows in eyes and lips.

But is that really true?

Once again, it's helpful to realize that truth comes in many layers. Expression has advantages as a way to learn about people. Nevertheless, it has just as many drawbacks.

When you rely on expression, you open the door for **deception**. At a young age, all of us have learned how to give a desired impression. It isn't even lying, necessarily, so much as slipping into an emotional space and conveniently deciding that this is the part of the truth to tell. Say you glare at your kid, Bobby:

"Were you just eating that cookie?"

Conveniently, Bobby remembers the microsecond between when he polished off the cookie and you entered the room. "No, Dad." he says. "I was just bouncing on the sofa."

A face full of innocence stares right back at you.

Oh well.

■■■

Apart from deception, expression has other disadvantages as a main way to learn from a person's face. Expression shows **mood**, and mood is a passing thing. Afterwards, reality sets in. How many times have you heard a friend's sad story begin with these words: "I trusted him because he looked so nice."?

"Nice," on a date or job interview, reveals precisely nothing about a person's long-term behavior. How about his personal style with power or intimacy or work?

To read information like that, you need face reading. Unlike expression, face traits can't be faked, which makes for a more accurate kind of information.

■■■

Most limiting of all, expression is **incomplete**.

"Eyes are the mirror of the soul," people say as they stare. Usually they're fooling themselves. Soul stuff is there, to be sure, but so is emotion. Usually folks are responding to emotion, not the unfathomable soul.

Consider this, though: For face readers, the entire face mirrors the soul.

How do you read faces now?

Here's a quiz to help you think about what it means to see faces as a face reader.
TRUE or FALSE? (Answers are at the end of this chapter.)

1. Observing a sales client's expression helps to put you in control.
2. Never trust someone with beady eyes.
3. Never trust someone with shifty eyes.
4. The facial feature people are most apt to dislike in themselves is their chin.
5. Men who grow beards may be hiding a weak chin.
6. People with fuller lips are sexier.
7. Intelligence shows in the shape of the skull.
8. People from the same ethnic group tend to look alike.
9. I can rely on my snap judgments about character from sizing up a face.
10. I know everything important about how my own face looks.

A new purpose for looking at faces

The first trick to seeing as a face reader is *intention*. What are you going to make important when you aim your eyes, your mind, and your heart? For face reading, you look at a person's physical face. As for your mind and your heart, it can help to actively desire to learn about people.

Please, I don't mean a tortured stance, as though in the throes of constipation: "I think I can. I think I can. I think I can." A simple wish is enough to make it happen. After making your wish, you can trust that it will come true. It's like the wonderful saying, "Let go and let God."

One reason our habits of looking at faces can be so limiting is that, along with our childhood education about census taking and so forth, most of us learned an underlying intention from the people who taught us: "I'll see just enough to show how clever I am."

The best face readers I've met have humility. That's not because their intention is, "I'll show how humble I am." but because they have aims like these: "I'd like to learn *about* this person." "I'd like to learn *from* this person." "I'd like to be of service *to* this person."

Having already mastered many ways of looking at faces, chances are that, unintentionally, you also have absorbed habits of the show-off variety. Even if they're unconscious—especially if they're unconscious!—such habits need to be broken.

So you may need to shake yourself up inwardly from time to time. Take a deep breath. Slow yourself down. What you're going to do now is face reading. The other ways of looking at people can wait until later.

Level with a face

As you prepare to read somebody's face, look from a straight angle. The same applies to how you can best study your own face in the mirror.

■ Don't look up to people. Don't look down on them. To see the truth, be on the level.

Seeing also involves taking time, especially when you are learning to see something new. For instance, it won't be enough to give a cursory glance and decide all that matters is that the face has "a big honker." If you're going to focus on the nose, pause long enough to see it properly. Ask: "How is it big?" and take another look. Which trait gave that first impression? It could have been any of these:

- Long nose length
- Large nose thrust from the side
- A pronounced arch that shows in profile
- Nose width at the bridge
- Nose width at the tip
- Nose width all the way down
- A nose that dramatically widens on the way down
- A chunky nose tip
- A large Priority Area II (See Index II for what on earth that means.)

Sound complicated? Don't worry. This book offers a systematic approach that will ease you into looking at face parts. Different physical features, like noses and ears, have their own chapters. Each **feature** contains several **categories**. Each of these contains **traits,** or items of **face data**. For instance, the *nose* feature includes the category of *nose length*. *Long* nose length is one trait. *Short* nose length is another.

Illustrations in this book group together different traits belonging to each category. To help you develop your eye for distinguishing one trait at a time, each picture within the set shows faces that are identical except for the face trait you're studying. In no time at all, you'll develop an eye for observing traits.

And each trait means something. Once you see it in somebody's face, the description for that trait will apply to each person you meet who has it. Zap! From now on you can read the Secrets of any face.

Earlier I joked about how kids see reality so clearly that magic tricks don't work for them. As you see faces more clearly, you also will see through illusions. It's a kind of magic that works better the older you get.

Q. God help me, I'm about as observant as a slug. Sure I want to read faces, but will I be able to?

A. If you're observant enough to read words on a page, you're observant enough to become a face reader. Think about this: Until face traits meant something, what reason did you have to notice them? It's like regular reading. Before you became literate, letters like b, d, p, and q were just lollipops. Face traits, themselves, are a kind of alphabet. Once you learn them, you're ready to read. And once you master this form of literacy, you'll be amazed at how effortless face reading can be.

Sometimes I'm hired to entertain at parties, pitted against a live band or a square dance, and still the face reading goes on. I've lost my voice, trying to squeak above the music. But I haven't had trouble eyeballing face traits or communicating their meaning. Face reading is like other skills in life. We're observant about what interests us.

Q. On behalf of all your students who are artists, I have to object. Color is such a beautiful thing about faces, all of the shades. It's God's paintbrush isn't it? Why not include it in your system of face reading?

A. On the receiving end, it's nice to be admired by an artist like you. But for every pure heart that's bedazzled by the sheer beauty of your skin tones or hair color, aren't there dozens who use the shade of your skin as an excuse to categorize you, then not really see you at all?

Q. How about looking at color even if we never say a word? Why shouldn't we keep on loving those colors?

A. By asking you to eliminate color as something to look for in face reading, I'm not saying never to enjoy it the rest of the time. You can paint people as nudes, too, but surely you don't ask everyone you meet to disrobe, just to enhance your artistic pleasure. Think of physiognomy as going on a short-term Color Fast. When you disrupt your normal intake of faces as mostly color, you'll open up your ability to notice other equally beautiful things about the physical face.

How do you read faces now?

ANSWERS

1.   FALSE. Paying attention to your client's expression sure beats paying no attention at all. But you're more apt to *respond* to her emotions than actively change them. To turn a mood from negative to positive, take charge of the conversation by getting on that customer's wavelength. For instance, read faces for eyebrow shape and ear angles.

2.   FALSE. What exactly are beady eyes, anyway? The overall impression "beady eyes" could be triggered by any one of these: small eye size, close-set eyes, deep-set eyes, or puffs over the eyes. When you learn to interpret each of these traits, one by one, you'll discover their meanings, which are probably not what you expect.

3.   FALSE. Unwillingness to look you in the eye is not a reliable clue to dishonesty. Reasons for "shifty eyes" include shyness, sexual insecurity, and depression. In fact, Americans from different cultural backgrounds are sometimes taught to avoid eye contact as a mark of *respect*.

4.   FALSE. According to a survey in *Psychology Today*, 30 million Americans dislike their chins, but 60 million hate their noses. Here's a more vital statistic, though: According to my ongoing survey of client reactions, for 99% of people who learn the inner meaning of face traits they dislike, guess what happens? They gain a new respect for their physical faces.

5.   FALSE. By growing a beard, a man has the opportunity to change the shape of his chin. With face reading, what you see counts. And thanks to free will, our faces change in many ways. Beards are one of them. When a man covers his chin with a beard, he transforms it. Inner personality changes accordingly.

6.   FALSE. Anybody can be sexy—or not. (You've done better some days than others, haven't you?) Here's a more reliable way to read somebody's lips: *lipfulness* relates to self-disclosure. The fuller the lips, the more readily a person shares personal information.

7.   FALSE. Phrenology, which gauged IQ by reading the bumps on the head, was often used as a way to brand people as good or bad, and its accuracy has been discredited. Face Reading Secrets is used as a way to add depth to our understanding of people, not take it away; it has nothing to do with phrenology, superstition, or determinism. (Common sense tells you the front of a man's face ought to be a heck of a lot more informative than the back of his scalp.)

8.   ONLY IF YOU DON'T LOOK VERY CLOSELY. Although a few traits, like skin color and hair texture, may be enough for stereotyping purposes, ethnic similarities are not a significant part of Face Reading Secrets. When you learn to read faces properly, people look less stereotyped, more individual.

9.   FALSE. Such judgments are usually incomplete, misleading, or self-fulfilling prophesies. Improve your batting average, and with it the quality of your relationships, by reading faces.

10.   MAYBE. Society teaches us to look at faces in ways that are both limited and limiting. We're obsessed by coloring, complexion, wrinkles, expression. As you learn face reading, you'll probably find many things about your own face you never noticed before. And you'll discover that all of them are highly meaningful.

■■■

4. Eyebrows

All of us are familiar with the dance of small talk. We put strangers through their paces by discussing neutral topics like weather. Sometimes this is just a way to put people at ease. But for someone like you, I'll bet another agenda is going on as well: you sincerely want to learn about the person. If psychiatrists can use ink blots for Rorschach tests, why shouldn't you use a cloud? When you talk about obvious subjects like weather, it's a way to study less obvious secrets about human nature.

Especially because you're curious about people, I'm delighted to introduce you to eyebrows, which you can meet from now on whenever you face a new person. And you'll want to. One minute of brow reading can tell an experienced face reader as much about thinking patterns as one hour crammed with mere small talk.

Hair? Where?

Distribution of hair on eyebrows is a vital statistic. To read it, start near the nose, then work your way out toward the ear. Examine one brow at a time.

- **Starter** brows are the most common trait. They come on strong at the start, then fade away. By the end, you'll find scanty hair or none at all.
- **Ender** brows do the opposite. However much hair is in the eyebrow close to the nose, that amount increases on the way to the ear.
- **Even** brows show the same amount of hair from start to end.

Q. What if the brows are thick or thin?
A. That's a different category: amount of hair.
Q. How about whether the brow looks arched?
A. Oops, that's a different category, too: eyebrow shape.

Q. Well, how about the color of the eyebrows? Can't brows look fuller because they are darker?
A. Yes, but you, the discriminating face reader, are looking for one trait at a time, which is amount of hair. Coloring doesn't count.

Q. How about makeup?
A. Not to worry and, especially, not to wash! When you take a good face reader's look, you'll see through the makeup, believe me.
Okay, mirrors up, everyone. What do you have?

Distribution of hair reveals how a person handles details. The pattern that shows on one physical eyebrow parallels the pattern that will show with one real-life project.

Starter brows go with a *talent* for starting new projects. It takes a special kind of enthusiasm to get something new off the ground. The *potential challenge* involves losing interest after the project is underway. Until you learn the *life lesson* of balancing your drive for creativity with the steadfastness needed to do justice to your ideas, here's what's likely to happen:

DISTRIBUTION OF HAIR
(in eyebrows)

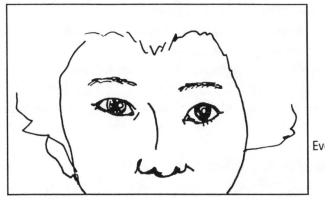

Even

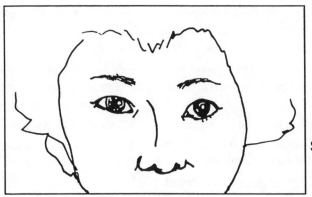

Starter

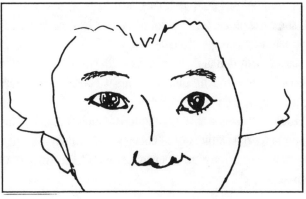

Ender

- If your brows thin out *halfway* across, typically you'll lose interest halfway through a project.
- If your brows thin out *three-quarters* of the way through, three-quarters of a project is as far as you'll get before you feel as though you're slogging through a marsh of boredom.
- If your brows fade out a mere *quarter* of the way across (as mine do, to the horror of Timothy Mar, as described previously), yes, you may have a major challenge with follow-through.

Why does this loss of momentum occur? On the positive side, people with starter brows generate more ideas for new projects than the other brow types. Once you've done enough of a first project to see where it's headed, your creativity draws you to explore the next project on your list.

Maybe the folks with these visionary brows aren't the best to depend on for details, but turn to them when you need a brilliant inspiration. Three innovators with starter eyebrows are Thomas Edison, Florence Nightingale, and Louis Pasteur. And although *Siang Mien* disparages people with starter brows, saying they won't accomplish much in life, Herbert Wexner hasn't done badly. He's the retailing whiz who created The Limited. Subsequently he acquired a few other little businesses, including Victoria's Secret, Lane Bryant, and Henri Bendel.

Explorer Matthew Henson's starter brows may have given him the initiative to put on all that cold-weather gear and head out on his polar treks. And, speaking of ice, let's not forget starter-browed Bonnie Blair, America's greatest female speed skater yet.

Strong starters can definitely be winners. They just have to try extra hard on their follow-through. They also might consider collaborating with the folks who have ender brows.

Ender brows represent a talent for following up on details. The farther you get into a project, the more details you can find to fix.

Can you, therefore drive yourself crazy as a never-ending perfectionist? Well, yes.

Procrastination can be a problem, too. Now, I don't mean all forms of procrastination, because there are so many varieties. Enders specialize in a particular kind of inertia. It's reluctance to start a new project. And it occurs because enders know what they're in for. People who have these eyebrows know there is no such thing as a quick 'n dirty job. One ender man of my acquaintance took three years before he was ready to straighten up his bedroom closet. Then it took him six hours. The job was perfect, of course.

Enders, once they hit their stride, are dynamite. Almost literally. *Siang Mien* notes that they make excellent soldiers—just the extra ammunition to have around during a drawn-out battle. This holds especially true if the eyebrows are set in a diamond-shaped face with prominent cheeks. You've seen such a face on TV. It belongs to William Schatner, brilliantly cast with these face traits, considering that his role is to protect the Starship Enterprise as long as the reruns endure.

Fortunately, ender eyebrows can be helpful in peaceful occupations, too. Witness the craftsmanship of cellist Yo-Yo Ma and of Kenzo Tange, the dean of contemporary Japanese architecture. And golly! Let's not forget to mention memory trainer Kevin Trudeau.

Gabriel García Márquez is the owner of strikingly thick enders. They riveted my attention when I saw a feature story about him in *The Washington Post*. Sure enough, the caption next to his face said, "The Novelist Has Spent a Lifetime Describing the Big Picture. And All His Days Getting Down the Details."

Incidentally, even if the only face category you ever learn to read is distribution of hair on eyebrows, I can guarantee that from now on you're going to enjoy your daily newspaper much more than ever before.

Even brows, the last item on this particular list, would never be left out by someone with this trait. You know, if you have these brows, how well you handle details. Ask Augusto Failde, who benefits not just from enders but from startup hairs, a relatively rare trait you'll read about later. Another even-browed success story is Norm Miller, who worked his way up from the ranks to become CEO of Interstate Batteries System of America.

With even brows, your thought process flows smoothly. You get an idea, develop it, and work out all related details. "No problem," you think. "No big deal."

But, of course, on The Learning Planet, there is a catch. It's a little potential challenge that comes up sometimes when a face shows talent: *a lack of tolerance for the rest of humanity.* We wonder what's wrong with folks who aren't good at something that's a snap for us. For instance, if you have even distribution of hair on your eyebrows, it's so easy for you to deal with details. Therefore, you may assume it's easy for everyone else, too, and find yourself grumbling: "What's wrong with that lazy slob—is he a space case or what?" or "How come she's always bogged down with details? Why can't she just handle them and move on, like I do?" Grumble, grumble—that's a lack of tolerance for the rest of humanity. Believe me, if others had your talent, they'd be glad to use it!

Q. How about pickup lines and other dating tips? Couldn't you have one different set for each of the brow whatchamacallits?

A. Ooh, your creative starter brows may be showing! For building friendships, yes, you can take a tip from distribution of hair. Discuss detail differently, depending.

Let's say, for instance, you and a would-be date are taking a stroll near a downtown construction site. Here are the lines I'd suggest you use to evoke fellow feeling from her eyebrows:

- To a starter: "What a lot of work. Do you think they'll ever finish?"
- To an ender: "I respect people who can tie up all the loose ends on a job like that, don't you?"
- To an even: "I hope whoever's in charge of that mess can find some competent people to clean it up afterwards. Have you

noticed how hard it can be to find people with what it takes to follow through?"

Q. You're not saying I ought to take all prospective dates by a construction site, are you? There's a bigger point, right?
A. The principle for getting closer to someone is to relate to that person's mindset. If you joke about the challenge that goes with a particular face trait, you're likely to win some points.

Congratulations, you've completed your first category. This is the sequence we'll follow with each subsequent trait: learn the choices within the physical category, find out what you have, then learn what each trait means, complete with examples. Before moving on to our next feature, let's pause to consider something all face readers notice, sooner or later.

Something VERY important

As your skill develops, you'll start to notice something interesting. The version of a particular trait on a person's face can be extreme or not. It's helpful to notice when a trait is a **VERY** because the more extreme the physical trait, the more extreme the inner significance. For thousands of years, face readers have used this rule:

■ VERY extreme physically = VERY extreme inwardly
To summarize:
■ VERY = VERY
By contrast:
■ Somewhat visible physically = somewhat important inwardly
And, for all practical purposes:

■ Only slightly visible physically = not worth reading. *

Q. Just how does a person learn to spot the VERYs?

A. First you'll get an idea of different traits from the illustrations and descriptions in this book. To make the transition to flesh-and-blood faces, look in the mirror and examine the traits on your own face. Next turn to other people, preferably several at one time, so you can compare their traits. Gloriously, it will dawn on you how different these traits can be.

For instance, you'll go hunting for eyebrow shape. Looking only at eyebrows, looking only at shape, leaping from one face to another, eventually you'll say something like this: "Aha! John has curved eyebrows while Jane's are straight."

Once you learned to identify traits, your next step is to develop an appreciation for VERYs:

Shape is one kind of VERY. To eyeball this kind of VERY, *compare two people* who have the same trait.

Eventually you'll see a face across a crowded room and it will thrill you—not because it's some enchanted evening and you've fallen in love at first sight but because you've found a second person in the room who has curved eyebrows. That means you can start comparing this person's amount of eyebrow curve with the amount of eyebrow curve on the first person. Whose eyebrow curve is more VERY?

Maybe Jack's curve more than Jim's. Some curved eyebrows, you'll realize, are extremely curved, while others fit into the curved category but curve only slightly. Bingo! The realization will hit you how a shape can be a VERY.

Size is another kind of VERY. Tracking this aspect may make you dizzy at first, as if riding backwards on a subway, because you won't just be looking for big versus small, but focusing on VERY big versus somewhat big—or VERY small versus somewhat small.

---

* Go on to another part of that person's face. Unless you're playing with Monopoly Spice Cards.

To see this most easily, *follow the proportions within one face*. So stop comparing Jack with Jim and do one face at a time. Let's say you have graduated to earlobes. Don't decide if Jim's earlobes are large by comparing them Jack's. He may have larger features all around. Instead compare the size of Jim's earlobes to the other proportions of Jim's ear.

You get the idea. Some faces don't show a single VERY, either of size or shape. At the opposite extreme is a face like Ross Perot's, where you'll find loads of VERY's. Some faces show 'em, some don't. It's that simple.

Eyebrows through thick and thin

Amount of hair on eyebrows means the overall amount of hairiness.

- **Thick** brows have oodles of hair.
- **Thin** brows have the opposite of oodles, whatever that is. Ah-dles?

Q. Since the brows could be starters or enders, which part counts for reckoning the amount of hair?

A. Look at the overall hairiness. Could you imagine the person you're reading with much thicker brows? Then the brows would be thin. If it's easier to imagine the person with much thinner brows, they're thick.

Q. What if you have no imagination?

A. Say it isn't so! Imagination is your birthright. Eventually, you'll claim it. Meanwhile, you can become a collector. Look at 15 people's brows, emphasizing the category "amount of hair." You'll build up your personal database mighty fast.

EYEBROW THICKNESS

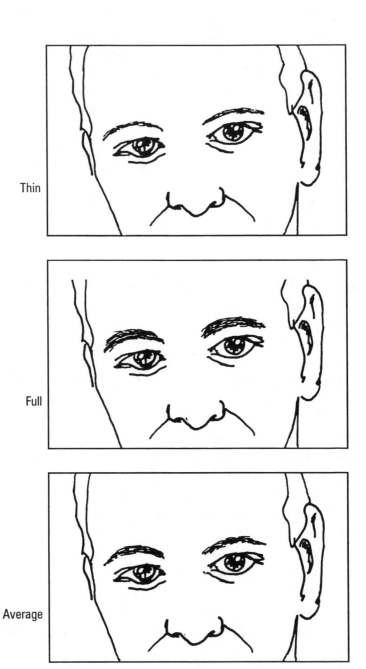

Thin

Full

Average

Q. What if you look at your eyebrow hairiness and find that you're not a VERY in either direction? What if your thickness is more of a sort-of?

A. Don't bother to read this trait for yourself. Skip it. Until you're experienced as a face reader, don't attempt to interpret any trait that is neither here nor there.

Amount of hair in a set of eyebrows shows how much detail a person feels comfortable handling at one given time.

Thick brows are a mark of intellectual power. Shucks. I know if this description applies to you you're probably casting your eyes downward and doing the time-honored squirm of modesty. If it's any consolation, people with thin brows can be just as smart. It's just that your personal styles are different.

Specifically, thick brows show that can juggle many projects at once. And if your brows are also even or enders, you'll keep details for each of the projects remarkably well under control. Furthermore, if you excel at debate (which would show in a persuasive lip trait we'll discuss later), you can cause jaws to drop in awe at your intellect.

Your only challenge is overwhelming people. Avoid telling friends about *all* the irons you have in the fire... your buddies/co-workers/employees may seethe with jealousy or faint from the blaze of your mental magnificence.

In the case of illusionist David Copperfield, thick even brows can be downright magical. Perhaps he has used them to set off fires; certainly there's no question about the man's ability to pull off fancy tricks, and plenty of them. Once a client with a less stellar career consulted me because he was thinking of getting eyebrow implants. Joe understood about the reciprocal relationship of the outer face and the inner self. He had high hopes for how he would change if he gave himself Einstein's VERY thick right eyebrow— which, indeed, must have been helpful for the great physicist's career. (Why not Einstein's left brow too? He thought he'd try one like Oprah's, enterprising man!)

I didn't recommend eyebrow surgery. (Can you see the TV commercials? "We're here from the Eyebrow Club for Men.") Whatever your eyebrow endowment, it has advantages.

Thin brows, for instance, go with mental intensity. Although you can push yourself to juggle a multitude of projects, you'll be more effective sticking to one at a time. Executive Steven Covey knows how to make best use of this talent. As the author of *The Seven Habits of Highly Effective People* he teaches how to organize and execute around *priorities*. That's the name of the slim eyebrow game.

Q. How would you apply eyebrow thickness to making a sale?

A. People with thick brows despise oversimplification. You'll gain their respect by presenting your sales points in great detail. By contrast, people with thin brows will prefer the simple version; they'll respect you more if you summarize what is most important.

Q. 'Fess up. Aren't you really saying that people with thick brows like mine are, quite simply, smarter?

A. No. Quality of judgment, originality of thought, and other facets of intelligence aren't involved one way or another. Thick brows mean a love for complexity. Thin brows mean a love of simplicity. Make the difference as simple—or complicated—as you like.

Eyebrow shape

Eyebrow shape refers to the geometric pattern formed by each brow.

- **Curved** eyebrows (sometimes called "arched") form parts of a circle.
- **Straight** eyebrows look, more or less, like a straight line.

EYEBROW SHAPE

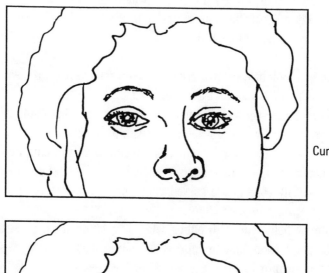

Curved

Straight

Angled

■ **Angled** eyebrows contain a hinge, where the hair changes direction. Most (but not all) angled brows have their hinges toward the end of the brow.

When you look at your own brows to see what you have, remember to look on the level, not upward or downward.

Eyebrow shape shows a framework for thinking. What kind of details do you, typically, notice when you're with people?

Curved eyebrows suggest that you specialize in noticing details about people's feelings. This shape is one of several facial signs of emotional sensitivity (others are curved chins, curved lower eyelids, and large inner ear circles).

Sensitivity helps you with either sales or relationships, especially when the person you hope to impress also shares this trait. The degree of curve is proportional to the focus on feelings. Owners of VERY curved brows are like magnets for emotions. In their presence, it's not enough to say "I'm fine. How are you?" You may as well come right out with your true emotions, because the owner of curved eyebrows is going to find them out anyway.

Q. Is that what you'd call our challenge with these brows, that we have radar for what's going on with people?

A. No, the challenge concerns what happens when your own feelings get hurt. Where do you normally shift attention to help yourself feel better? To feelings—so you keep coming back to the bruise. Compared with the other two eyebrow types in this category, it's much harder for you to lighten up during times of emotional upheaval.

Owners of VERY curved brows like yours are especially vulnerable. That's the price you pay for being so perceptive. However, it may console you to know that *Siang Mien* observes that such brows, when also thin, denote passion. This makes sense, considering that ultra-thin brows, with any eyebrow shape, suggest a one-track mind. Thus, VERY thin and curved brows suggest someone who is particularly effective at dealing with one project at a time, plus the object of attention is most likely a love relationship. So, yes! Of course you'll have passion potential.

Q. Isn't your interpretation sexist? After all, everyone knows that women have curved brows. Men's brows are straight.

A. Ouch! You've bumped smack into a stereotype. This one is easy to get rid of, luckily. Your assignment, if you'll choose to accept it, is to start looking at real people. Look them straight in the eyebrows.

Dancer/actor Gregory Hines, has brows that are both curved and full. His incredible tap dancing expresses both the sensitivity and the complexity you would expect from his brows.

Paul McCartney has VERY curved brows. More than the other Beatles he has specialized in composing love songs.

Straight eyebrows show a bent toward noticing ideas. It could be devotion to a cause, intellectual curiosity, or a "passion" for logic. Trekkies, remember Mr. Spock? In real life, actor Leonard Nimoy's brows are curved. But a stroke of makeup genius gave his character ruler-straight brows.

Q. His brows were cute, but isn't the term "genius" a little strong?

A. Maybe, but consider the character's major problem. Spock was supposed to be part Vulcan, part human, resulting in conflict over being excessively logical. This, in fact, is exactly the problem that can go with straight brows. A person can be so involved in gathering information, ideas, and discoveries that others may find him heartless.

Excessive heartfulness isn't likely a problem, at least. Recently I had a conversation with Blake, a six-year-old friend of my son's who handles disappointments with amazing self-control. Blake also shows VERY straight brows. I couldn't resist asking him, "What do you do when you're upset?"

"That's easy," he said. "I count to five. Then I say, 'There's no reason to be upset, is there?'"

Just try doing that if your eyebrows are VERY curved, rather than VERY straight!

Angled eyebrows show a managerial mindset. Part of the person is always detached, asking questions like these: "Is this conversation working for me?" "Is this person wasting my time?" "What do I really want from this situation and how can I get it?"

With a deep eyebrow angle, the person won't hesitate to jump in and change the flow of the conversation. Confrontation may even be considered fun.

Scary for the rest of us, though, isn't it? Even when the trait isn't VERY extreme, and confrontations thus are kept to a minimum, the potential challenge with angled brows is intimidation. Others can feel when they're being watched; detachment can arouse suspicion.

But surely that's a small price to pay for a big strategic advantage. Managers thrive on detachment. And the profession where Americans seem to value angled brows most is broadcast news, according to my fellow physiognomist R. Neville Johnson. On our news anchor teams, Neville points out, the heavy hitter is usually a man with at least one VERY angled eyebrow. I guess we enjoy the Peter Jennings and Sam Donaldsons because they revel in conflict. Watch how they spice up a broadcast by taking charge, interrupting and dominating, charmingly or otherwise.

Q. Even though I don't have that managerial mindset (being of the straight-browed persuasion, as you can see) a light bulb is going off in my head. We should be able to use brow shape to make sales, right?

A. You're right. It's a matter of viewpoint.

- For a customer with curved brows, emphasize feeling-related sales points: "Don't you feel bad when you have company over and they can't see a clear picture because your TV screen is so small? Imagine how you can relax once you own this home entertainment center."

- For straight brows, make sales points and *say* you're making points: "First, you'll notice that, on this screen, you can see the whites of their eyes when they shoot. That's because the system has Whoopdedoo." "Second, notice the clarity of the screams in this movie. That's the trademarked sound...." and so forth.

- For angled brows, emphasize how the product will help your client stay in control: "How would it change the way you entertain if you had a screen this size?" "What effect would it have on your guests?"

You see, every one of those eyebrow hairs can tickle your imagination. Keep the life in your sales pitches by seeing the life in your customers.

Eyebrow height

While you're catching sight of all the traits nestled in eyebrow hair, don't miss **eyebrow height**, the relative amount of distance between brows and eyes.

- Most people are **middlebrows**, with a space between brows and eyes that you will come to recognize as moderate.
- **Lowbrows**, by contrast, wear their eyebrows close to where they blink. With an extreme lowbrow, it looks as though the brows are tumbling into the eyes.
- **Highbrows** show a big distance between eyes and brows. At first

glance, folks with highbrows may look as though they are raising their eyebrows. They're not.

Q. How can you tell?

A. Time will tell. Highbrows remain uplifted throughout your entire conversation. Middlebrows and lowbrows relax eventually. To simulate the highbrow look, they will have to be heaved up again.

Q. Highbrow, lowbrow—aren't you getting a bit snobby in your terminology?

None of these terms, of course, refers to culture. Two examples from the world of music: Dolly Parton has highbrows while Victor Borge had lowbrows. No face trait, brow height included, dooms a person to listen to any one kind of music. *Eyebrow height* turns out to be about the timing for expressing ideas, a.k.a. verbal spontaneity.

Those of you with *highbrows* have a secret weapon. You're comfortable keeping ideas to yourself. Although you don't literally hide thoughts in the space above your eyes, you must use some kind of inner mental compartment—something that works like a safe deposit box for your plans, keeping you from blabbing about new business ventures until they are well established.

When an important conversation is coming up, you can rehearse it to perfection. No other brow height can match you in this regard. And keeping your own counsel has obvious advantages for every aspect of life. The only potential challenge is appearing aloof, but that may be a small price to pay for your strategic advantage.

Dr. Martin Luther King, for example, awed his followers. And in true highbrow style he created a huge political momentum before telling the world outright, "I have a dream."

A *lowbrow* would have talked about his dreams right from Day One. Lowbrows have a gift for spontaneous timing. Forget the advice, "Think before you speak." Rehearsing conversations in advance will make the

EYEBROW HEIGHT

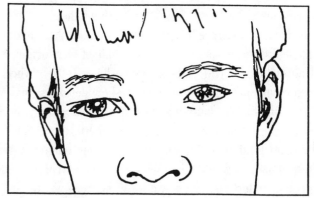

Middlebrows

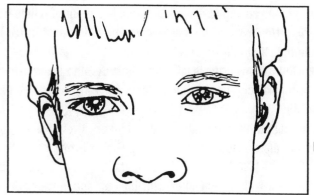

Lowbrows

Highbrows

words sound stale. If you're a lowbrow, you know your ideas are like bread that pops out of the toaster, best when fresh and hot.

You spontaneous talkers are happiest in occupations that value your ready wit, like talk-show hosting. Take the example of Merv Griffin, who capitalized on his spontaneous style to rev up his personal "wheel of fortune." Before making millions as a game show developer and talk show host, Griffin worked as an actor. In his autobiography, he recounts how he caused problems for his fellow performers. Since he could never resist ad libbing, his speeches came out differently every time. The rest of the cast would miss their cues. To an eyebrow reader, it's no surprise that Merv couldn't play a show the same way twice. The man's brows dip so VERY low, they're practically eyelashes.

Lowbrow boxing champ Muhammad Ali made a point of selling himself in the ring. His brow height suggests that he didn't think twice before proclaiming, "I am the greatest!"

One notorious TV lowbrow is talk-show host Geraldo Rivera. He has described his approach to reporting in this way: "I just try to react and put it on the air."

By capitalizing on his personal style as a thinker, Rivera has the right idea (however questionable his taste may be). Lowbrows of all tastes will succeed most when they specialize in immediacy, personal involvement, expressiveness. Just remember, blurting puts you in your power.

As for *middlebrows*, timing is not an issue. You're flexible. In one situation you'll practice beforehand. Other situations, you'll tell it like it is, no fuss, no muss. Your only question may be: "What's with these other silly people?" After all, you're not apt to have a lowbrow's problem of letting cats out of their bags. Neither do you run a highbrow's risk of appearing secretive. Your only problem is that perennial affliction of the fortunate, a lack of tolerance for the rest of humanity.

Q. I wouldn't dare to let myself blab. Lowbrow or not, I'd lose my friends or my job. Hasn't anyone told you that saying what's on your mind can be dangerous?

A. Because of something else that shows in your face, you have good reason to hesitate. Sometimes a person's talent for spontaneity makes quite a contrast to challenges that show in other face parts, and your VERY thin lips point to one of these challenges.

Others are a short mouth, vertical forehead furrows, puffs, and down-angled eyes. All will be discussed later, so you should have no trouble figuring out how to get around the challenge with using your gift for spontaneous speech.

Q. Is it complicated, then, figuring out how to use the brow height category to be better at sales?

A. Actually, it's simple. Pay attention to your personal style and go with the flow. Specifically, if you're a lowbrow, give yourself license to speak your mind right away, even though your boss hasn't told you to. Your boss may not be a lowbrow.

And if you're a highbrow, relax into the timing that suits you best. Don't force yourself to chat when your natural mode isn't chatty.

Special eyebrow talents

For special fun, check out the **special eyebrow talents** that can show in eyebrows.

- **Wild hairs** are the UFO's of the eyebrow world. They land hither and thither, sometimes long and curly, sometimes thick or differently colored than the surrounding hair. Their meaning is as intriguing as their appearance.
- **Contradictory hairs** grow towards each other, sometimes even tangling each other up.

SPECIAL EYEBROW TALENTS

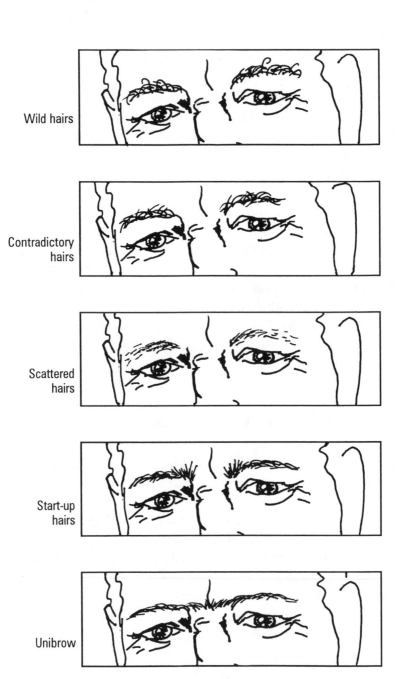

Wild hairs

Contradictory hairs

Scattered hairs

Start-up hairs

Unibrow

- **Scattered hairs** space themselves out like folks in Montana who feel their neighbors are encroaching if they live closer than 50 miles away.
- **Startup hairs** grow straight up, in contrast to the rest of eyebrow hair which grows sideways. When you find these special hairs, they will be at the start of a brow—hence their name. While, technically, most brows begin this way, seldom are the startup hairs numerous enough to form a definite clump.
- **Unibrow** is the affectionate nickname given when two eyebrows merge into one, due to hairy enthusiasm at the top of the nose.

Special eyebrow talents relate to unusual thinking patterns.

Q. Come on, isn't everyone's thinking unusual, at least to the person who's having the thoughts?

A. With these special eyebrow traits, we're spotlighting patterns that are relatively rare, even more than the sense of uniqueness that inspires each of us personally. I'll never forget the student who came up to me after I gave a meditation class at the University of Miami. It happened 26 years ago, but I can still hear her voice as she confided in tones of deepest secrecy: "I'm not like other people. I have thoughts that I never say. These thoughts are hidden inside my head."

Wild hairs symbolize wild ideas. They can result in outrageous creativity, as in the case of Albert Einstein or Warren Buffet, who has been named by *Forbes* as the richest person in America. Pluck such hairs at your peril.

Contradictory hairs show a more iffy talent. You have a high tolerance (maybe even an attraction for) conflicting ideas. Such hairs have punctuated the career of Donald Trump.

Scattered hairs represent scattered thoughts, a challenge to consistent follow-up. But the pattern of having extra, unrelated afterthoughts can be valuable, too. Einstein again--need I say more?

Do you know anyone whose *startup hairs* show? It's the look made famous by model/actress Brooke Shields. And it symbolizes intelligence. (Shields is, after all, a Princeton grad.) Specifically, visible starts to eyebrows symbolize conscious access to thoughts and feelings at an early stage. Before embarking on a new project, the rooted one will anticipate potential problems that would escape others. And the potential problem for the startup eyebrow wearer is being considered a wet blanket because of all the times you say, "Hold on. There could be a problem."

The fact that you generally happen to be right may not win you popularity points either. Still, it's an enviable trait. For instance, consider how Augusto Failde has benefited from his discriminating taste, launching one successful cable network after another, including Latino Entertainment Television.

As for *unibrows*, they go with nonstop thinking. Typically, the mind doesn't turn off. Insomnia may be a problem. Therefore, a unibrow is the one physical face trait I recommend changing. Tweeze. Try electrolysis. Or rent a tiny lawnmower. Because face traits and personal style are interconnected, calming down nonstop brows may help your mind to relax.

Q. Are you saying I could have insomnia because my eyebrows grow together?

A. An outer physical trait doesn't *cause* an inner aspect of personal style. It's a connection. More accurately, it's a **reciprocal relationship**, meaning that if you change the inner person, the outer face changes. (This long-term kind of change is by far the most common.) But when the outer face changes, through cosmetic surgery or so-called accidents, the inner person changes too, right away.

Q. What's an example of changing from the inside out?

A. Over time, depending on your choices and values, your face will physically alter in ways that correspond to your personal style. It's highly specific. For instance, when I became a mother, my eyelids changed in a way that reflected a new style of intimacy. As a face reader, you'll notice plenty of changes you never noticed before.

Q. Is it cheating if you pluck your eyebrows?

A. Whom would it be cheating?

Q. You know, the way you're supposed to look.

A. Short of wearing your head on your shoulders, your ears on your head, and so forth, I don't believe in a pre-ordained way people are supposed to look. What you wear, or create, on your face has an inner meaning. That's what you are learning to read. Faces don't appear by decree. They evolve.

Q. How about cosmetic surgery? Wouldn't you call that cheating?

A. Cosmetic surgery is a good example of how people change on the outside, then change on the inside.

Q. I always thought the changes from nose jobs and such were based on having people respond to you differently. You know: With a nice new nose you look better, people treat you better, you feel better.

A. There's more to it than that. When you change the outside, you alter the inside—and in ways you can predict by reading this book. A nose job will win you points from people who value a certain style of nose; however it could result in your passing up the chance to do work that is highly original and important. Cheek implants may make you look more imposing, yet adapting to your new power style may be more than you bargained for, deep down.

Even if the physical operation you pay for is completely successful, you'll have inner side effects. They're inevitable, due to the reciprocal relationship between the outer face and the inner person. Cosmetic surgeons have hired me to advise them on how their procedures change people on the inside. Surgeons worry about malpractice suits.

Their customers, I believe, should worry more than they do about the inner consequences of treating their faces as if they were Play Doh™.

Any cosmetic surgery will have unintended consequences. For many people, surgery is a good choice. For others, keeping an inner-based talent may be more important than the social aspect of looks. One thing's for sure: Cosmetic surgery is a far more complex choice than most folks realize. As a face reader, you'll be in a position to understand this more fully.

Q. With the kind of sales I do, I'm under a lot of pressure to look young. Like a lot of guys, I'm not into vanity but I am into reality, so I'm looking at plastic surgery for job security. What do you think?

A. Henry David Thoreau joked, "Beware of all enterprises that require new clothes." I'd say the same of any enterprise that demands a new nose. As a physiognomist, I flinch at the growing number of ads and magazine articles that tout vanity surgery. Nobody pays to advertise a contrary view; where would the profits be?

Well, face reading offers a spiritually-profitable contrary view. You can use physiognomy to counter being manipulated into making vanity surgery the norm. Consider this: once American women wore corsets, then they wore girdles; now we're free to wear neither, but have internalized them instead. The eating disorders we have today are bad enough; do we really want a future where women (and later, men) follow fads implemented by surgery instead of cosmetics?

Choosing vanity surgery contributes to this kind of social pressure. So, since you asked me, I recommend that you just say no. What kind of "security" can come from erasing part of your face? Cosmetic surgery helps to score social points but can be deeply confusing to the soul.

If you must change something, why not experiment with your eyebrows? There's good reason why they're the easiest part of the face to change. As you learned in this chapter, eyebrows relate to thinking patterns, and flexible thinking helps us stay young where it counts, inside.

5. Ears

Pssst... when you're ready for deep and useful secrets, turn to **ears**. No other part of the face tells you more about how a person designs reality. These profound patterns are largely unconscious. Nevertheless, I think you'll recognize yourself in the following categories.

You may even encounter a level of truth so deep, it's eerie.

Ear length

The first secret that ears can tell you relates to the category of relative **ear length**. Yes, I am boldly beginning this chapter with the hardest part first. How on earth can you gauge such a relative thing as ear length? Start with you, and you alone, in the mirror. (And look at your face on the level, remember, with that mirror neither higher nor lower than your face.)

Behold the length of your ears! Compare that to the length of your face, from forehead to chin. How many ears could you line up, end to end, before running out of face space?

■ Is your answer three or four? Then you have magnificent **long** ear length.

- Could you line up seven, eight, or even nine of the cute little things? Then you qualify as having **short** ear length.
- Should you be able to fit in five or six, you have irreproachably **medium** ear length.

Q. Oh, I know I'm not going to be good at this. In high school biology, I was the one who couldn't see a single darned thing in the microscope. What if measuring anything, even ear length, gives you the creeps?

A. Then forget the formal method. You're allowed to take a wild guess. Given the rest of the face, do the ears look large, medium or small? Whadda you think, huh?

Now is as good a time as any to remind you that face reading is intuitive, even the part that involves assessing the relative size of physical traits. When you feel like you're in the shoe store, stepping into their strange, guillotine-like device for measuring foot size, maybe your feelings are trying to tell you something: lighten up! Approximate size will do. Anyway, the more ears you read, the easier you'll find your way around the category.

Q. Big ears? You bet they're big. They're the bane of my existence. See how they stick out?

A. Get a grip. Just about everyone has developed a big emotional charge about some part of the face or other.

Consider this: a facial feature can be big in many ways. In your case, yes, your ears angle out a lot, which will make your ear angle trait a VERY. But we haven't gotten there yet. We're looking at a different category now—ear length. On you, that's medium ear length.

Q. Okay, you're right. The angle is the big part, not absolutely everything about my ears. Who would have thought?

Ear length tells you how much information a person unconsciously prefers to deal with. This amount, like ear length itself, is relative.

EAR LENGTH

Short

Long

Medium

Long ears go with exceptional listening ability. Examples are Lyndon Johnson, the "wheeler-dealer" president; humanitarian Albert Schweitzer; and multi-level marketing kings Richard DeVos and Jay Van Andel, who started Amway in their basements. (Their little company is now worth over $3.5 billion.)

What could possibly be a challenge for someone who soaks up information the way dry sponges slurp up water? Getting soaked, that's what. Maybe you're familiar with this challenge. Even after you've heard all you want to, unconsciously you can't stop taking in more. Eventually, you may become confused about what you, personally, think—as opposed to all the information that has seeped in from other sources.

Still, the advantages of long ears are many, including skill at crossword puzzles... or any activity that draws on general knowledge.

By contrast, people with *short* ears don't just collect information, they take it seriously, even personally. Overload alert, if you're in this group! Your potential challenge is to fill up faster than others. Then you shut down and stop paying attention, no matter what others may be trying to tell you. (It may be hard to admit to yourself that you might do this; if necessary, ask someone who knows you well for a second opinion.)

What's wonderful about your cute short ears, however, is how well you use what you do take in before shutting down. Charlie Chaplin never missed a trick that might be used by his Little Tramp. Peter Sellers' comedic ear has yet to be equaled. Michael Jordan has made excellent use of each perception that comes his way, whatever the sport.

As for *medium* ear length, you're flexible in the listening department. Sometimes you'll take in data like crazy. Other times, you'll choose to turn off. Overwhelm (at least regarding unconscious listening) doesn't weigh you down much, does it?

Nice flexibility, friend; your only related challenge is that small problem, a lack of tolerance for the rest of humanity. Why do some people stop listening so easily? Why do others make themselves sick and tired, they're so darned available to listen to anyone who crosses their path?

Q. So might this explain why my wife refuses to take our kids to the circus? She claims it exhausts her. My wife's ears are like little seashells.

A. Yes, the trait that shows in her ear length might be involved. What I'd recommend is that you take her at her word whenever she says she's tired of being with people and needs to be alone. Remember, it's not about you. It's between her and her ears.

Ear position

Now ear this.... Unless you're familiar with Jenkins' ear * or the self-amputated ear of poor Vincent Van Gogh (may you never have such a bad day!), you'll think of ears as having only one possible position: the side of the head.

Now, however, we're going to consider the possibility that **ear position** has more to it than either being near to your cheek or else, whoops, not. Where, relative to the rest of your face, do your ears hang out?

To see this category, you'll need to line up a couple of mirrors so you can inspect yourself in profile. You also may need, temporarily, to rearrange your hairstyle. (That goes for all the rest of the ear traits in this chapter, actually. By some strange, hairy coincidence, covered-up ears are hard to read.)

- Occasionally you'll find **high** ears, with tops that reach above eyebrows, while lobes don't reach the tip of the nose.
- More common are **low** ears, with earlobes below the tip of the nose. The top of the ear may not reach as high as the eyebrows.
- Most common of all are **middle** ears, fitting neatly between the highest part of the eyebrows and the nose tip.

* Reputedly it started a war after being cut off. Neat trick! For details, check your British history books.

EAR POSITION

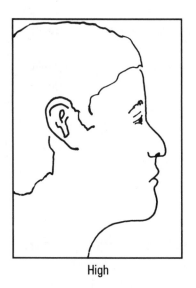

High

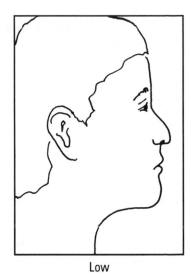

Low

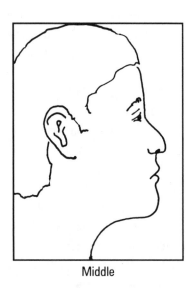

Middle

Q. Wow! I have no trouble seeing this trait from the front, but the peculiar thing is that I seem to be able to shift my ear position. Sometimes my ears seem high, other times low. Does this point to a special talent?

A. No, but you have discovered what's wrong with trying to read this trait from the front. Sure you'll see something. But it will hinge on how you angle your head. When you look up or down, you'll change your apparent ear position. That's why I recommend that, rather than approaching this trait frontally, you view it from the side. This enables you to use two stable reference points, the top of the eyebrow and the tip of the nose. From this perspective, ear position won't change.

Q. Golly, do you mean that this trait will never, ever change?

A. Expect it to possibly change, sure, but in a matter of years, not seconds. When ear position flips back and forth, either you're being treated to time-lapse photography or you're watching a cartoon. Otherwise it's because you're doing that naughty frontal ear viewing trick.

Ear position is one of the most practical traits you can read, especially if you work in sales. It reveals the speed with which someone makes decisions.

High ears signal a quicker than average speed for processing information. High ears belong to the legendary computer entrepreneur Steve Jobs, as well as to many who are most comfortable working at the rapid speed required to design computer software.

Sir Charles Drew, a leader in the preservation and storage of blood, had high ears and large fangs (just kidding about the fangs). Other innovative high-eared types are J. Craig Venter, who has spearheaded the use of automated gene sequencers; earlier-generation geneticist James Watson; town planner Sir Patrick Geddes; and composer Edgard Varèse. John Steinbeck used his high-speed intelligence for prolific novel writing; Wilt Chamberlain used his for basketball; Midori has used hers to become a violin prodigy.

Once upon a time, at a party, * my attention was flagged by a man with the highest-placed ears I've ever seen:

"Hello," I told him. "You have the highest ears I've ever seen. Do you learn things unusually fast?"

"Well," he returned without skipping a beat. "I do speak 18 languages."

What's the downside of up-hoisted ears? Impatience can be a problem. You get the point, already. Why doesn't the person who's talking to you keep moving? (Answer: she doesn't have high ears, so her mind doesn't move that fast.)

Another potential challenge involves your urgent need for closure. Yes, you make good decisions at top speed, but stalling drives you nuts. Sometimes you may rush into a decision based on incomplete data just because you can't stand waiting another minute.

Such a problem is not likely with your opposite ear type, a person with *low* ears. Here's someone who may have a slower speed of intelligence. Please note: The amount of intelligence may be just as great as with other ear positions. Timing and style are different, that's all.

Decisions are made in a different manner as well. More than anything else, low ears mean that your need for wisdom is greater than your need to get the decision over and done with. To put this a fancy way, you have enough inner strength to delay closure. Here's how I think you operate, at your best:

■ First you gather data, and the research phase may last for years if you have your way.

■ Second, you evaluate—a word that should be spelled *evalu-wait*—because waiting is exactly what other people will do while you make up your mind.

---

* No question about it, face reading is the ultimate tool for introducing yourself to others at parties. Instead of bursting forth with clunkers like "Haven't I seen you somewhere before?" you can intrigue your potential dates by saying "I've NEVER seen you anywhere before, or anything remotely like you—at least when it comes to your ear position (substitute whatever face trait you're ogling). I'm a face reader. May I tell you what I think it means?"

■ Finally you arrive at your decision. It had better be good because odds are you are never going to want to change it, not after all you've been through.

Yes, some might consider it a challenge that once you've made a decision you're about as flexible as the rock of Gibraltar. But here's what you can tell the grumblers:

In making my decisions, I emulate those who have demonstrated the political wisdom of low ears. *

As you high-eared readers may have guessed by now, being a low-eared decision maker can bring a distinct advantage. Say you've just been elected President of the United States. How nice! But as you'll soon become aware, the president's honeymoon with the electorate shortens every four years. With the press, you'll have, maybe, two hours of politeness before all your decisions are criticized like crazy. Therefore, consider the statistical advantage if you can make, say, *half* the number of decisions of someone with high ears.

Presidents Reagan, George H. and George W. Bush may have gained some advantage from their relatively slow speeds for making decisions. By contrast, consider President Clinton's plight, related to his high ears. Sure, intellectual celerity helped him earn a Rhodes scholarship, which set him on the path to high office. Later, when he was in the White House, high ears signaled eagerness to make quick decisions personally and politically and, with this, vulnerability to criticism.

As for you lucky readers with *middle* ears, no such problem for you, only the usual lack of tolerance for the rest of humanity, specifically the hasty and the dawdlers. Otherwise, flexible intellectual timing can be an entirely positive asset. Interestingly, it's very common among professional baseball players. Great ones come to mind, like Mark McGwire, Willie Mays, Rickey Henderson, and Orel Hershiser.

* Considering that most folks don't use the word "emulate" when making wisecracks, that ought to show 'em. If pressed, you can go on to list historical figures who have held high political office. Confirming my theory that low ears bring a teflon effect, consider that Reagan has by far the lowest ears of any American president. Only Millard Fillmore and Franklin Pierce come close to the Gipper's gravity of ear.

The talent that shows in middle ear position also has helped billionaire Marvin Harold Davis to earn a reputation for uncanny timing, whether in oil, Los Angeles real estate, or hot property from Twentieth Century Fox.

Q. Help me out here. I'm trembling on the verge of something important. How can I make use of knowledge about my own ear position to improve my relationships with others?

A. You're onto something here, all right. To benefit from reading this trait, first pay attention to what you've got. Then adjust to your friend's wavelength.

- Do your ears hang low? Give some friendly reassurance that you are, indeed, awake and listening. "There's a lot to think about here," you may say. When you're mulling over a decision, praise your buddy's patience. Remind him, if necessary, that you take a long time because you value the wisdom of a decision more than speed—which happens to be true. And it's nothing to sneeze at.
- Do your ears hang high? Then show mercy and slow down the lightning speed with which you leap from one edge of thought to the next, possibly leaving in your wake the rubble from a marathon of mixed metaphors.

Ear angle

How far do your ears stick out from your head? That's the clue to another secret.

One way to gauge **ear angle** is to use the pencil test. This demands a certain amount of coordination, but I'll bet you're up to it. First, poke your hair away from your right ear. Hold your mirror in your left hand

EAR ANGLE

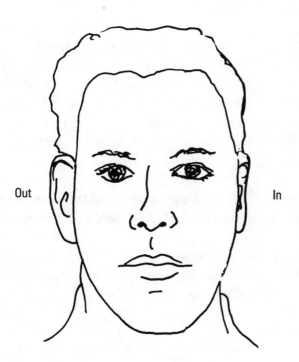

Out   In

so you get a straight-on front view. Grasp a pencil, point side upwards, in your right hand and slide it in back of your ear.

Did it make your ear wiggle?

- **In**-angled ears will flap to make way for the extra thickness.
- But **out**-angled ears don't need to move a bit. In fact, some ears are so VERY out-angled you could fit two, three, or even four pencils in back without making any visible difference. (It's not that I recommend this trick as a new form of storage. Even if your space for office supplies is limited, this test should be a one-time thing.)

Q. Easy for you to joke about my Dumbo ears! Has it occurred to you that talking about face parts like these could be insulting?

A. Actually I take face parts at least as seriously as you do, though with a different perspective. You, like many people, have been criticized unfairly or even ridiculed. Regaining your rightful self-esteem is part of your mission in life.

As for me, my mission includes freeing Americans from using animal names—unless referring to animals. Sensitivity to hurtful language has grown dramatically during our lifetimes, but one holdout is the nasty names folks unthinkingly use for face parts. Few people today would dare to make fun of someone for being physically disabled, let alone "handicapped," yet folks who are otherwise kind still make fun of so-called "Dumbo ears," "Chipmunk cheeks," or "Pug" noses.

Next time you catch somebody making fun of a face part, try the face reader's retort: "And did you know which magnificent talent goes with that trait?"

Face reading would be worth studying just for the sake of being able to tell them.

Ear angle relates to how a person deals with social conventions. Imagine that the airwaves in this room are filled with messages from society: "Dress like this." "Sit like that." "Don't speak until you're spoken to."

Social scientists can (and do) have a field day studying all the folkways that bombard us, often unconsciously. To understand where ears fit into this picture, think about all the people in the building where you are now. Imagine that everyone has been issued a catcher's mitt to pick up these messages—two catcher's mitts, in fact.

For people with *in*-angled ears, it's as though all messages are caught immediately and tossed, splat into the brain. Picture heads nodding, "Yes, I get it" along with each catch. Behaviorally, you'll find that ears laying flat against the head go with a strong desire to belong, even if that requires following silly codes of conduct.

Tact is one name for this gift. Social radar is another way to put it. If you have this ear angle, give yourself credit. Isn't it true that you notice the subtlest of nuances when it comes to manners, dress, and other ways that people display their Interpersonal IQ? Even when you choose not to conform, the choice is deliberate.

In work situations, you benefit from your ability to fit in wherever you go. Fit in? Hey, you *melt* in... like butter on fresh hot corn.

So what's the challenge? How deeply can you respect people whose manners are terrible? Even if you work at being non-judgmental, admit it. You'll see some weirdo acting out on the road or at a party and inwardly your respect for that person will plummet.

Maybe the real problem is that your own good manners come so naturally, it's hard to consider them a personal achievement. Face Reading brings perspective: other people aren't necessarily clods— they simply lack your gift. For additional consolation, know that your ability to fit in can greatly help your career, especially if you work in professions that are traditionally conservative.

Say you'd like to be a Supreme Court justice. In-angled ears appear to be a job requirement for its most conservative members, Rehnquist, Thomas, and Scalia.

Swing justices show some angle quirks. O'Connor's *right* ear—revealing personal style with work—angles in. But her *left* ear is an outie. Kennedy's ears are mixtures, too, in the opposite direction. Soon you'll read about the meaning of having two different things happen in one face. The simple interpretation for now is that both Kennedy and O'Connor send themselves mixed message when it comes to their desire to conform to the highly conservative Rehnquist court.

(Relatively liberal Supreme Court justices Stevens, Breyer, Ginsburg, and Souter have out-angled ears. Two apiece.)

Ear angles, like other face parts, don't dictate loyalty to any legal philosophy or political persuasion. They show the urge to *belong* to the social group of one's choice. Souter, the high court's most VERY in the NOT in-angled department also has extreme ear tilt—indicating an outsider's perspective on society. President George H., if only you had checked with me before appointing the allegedly conservative Souter! I could have warned you not to try to predict the man's opinions.

In-angled ear folk, when not doomed to a life of decorum on the Supreme Court, may delight in ridiculing conservativism. One of my favorite examples is Matt Groening, creator of "The Simpsons." Wacky, yes. But conservatives have praised this show as one of the best examples on network TV of strong family values.

In days of yesteryear, English novelist Charles Dickens also specialized in depicting eccentricity. When you register every social nuance, eccentricity is easy to notice, but you wouldn't dream of acting that way yourself. Although Dickens depicted eccentrics galore, his plots rewarded those whose actions conformed to Victorian values. Another in-angled example is W.S. Gilbert. His take on propriety produced the wittiest comic operas in the English language.

Of course, the staunchest conservatives find little humor in nonconformity. Traditional *Siang Mien,* I suspect, comes from conformists without a shred of humor. Its assessment of out-angled ears is typical: "People whose ears stick out have emotional problems. The closer ears stay to the head, the better."

Maybe that was true 3,000 years ago, in China. By all accounts, it wasn't a society that welcomed free enterprise. If you didn't adapt well to following protocol and position, you wouldn't go far. And that, in itself, could have been enough to cause emotional problems.

Today's American culture, however, *rewards* people with out-angled ears. Aside from the extreme example of Ross Perot, we can find many instances of self-made entrepreneurs who benefit from their reluctance to conform to society's expectations. Yes, it's true that *out*-angled ears go with behavior where you automatically do what you want. Only afterwards do you find out what other folks were expecting and deal with the challenge of damage control.

Cross-dressing, in-your-face, Dennis Rodman may not be your typical basketball star, but for someone with VERY out-angled ears he's not that unusual.

Business, even more than basketball, rewards nonconformity. For instance, the leading edge of American science today is study of the human genome. And right on that edge you'll find Human Genome Sciences founder William Heseltine. Long before it became fashionable to focus on this research topic, Haseltine followed his personal genetic (and soul-driven) programming for outies.

Other wildly successful entrepreneurs with out-angled ears are Jeff Bezos, founder of Amazon.com; Michael Dell, founder of Dell Computer Corp (right ear out-angled only); and David Kelley, producer of the iconoclastic hit TV shows "Ally McBeal" and "The Practice."

If you, too, have out-angled ears, even if you *appear* to fit in, you'll do it only as a deliberate choice, keeping up appearances because it serves you. Should you aim to flout convention, you'll do that even better. When it comes to other people's expectations, your motto could be that of Alfred E. Newman, "What, me worry?" The hero of *Mad Magazine* has been drawn with the perfect VERY out-angled ears.

In (more or less) real life, J. M. Barrie had the perfect ear angles for creating Peter Pan, the boy who refused to grow up and conform to expectations of an adult. Influential adult rebels include Mahatma Gandhi, leader of India's nonviolent revolution, and Robert Goddard, pioneer of American Rocketry. Would Ollie North have given the same shredding instructions if his ears stuck out less outrageously? If ever there was a man with Contra ears, it was North.

Folks with *moderate* ear angles, whose ears refuse to fit into the categories of in- or out-angled, don't have the previously described issues around conformity. At worst, they may come up with a case of lack of tolerance for the rest of humanity.

Ear proportions

How good is your sense of proportion? Let's apply it to ears, for a change. **Ear proportions** vary considerably from person to person. To evaluate them, you'll need to tell apart the following:

- **Earlobes**—they're simple. You recognize them already, especially if you hang earrings from them.
- The **outer circle**, farthest from the head, may be new to you. It's the easiest part of your ear to pinch, next to your earlobe. And the sensation when you pinch it * is quite different. Compare the two sensations and you'll feel what I mean.
- You may have to do a double take before you recognize your **inner circle**. That's an indented area that includes the earhole. To pinch the inner ear circle, you really have to grab onto the ear: index finger on top, thumb underneath—at the spot where the underside of your ear meets your head.
- Inner and outer circles are separated by a fleshy **border**, a curved ridge where the skin folds over like pastry at the rim of a well made pie. This border can be clear and well defined, or the

* Gently, please. No aspect of face reading is supposed to cause pain.

reverse. When you pinch it, again you'll have a different sensation. Because of the folded-over aspect, it's the *hardest* part of your ear structure (along with the outermost part of your ears, the edge of your outer circles).

Got all that? Practice poking the various parts of your personal ear equipment. Unless you have VERY out-angled ears, you'll need to tug on your ear and bend it sideways to hold it up to a mirror. See if you can find the border between your own inner and outer circles. Is the border defined or low-profile? And do you notice that the inner circle is next to, but not the same as, the hole that leads to your true inner ear? Borders are especially fun to notice. See if you can follow yours from the bottom of the inner circle, then upwards and around as it curves to form the shape of your inner ear circle.

Q. Have mercy! This reminds me of the maze puzzles I give to my kid.... Okay, I've followed the border around and I think I get the difference between inner and outer ear circles. But I'm wondering if my border counts as part of the outer circle, given the way it folds over?

A. Excellent point! Evidently you're a whiz with mazes. Nothing on the face is harder to understand, physically, than ear proportions, so more power to you. Once you have grasped the concept of ear borders, plus inner and outer circles, your next step is to develop an eye for whether the border becomes part of the inner circle or outer circle. In some cases, the border sticks out on its own, belonging to neither camp. It's then a protruding ear border. All these fine points are significant.

Q. You say they're fine points. Is it okay to skip them if we're new at this stuff? What if the in's and out's of ears are starting to make you seasick?

EAR PROPORTIONS

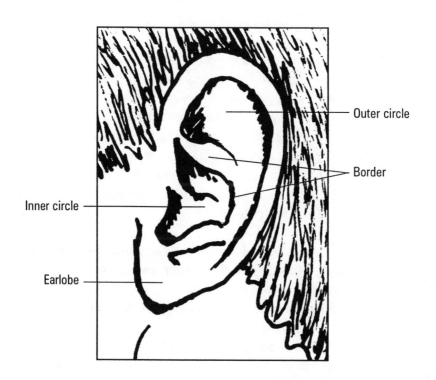

Outer circle

Border

Inner circle

Earlobe

A. Sure. Skip this section until you reread the book. Otherwise, here come the facts of life about **ear circle proportions**.

- **Large** inner circles generally go with **small** outer circles. After all, there is only so much ear space to go around.
- Conversely, **small** large inner circles go with **large** outer circles.
- Or the inner and outer circles may have **equal** proportions.

Okay, what's going on with *your* ear circle proportions?

Ear proportions are worth the trouble it takes to find them because they tell you about unconscious ways a person sorts through reality.

Yes, being human, we make reality manageable by specializing in different layers of it. (People who don't do this successfully live in a state of chronic overwhelm and may even be diagnosed with autism, schizophrenia, or other forms of mental illness.)

Most people, however, sort through reality in a pretty consistent manner. Although unconscious that we are doing this, we do it well. In fact, we do it so well that most folks assume their version of reality is It: The One True Reality. Nevertheless, face readers have the privilege of discovering different realities. We can even discern, straight from ear proportions, which reality a person is likely to believe in most.

Here's how: *Inner circles* symbolize paying attention to subjective reality, like feelings, spirituality, and philosophical belief. *Outer circles* symbolize paying attention to so-called "objective" reality, like facts about who did what, when it happened, and where. Newspapers cover objective life. Literary magazines and the like are about the subjective version.

Who typically writes for the more arty publications? Often it's folks with *predominant inner circles*—they are the world's poets, artists, and philosophers. For these deeply sensitive people, events tend to be metaphors. Think of John Bradshaw's efforts to popularize the concept of the Inner Child. Someone with equal and opposite ears might bluster: "What child? Heck, you're 40 years old if you're a day."

So you'd rightly expect huge inner circles on a W.B. Yeats or a Bertrand Russell, not a George Washington. Our only President yet with larger inner circles than outer was Franklin Delano Roosevelt. When he created programs named New Deal and Social Security, even his language was symbolic. How appropriate!

The potential challenge with this trait is being too self-involved. You may not believe in "reality" much, apart from your interpretations. For instance, consider this story from one woman whose outer circles are so small, they're practically non-existent:

"When I was five," Sally said, "I told my mother in no uncertain terms: 'If I'm not interested in people, they're not even in the room, and that's that.'"

Nobody likes to be ignored. Someone with VERY predominant outer circles will find it hard to respect a person who doesn't believe in objective reality.

Predominant outer ear circles reveal a practical talent. Think of Mark Victor Hansen, the motivational speaker who put anecdotes into *Chicken Soup for the Soul*. Or more picturesquely, bring to mind Betty Edwards, the art educator who encourages students to look before they put pencil to paper, avoiding stored up symbols and shortcuts by *Drawing on the Right Side of the Brain*.

It's not all roses and still-life arrangements, though, having big outer circles. Inner life may not be valued. Remember when presidential hopeful Michael Dukakis debated George Bush? When questioned about how he would react if his wife were raped, Dukakis stunned the nation with his unemotional response. But nobody would have been shocked if they had taken the precaution of reading his ears. I've never seen a more VERY example of predominant outer circles.

Like politicians, professional athletes depend on their objectivity, and large outer circles are common, for example, home run hitters Babe Ruth and Ted Williams. Jockey Steve Cauthen belongs to this group. Off the playing field, a great example of objective-dense ears is explorer Thor Heyerdahl, part athlete, part explorer, part anthropologist.

Although folks with big outer circles may have a challenge with sensitivity, they can enjoy tremendous career success because of their grip on facts. Practical, scientific, organized—these are just some of the attributes that go with this trait.

Some of the ears you'll meet will have *balanced inner and outer circles*. This represents a talent for balancing inner and outer experience. If you have this, friends may have praised you as a sympathetic listener who makes use of what you understand in a practical way.

Dr. Abraham Maslow had ears like this. Fittingly, he's the psychologist who decided to focus on well adjusted, self-actualized subjects rather than the mentally ill. He realized that peak experiences (moments of deep subjective fulfillment) can become a basis for achievement in objective life. Maslow heard the whole story.

Q. How about borders? Mine seem to be on partial vacation. Should I worry?

A. *Ear borders* represent a wall that separates inner from outer life. *Low-profile borders* aren't a cause for alarm, but they do go with taking objective matters personally, also assuming that your personal truth has universal meaning.

Q. Unlike most human beings? Come on, don't we all do that?

A. You're right, but folks with low-profile borders do it more often. No doubt James Thurber's wacky creation, Walter Mitty, had no ear borders at all. Like Mitty, you're stuck with an active imagination. You may as well learn to enjoy it.

A real-life example of someone with low-profile borders is James Whistler, famous for his painting "Arrangement in Grey and Black," better known as "Whistler's Mother." The artist's ears had very deep inner circles with blurry borders, which may explain both his problem with extreme over-subjectivity (which resulted in some unfortunate lawsuits) and an incredible sensitivity to nuances of light (responsible for his fame as an artist, which has endured even longer than the interminable lawsuits).

By contrast, Ralph Waldo Emerson's ears had large inner circles with VERY *well-defined borders*. His essays proved him to be a master at validating spiritual experience, then helping people to change contexts and apply their wisdom in objective, practical ways. Reread his essays with that in mind and you'll find example after example.

When the circle on the inner ear is defined with a VERY clear border, it's like sticking a big sign on the lawn to your house to warn passers-by, "No trespassing." Upon that person's psychic property, public and private spaces will not overlap. Such people are good at keeping their personal insights in perspective. Poet T.S. Eliot had huge inner circles protected by monumental borders. This built-in sense of propriety helps you to understand how he could have written a line like, "Do I dare to eat a peach?"

Inventor Alexander Graham Bell's VERY large inner circles were protected by an equally well defined border. How appropriate for the man who invented the phone to set a personal example of deep, but balanced, listening ability.

As for the rare talent of *a protruding ear border*, that symbolizes fascination with the boundaries between what is public and what is private. You can watch this talent perform right on your TV screen. Just tune in Oprah, the woman who has single-mouthedly transformed talk on TV. Consciously or not, her mission has been to take closely held feelings and broadcast them loud and clear.

Denial won't work around this lady. No wonder Oprah Winfrey has chosen guests whose revelations smash viewer's boundaries. From her own life, alone, Oprah has opened up taboo topics like sexual abuse, teenage pregnancy, and the ups and downs of weight loss. Her gift is to create a forum where it is safe to acknowledge the truth, even if it seems complicated, inconsistent, or messy.

Q. My grandmother told me that large earlobes mean wisdom, and that's why the Buddha is often depicted as having them. Someone else told me that large earlobes mean long life. Which of these is true?

A. The truest part of anything you've said is that, yes, Buddha statues and paintings traditionally have long earlobes. Regarding the longevity part of your question, I'd suggest you research that one at your nearest morgue. As for the wisdom part, large earlobes do mean wisdom but small ones do too. Each specializes in a different kind of wisdom.

For interpretation, it helps to know that *earlobes* symbolize paying attention to physical reality.

Q. But I thought the outer ear circles were about facts. Isn't that the same thing?

A. Actually, no. *Factual reality* is about the heft, the sweat, the mass, the clothing, the data about being in physical form. For instance, Taylor has a hobby of collecting baseball statistics. These are facts—outer ear circle stuff—about home runs, stolen bases, and the like.

By contrast, *physical reality* is about the visceral side. What's the condition of the Astroturf? How do the uniforms fit the players? Who on the team seems to take the greatest delight in spitting? Because of the earthy associations with earlobes, let's reserve a fuller discussion of them for the chapter on "Sex."

Asymmetry alert

Now that you've uncovered two sets of facial mysteries, both eyebrows and ears, you're no longer a novice face reader. Information is starting to peek out at you from formerly unexpected face parts. Believe me, your fun is just beginning. Because your sleuthing ability is growing apace, now is a good time to enhance your skill with an extra nuance. Who would have guessed this: Some of your most impressive detective work will involve something many people either feel secretly ashamed of, put in denial, or simply don't see.

To put it bluntly, people are lopsided.

Before you gasp in horror and run for cover under the nearest paper bag, you need to know that, to a face reader, lopsidedness isn't necessarily bad at all. It's fascinating, revealing, and very human.

Face readers even have a technical term for it: **Asymmetry**. Category-by-category and trait-by-trait, faces show differences between one side to another.

Yours does, for instance. Prove it to yourself. Look in a mirror. Cover one side of your face with a sheet of blank paper. You'll see one eyebrow, one eye, half a nose, a nostril, and so on.

Now move the paper to cover the other side.

The right and left sides are so different, they could belong to different people.

Q. How come? And should I run, screaming, to the nearest plastic surgeon?

A. I hope not. *Asymmetry* is not a mistake. Rather, it's a process of evolution. Baby faces almost always start off symmetrically. Change develops gradually. And every change has a reason.

The *right side* of the face represents your public self—the first impression you give to others and how you come across on the job. The *left side* reveals your private self, how you function with family and friends.

Babies don't have much privacy. Even drool becomes a shared experience. But as we grow up, we gain skill at presenting ourselves in public. One word for this is sophistication. Another is self-protection. During your teenage years, I'll bet you learned the hard way to develop a social facade. Confucius, or somebody, should have said:

"He who wears a heart of mush on his sleeve will be treated like someone whose shirt has oatmeal stains."

Therefore, out of self-defense, people develop two different ways of acting: a public version, for strangers; a private version, for friends.

And here's the fascinating part. Where your two styles differ, precisely at the corresponding face part, that's where your face shows asymmetry. As an advanced face reader, you'll want to compare and contrast. But for now, the way to deal with asymmetry is far simpler:

- For **business** applications, read the right side of the face.
- For **relationships**, read the left side.
- And always, when you're viewing right and left on a person opposite you, remember to flip sides mentally, as if shaking your right hand with the other person's right hand.

Q. Am I the only one to feel overwhelmed? Now there's asymmetry on top of everything else. How will I manage to put it all together?

A. With patience—although I'm giving you an overview now, developing skill at face reading takes time and practice. Here's the typical sequence of development:

1. Shift gears with the intention to do a face reading. You'll look for physical face trait information exclusively, so let distractions (like lipstick on a woman's teeth or your favorite old face watching habits) wait until later.

2. Slow down enough to look at one trait at a time. Don't panic. Ears and other face parts will usually wait for you in a rather serene manner.

3. Read one side of the face at a time until you feel ready to deal with asymmetry. For business applications, read the right side of the face. For relationships, read the left side.

4. Notice if the trait you have found is a VERY, which will have bearing on your interpretation.

5. When you feel ready, add depth to your reading by taking asymmetry into account.

Q. Would you please give an example of interpreting asymmetry?

A. Okay, let's consider you. Did you ever notice your different ear positions?

Q. You mean there's a reason why my eyeglasses tend to slope to one side? Gee, you're right. The left side is low, with the lobe hanging below my nose tip. But the right side is high, above my eyebrow. Oh my God! So, what gives?

A. When you work, you make good, quick decisions. But for personal choices, like whether to stay at that job, or where to live, I think you're much more thorough before you make up your mind.

Q. You're absolutely right. Funny, the way I always explained it to myself was that with decisions about my personal life, I'm spending my own money, so I'm more careful. What do you think about that kind of interpretation?

A. Life has many levels. As a thoughtful person, you can't hear that too often. The advantage of interpreting from the face reading level is that the meanings add up. Just as you want to accumulate savings in your personal bank account, face reading helps you to accumulate wealth in your wisdom account.

From now on, when you meet people with low ears, you will understand something about how they make decisions. This will hold true whether they're rich or poor, big spenders or not. (And the spending aspect, you'll see, actually shows in a different part of the face.)

Since you work in sales, it will help you to learn how a prospect makes decisions, how that prospect spends money. Assuming that "people are careful when spending their money" isn't necessarily true. It's an aspect of personal style, and wouldn't you love to learn how to read it! It's in the chapter on noses. Before then, however, let's examine the most popular feature.

6. Eyes

The **eyes** have it. Most of the time they win our attention, whether we're gazing romantically at the color, searchingly for the expression, or with the soulful look we reserve for no other face part. Yet often the way we look at eyes limits us. How about the truths we can read if we gaze slightly elsewhere—*around* the eyes? The dry parts, the structure, can tell us a great deal about different aspects of outlook. The "truth" written all over someone's face with expression may cover up, or even blatantly contradict, the long-term truth of physiognomy.

Maybe it isn't romantic, but if I were single now, I'd go shopping for eyelids as much as for what I could find in the eyes of eligible partners. And, regardless of your marital status, you people watchers will find this face part a perpetual source of fascination—you'll be able to contrast expression (which people work hard to control) with a deeper reality (one that most people can't control at all).

Especially since you already believe you know pretty much all there is to see about eyes, this chapter will make you think twice, maybe even blink twice. Most amazing of all, you'll probably discover things you've never noticed before about *your own eyes*.

Lower eyelid curve

The amount of your **lower eyelid curve** is something a person seldom notices, unless you're a woman out to make a killer impression by swabbing each tiny lash with mascara. When you study this underrated aspect of eyes, you'll find you can change the shape of this curve pretty easily. Grab a mirror now and see for yourself by acting in two short movies, which I will direct.

Movie #1 is a melodrama called "The Pride, the Glory, and the Hideous Death." You, regardless of gender, have been cast as the beauteous heroine.

It's a silent movie and the plot is pretty predictable, so let's skip ahead to the final scene. Alas, you have been tied to the railroad tracks. Staring upwards, you happen to see the villain who is bending over you, ostensibly to gloat over your plight, but mostly so he can hear you deliver your final speech.

Emote as you read it:

"You beast! I trusted you. Now I realize how you lied when you said you wanted to use the deed to my property as a dance card. Of course, I refused your proposals of marriage. But you, terrible cad that you are, ignored my refusals. And then, even worse than confiscating my home and cattle, you did the unpardonable. You read my diary. How you will suffer some day, you ink blot upon the name of humanity!"

There you go. Dainty fists clenched, glare at the villain for all you are worth. Feel the indignation, the rage.

Good.

Now freeze your expression. Stare into your mirror and look at the shape of your lower lids.

Take a deep breath, shuffle your face parts back to normal. Now prepare for Movie #2, pleasant family entertainment entitled, "Lustful Frenzy in Valentine-ville."

This time you get to have your very own gender and sexual persuasion. Once again, you're the main love interest. And once again the plot is rather predictable: A meets B. They fall in love. They fight. Now their bubbling passion seems doomed to a low simmer, possibly evaporating to the point where it will burn the saucepan.

Not to worry, here comes the thrilling conclusion. Most unexpectedly, your co-star declares a hidden, hopeless, and passionate love for you.

Oh, did I mention that you get to pick your co-star? Make it someone droolingly adorable. Imagine yourselves together, neatly locked in an embrace. You're in the ideal position to probe for specifics:

So imagine yourself staring into your love interest's eyes as you ask the all-important question: "You say that out of all the people you've known in your life, I am the most attractive, intelligent, generous, kindly, creative, and downright saintly? Tell me, when did you first begin to notice?"

Emote, remember, emote.

Freeze. Check out your lower lids this time.

These scenes have much to tell you about lower eyelid curve. *

- Under certain circumstances, such as those in Movie #2, you can make goo-goo eyes. **Curved** lower eyelids can curve to such an extent that the English language has a special word for it, "rounding" your eyes. Generally you'll do this when you are infatuated, curious, vulnerable, or otherwise emotionally wide open.
- Under other circumstances, such as those in Movie #1, you can narrow your eyes. This creates **straight** lower eyelids, which reflect wariness, hurt feelings, suspicion, shyness, or other emotions related to a general emotional closing down.

* Assuming that you can scrunch up your face a lot when you act. Otherwise it's back to acting school for you, I'm afraid.

- Yes, there are advantages to eyes that are completely round (10 on a scale from 1-10) but there are equal and different advantages to eyes that are utterly straight (1 on a scale from 1-10). The same goes for eyes in-between, which are **moderate** regarding degree of straightness versus curviness (5 on that 1-10 scale).

You'll want to know the meaning of these different amounts of eyelid curve because each of us has a default setting, much like your favorite word processing software. Sure you could switch to 30-point type. But probably a more standard type size, like 12-point, will pop up on the screen and stay there until you change the setting.

Similarly, your lower eyelids have a default setting. And that's what I invite you to read right now. (As always, remember to look on the level. It's important.) On a scale from 1 to 10, how would you rate the amount of curve in each of your eyes?

Eyelid curve, when you're not acting, reveals how far you extend yourself emotionally to new people in your life. Your score for the right eyelid curve relates to how you deal with strangers at work. Left eyelid curve symbolizes your dealings with new people who are being auditioned as friends.

Curved lower eyelids mean the range of scores from 8-10, with 10 being the VERY version. With curved lids, you have great willingness to "be here now" with other people, even total strangers. Everyone is treated as a potential teacher and you're eager to learn.

President FDR exemplified this openness. He is said to have known 5,000 people on a first-name basis. If you look farther back in history, you'll find equal openness in gravity man Isaac Newton; Heaven and Hell expert, the poet Dante; and Noah Webster, America's first dictionary maker. A more contemporary example is Argentine human rights activist Adolfo Pérez Esquivel; he has managed to keep himself open despite all the suffering he's witnessed.

LOWER EYELID CURVE
(on a scale from 1–10)

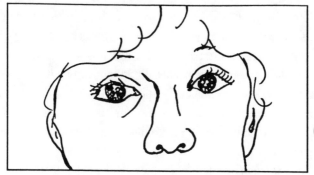

Curved (10)

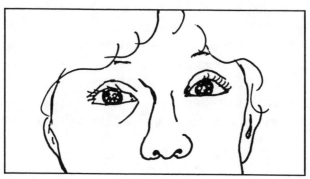

Straight (1)

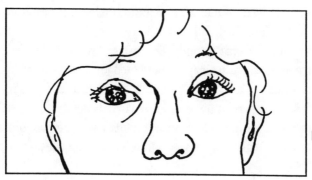

Moderate (5)

So what's the catch with curved lower eyelids? Gullibility, sometimes. Vulnerability, always. Childlike sensitivity can hurt, which is why so many people have chosen to grow out of it. Conservative spokesman William F. Buckley, Jr. has remained a 10, which helps account for his charm. Even when he wittily dispatches an opponent, one has the sense that Buckley has taken a gentlemanly appraisal prior to the verbal onslaught. He's even taken the unusual move, for a secular man of letters, of writing autobiographically about his life as a Catholic. If that isn't opening himself up, what is?

Those with *straight* lower eyelids have a distinctly different set of strong points. First, they tend to be excellent judges of which people would waste their time. Typically they evaluate strangers within seconds—and most get the gong. Why invest in people who are emotionally draining, scatterbrained, and so forth?

The challenge, of course, is the risk of being not only shrewd but judgmental. Some perfectly good potential buddies may wind up in the trash. But, back on the plus side, you'll never have a more loyal friend than a 1. If you have a set of straights, you know why. Given the tough test you ask people to pass, anyone who makes it will be a friend for life.

Just for fun, ask the next 1 you meet: "How long have you had your best friend?"

"Since kindergarten" is a typical response.

Ultra-conservative Rush Limbaugh may display the style and charm of a pit bull, but could his following be any more loyal? Probably they're taking their cue from him, a 1 in the lower eyelid department. Other politicians with VERY high wariness are former President George Bush and his Vice-president Dan Quayle, both noted for their extreme loyalty. The Reverend Jesse Jackson's lower eyelids may take you by surprise because the upper part of his eyes is so curved. Before face reading, one assumes that the top and bottom eyelids have equal amounts of curve. Maybe they start out that way, but this is a highly flexible part of the face.

When Hillary Clinton became First Lady, her default lower eyelid curve was a 10. By the time of her husband's second inauguration, a critical public had worked hard to whittle her down to size; Hillary's social trust certainly downsized... all the way to a 1.

Since politicians are criticized so routinely and brutally, it's not surprising that they develop such wariness. More surprising is how many movie stars who are specifically known for projecting an image of sexiness, are similarly unapproachable. Kim Basinger, Madonna, and Cher all follow the wary example of Marilyn Monroe.

As for men, you might expect to see "1s" on tough guys like Clint Eastwood and Jack Nicholson, but you may have to look twice to realize you're seeing it on screen idols like Tom Cruise and Luke Perry.

People with *moderate* eyelid curve (4-7) have learned some practical skills for self-protection. They close themselves off during the testing phase with new acquaintances but remain open enough to let through more friends than the folks with high wariness. Psychologist David Burns' claim to fame involves developing a Feeling Good strategy to combat low self-esteem and depression. He teaches clients openness, yes, but to a *manageable* degree. This follows the example of his moderate eyelid curve.

Q. How could I use knowing about eyelid curve to help my social life? Being single, I can use all the help I can get.

A. Look at your own eyes and accept the strengths of your personal style.

- If you're wary, don't demand that you make close friends instantly. The only way someone with 1s or 2s can do that is by falling in love with a fantasy. People must earn your trust, which is a perfectly valid way to operate.
- Conversely, if you're at the high end of eyelid curve, know that you may be a pushover for love. Slow down! Also, it won't hurt to check on yourself occasionally to find out if you're carrying

around hurt from disappointing relationships. That tender heart
of yours may often need healing.
- With a mid-range curve score, congratulate yourself on your
social adjustment. Don't expect all your dates to have developed
the same relative ease at dealing with strangers. Look 'em in the
eye and slightly downwards. The degree of curve will help you
figure out how to pace the relationship.

Puffs and lashes

Remember Puff, the Magic Dragon? Despite the upbeat tune of this song,
dragons aren't generally famous for happy magic. That certainly holds
true for the dragon-like puffs of skin that emerge over some eyes. Like
any face traits, they symbolize talent but, more than most traits, they come
with a definite price to pay.

Most folks don't have **puffs**. Don't confuse puffs with more common
eye traits we'll discuss later: small eyelid thickness, single eyelids, and
deep-set eyes. Puffs involve extra wads of flesh that start beneath the
eyebrow and cover up part of what's beneath.

- **Low-level** puffs cut off a bit of the eyelid.
- **Industrial-strength** puffs have grown to such an extent, they
cover up part of the eye itself.
- **None** is what you probably have. Above the eyelids, all is clear.
And even on a day when the areas above and below your eye puff
out a bit, you don't have dedicated wads of flesh that fall into
your eyelids or eyes.

Typically, the cause of puffs is self-neglect due to focusing hard on
other people due to pleasing them, helping them, earning money from

PUFFS

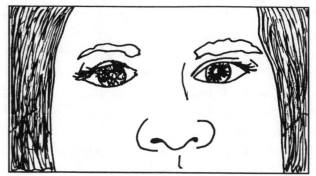

None

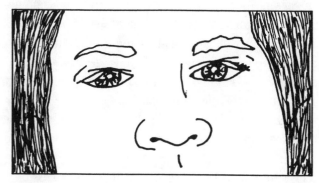

Low-level

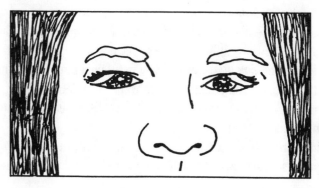

Industrial-
strength

them, etc. The puff-wearer does not pay attention to humdrum little messages from her physical body, such as "Give me a nap" or "Let me out of this office. I need to play."

When personal neglect continues, puffs expand. The whoppers that cover up part of the eyes symbolize a blindness to personal health. If you're tempted to run to the cosmetic surgeon for a fix, why not consider healing the cause of the facial cascade. Undiagnosed allergies, for instance, often create puffs. Acupuncturists, nutritionists, and homeopaths may help you listen to what you body has been trying to tell you, then remove the attention-getter. (This holds true whether your eyes show puffs above or bags below.)

Apart from possible health warnings, *puffs* demonstrate high involvement in career. They mark a person with drive, someone dedicated to achievement. Ironically, the challenge related to puffs may also contribute to success, though few would choose it voluntarily: irritability. One example is Joe Girard, called the world's greatest salesman in the *Guinness Book of World Records*. His face suggests he's a charming guy, but not someone to suffer fools gladly.

For *low-level* puffs, read low-level fussiness. Small mistakes meet with low tolerance. This can correct overly permissive management styles. Critics balance out the airy-fairies. So thank goodness for managers like Nancy Austin and Tom Peters, co-authors of *A Passion for Excellence* and co-wearers of modest puffs. Perhaps a somewhat larger version of fussiness helped actor John Wayne bluster his no-nonsense way into America's hearts.

Is it a coincidence that the pages of *Forbes* are peppered with photos of slightly puffed-up millionaires? I think not, but if you want to verify the effectiveness that goes with feisty puff temperament, why not ask their accountants? You could tell them you're a college student doing research on the Puff-erati. You need to know if their tempers match their bulging bank accounts.

An even more mixed blessing comes in the form of *industrial-strength* puffs, so huge that they may impede vision. Taken in context with the rest of the face you may read a passion for high achievement along with chronic cantankerousness, defensiveness, even selfishness and dishonesty—or you can read *all* of them in the face of Rasputin, the sinister monk from Russian history. In American history, many of our least popular presidents had their imperial puffs: Andrew Johnson, Ulysses S. Grant, Grover Cleveland, William Howard Taft, Benjamin Harrison, Martin Van Buren, and Millard Fillmore.

Admittedly, some folks wear even the most extravagant puffs with style. The puff point of view may be essential to their charm, disguising the unglamorous aspect of how hard these people push themselves to succeed. Would Sir Arthur Conan Doyle have created the same Sherlock Holmes if he hadn't, himself, been so darned persnickety? Imagine that rascal W.C. Fields not complaining! During World War II, Winston Churchill's puff-powered rage was a source of comfort to millions. Today politician Pat Buchanan's fans almost swoon when he exercises his curmudgeonly wrath. And ball playing legend, Cal Ripken, Jr., reassures fans every time he comes to work, puffs and all.

Q. Without meaning to sound sexist, it seem to me that men have the lion's share of these puffs. Is there some kind of feminine equivalent?

A. Grumpy, grumpy—all of us have our moments. And you're right that men are more likely than women to carry puffs, especially the industrial-strength variety. However, my sex makes up for the difference with **fine eyelashes**.

Eyelashes for humans are like whiskers for cats—sensitive probing devices. In the case of humans, we don't use them for physical probing. Nonetheless, our lashes reflect on our physiological sensitivity. The finer the lashes, the more high strung the person.

Anyone with *fine lashes*, therefore, is wired to react, whether it's being jumpy as a cat or barky as a dog... and I specifically mean one of those nervous-looking tiny dogs that can endear itself as a "lap dog" but also *bites*. Not that these ladies will necessarily chew you out, literally or figuratively. But a hair-trigger temper is possible. The talent is sensitivity, which can play out in delicious ways, too, such as a gourmet chef's exquisite sense of smell or an artist's eye for color.

Width of set

Here's your chance to figure out a face trait. Given that distance between the eyes relates to.... wait a minute. First you need to distinguish the physical trait.

- **Width of set** means how close eyes are to each other.
- **Close**-set eyes live like near neighbors, on either side of the nose.
- **Far**-set eyes space themselves more like distant cousins, one living close to the edge in one direction, the other located at the opposite coast.

Keep in mind, most people's eyes have **average** set, a trait that's not worth reading. So avoid squinting, mumbling, and desperately measuring with your fingers to get a fix on eye set width. Unless the closeness or distance seem obvious, go on to a different trait (also to a different person, considering that the stranger whose face you've been fingering probably has fled the room in fear for his life).

So what do you think about the meaning of *width of set*? It's got to be something about conscious outlook, but what?

Give yourself one point if you guessed width of perspective.

If you're calculating like fury exactly how many millimeters go with which eye set distance, you don't win any bonus points but probably you can give yourself credit for having *close*-set eyes. As if people with any other eye set would stop to calculate millimeters!

WIDTH OF SET

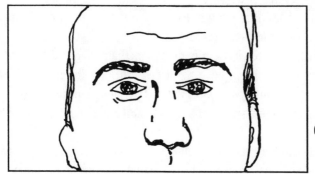

Close

Far

Average

When you have close-set eyes, you have a talent for focusing. With any aspect of life that matters to you, nobody notices more details. Nothing/nobody escapes you.

Therefore you excel at crafts or any medium where discriminating focus is required. Examples are silversmith Paul Revere, wordsmith William Safire, children's book author Dr. Seuss, unrelentingly gorgeous-voiced singer Kiri Te Kanawa, and amazing guitarist Mark Knopfler.

Golfers hear this: the only example I've found of a face trait linking to excellence in any human endeavor applies to your sport. It's hard to find a top-notch player without at least one close-set eye. Examples include Tiger Woods, Nick Faldo, Jack Nicklaus, Amy Alcott, and Tommy Armour.

Q. Why golf? Why eye set?

A. Golfers have to discriminate fine nuances of turf, of slope, of club. Guess the super-fine distinguishing abilities of close-set eyes pay off. Of course eye-set alone won't guarantee success at golf. You also have to be able to hit the ball.

What's the downside if you have these finely-tuned eyes? Beware of criticism. Since you're so good at noticing things, once you start finding fault, you'll be a champ. "Seinfeld," the hit TV show, generates a lot of fault-finding jokes, thanks to Jerry Seinfeld's VERY close-set eyes. Watching his show is one of my favorite forms of laughter therapy, but would I want to be one of his dates? Would you?

Q. How about relationship advice for those of us who have taken the plunge and married a close-set eyed husband?

A. Marvel at his surveillance ability. Laugh at the rest.

As for spouses and others with *far*-set eyes, don't expect yourself to cross every "t" crossed and dot every "i." You're doing well if you remember the periods at the ends of sentences. If anything, far-sets space out, especially if they also have starter eyebrows. Their special excellence, though makes any apparent vagueness worthwhile.

Here are rangers who see the whole forest. Think of far-set, far-sighted William Fulbright. When Chairman of the U.S. Senate Foreign Relations Committee, he took the lead in criticizing foreign military intervention. Margaret Sanger was far ahead of her time when she saw the need to make birth control available to all women. Author Marilyn Ferguson is the premier philosopher of the New Age. Far-set imagination has also guided science fiction writer Arthur C. Clarke, who's most famous for "2001: A Space Odyssey." Kurt Gödel is a cult hero for some mathematicians. Editor Grace Mirabella has created America's most graphically creative fashion magazine.

People with far-set eyes can display a knack for setting precedents. Composer Ellen Zwilich set one by being the first woman to win the Nobel Prize. Paul Laurence Dunbar became the first African-American author to gain national renown.

Q. Which would you say are more romantic, folks with far-set or close-set eyes?

A. Far-set-eyed dates are more romantic but close-set mates will be more practical. Assuming your romance lasts a while, that quality's going to seem pretty lovable, too.

Depth of set

While scanning eye set in the mirror, **depth of set** is worth your notice as well. You'll see it most easily from a profile view. Locate the eyebrow. Beneath it you'll find the top of the eye socket. Aren't you glad our eyeballs don't need to be changed periodically like light bulbs! When yours was installed, how did it angle?

- At one extreme you'll find **deep-set** eyes.
- The other extreme is **protruding** eye set.
- Most eyes have **average** set, a trait not worth reading.
- Glazed eyes? That's probably temporary, brought on by excessive time with **TV** set.

Q. Aren't bulging eyes caused by a thyroid condition?
A. They can be. Remember, though, how life has many layers. What matters, from a face reading perspective, is what a trait means. So take concerns about protruding eye set to a doctor but, as a physiognomist, learn about the trait's inner significance.

Depth of set reveals involvement about participating in a conversation. This is one trait that often carries over directly into body language. The owner of *deep-set* eyes enters into conversation casually, as though leaning back in her chair as she listens to you. This mirrors a laid-back involvement. I'll warn you, it also reflects a fine bluffing ability, and not only for poker.

What's the person's inner reaction? That's anyone's guess. Behind that polite smile, your friend may inwardly be rolling her eyes. Typically, the secret emotion ranges from cautious skepticism to silent ridicule. Deception isn't necessarily involved. There's just a gap between what is felt inwardly versus what is outwardly acknowledged. Ever wonder, for instance, what goes on inside the head of deep-set Regis Philbin on "Who Wants to Be a Millionaire" while he asks, "Is that your final answer?"

Q. Great, so how do I sell to someone with deep-set eyes?
A. Get to the point. Back it up with as many facts as possible.

Certainly you wouldn't have wanted to waffle in front of the inscrutable anthropologist with the deep-set eyes, Margaret Mead.

Or talk a lot in front of reporter Bob Woodward—maybe he went too far in ridiculing Hillary Clinton's strivings for spiritual peace when in the White House, but any physiognomist could see a clue to his

DEPTH OF SET

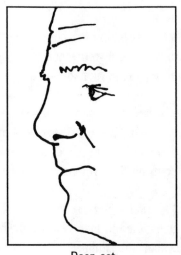

Deep-set

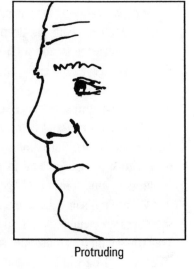

Protruding

Average

modus operandi. Deep-set eyes reveal that, as an interviewer, he would be an expert at hiding his journalistic intent.

The challenge with the deep-set trait is letting too large a gap develop between the facade you're projecting and your inner truth. Once the distance grows too great, you'll lose an important kind of authenticity.

On the positive side, this eye set goes with a reserve that can be especially helpful for sales or other aspects of business. I love this comment from Samuel Curtis Johnson, a man of deep-set eyes and personality who was instrumental in diversifying the products of his family business beyond Johnson's Wax:

"We are polishing the floors and furniture, cleaning the rugs, killing the bugs, sweetening the air and waxing the old man's car. And whenever you get bit by a mosquito, remember, I'm smiling."

Sure he'll be smiling on the inside, but will he let it show? By contrast, someone with *protruding* eyes will let you see every inch of that smile. High involvement is the preferred style. Body language may show someone literally sitting on the edge of her seat. If you are in this category, you know that your obvious interest in the conversation is nothing compared to your inward state. You are truly, totally, there in the moment.

Here's a word to the wise: when someone with this high involvement speaks, don't interrupt. Otherwise your words will be interpreted as an Archie Bunker-like command to "stifle yourself." Yes, with her protruding eyes, actress Jean Stapleton was perfectly cast as Archie's wife, Edith, in the classic TV sitcom. An even more famous wife, former first lady Barbara Bush, showed a high degree of personal involvement when talking with people. Her engaging personality reflected her inner engagement.

Eyelid structure

If you were with me in a class right now, I'd invite you to join me for a break. In my Professional Face Reading program, one of our more diverting entertainments is to walk around the room making faces at one another.

Compared to kids, grownups can be pretty inhibited about smooshing eyebrows towards cheeks; taking full advantage of the 700 or more ways you can shove out your lips; exploring the special humorous effects you can create when you let your fingers get into the act of face making; plus the delicious assortment of ways to twist your lips and nose over to one side of your face.

Try making some faces right now, if you dare. It's good for you. Don't believe what you may have been told as a kid, "Stop making that face or it will freeze forever."

However, even the most uninhibited grownups are not likely to experiment with one face-making trick that is exceedingly popular with kids. Next time you're driving with a back seat full of youngsters, watch in the rear view mirror when they start to turn their eyelids inside out. *

Adults generally ignore eyelids. Many of us haven't yet noticed that **eyelid structure** for humans comes in two different varieties. Yes, when you observe how the skin of the eyelid folds down from the brow bone, you'll find either:

- A **single eyelid**, where the skin connects directly from brow bone to eye, or
- A **double eyelid**, that folds over to form a crease at the eye socket.
- Should you find a **center** fold, you're looking at pinup pictures in some magazine. Honestly! Come back to face class.

* Considering that we adults don't have kid's super-flexible bodies, this form of recreation might be dangerous for us; I am NOT recommending that you try this trick, no matter how liberated your inner child.

EYELID STRUCTURE

Single
eyelid

Double
eyelid

Q. Does what you call single eyelid contribute to having slanted eyes, like someone from China?

A. Here's the funny part—though typically a discussion of "slanted" eyes is more offensive than humorous if your eyes are the ones under discussion—so-called "slanted" eyes aren't slanted at all. At least, they're not slanted more than eyes that aren't dark brown and set off by skin with a golden undertone. Assuming you're human and own a couple of eyes, they are going to have an angle or slant. So do your mouth, your eyebrows, and other face parts. When we look more at eye angle in a later chapter, you'll discover that angle is entirely different from eyelid structure.

When you're brave enough to look, really look, past the stereotype, you'll find nothing unusual at all about eye angle in your Asian-American buddies. What you may find is a single eyelid fold. In America, as compared with certain parts of Asia, having this trait puts you in a minority group. If you're not in this group, stare discreetly at the next person you meet who is. You'll finally come to terms with the trait.

Eyelid structure, like eyelid thickness (which we'll turn to next) gives information about your outlook on life.

Single eyelids go with the expectation that, as a person, you're closely connected with others. By contrast, *double eyelids* go with the assumption that you are, first and foremost, separate.

Is it a coincidence that America, the land of the free and rampantly individualistic, was founded by people with double eyelids? Is it a coincidence that Japan, a country founded by people with single eyelids, places such value on getting along?

Ooh, I think not.

The single eyelid way of life may involve nuances of bowing that would seem mighty alien to your typical native of Washington D.C. Ever since the Declaration of Independence, community has not been our top priority. Yet Asian-Americans have enriched this country for generations, and a single eyelid perspective is a highly significant, though often ignored, part of this contribution. Ask the great enlightened sages from every corner of the world. We are family. Awareness of oneness with others leads to a profound kind of spiritual learning.

Still, living with single eyelids doesn't necessarily mean that you have attained total spiritual enlightenment. Instead you may, frankly, feel burdened by all your obligations to older brother, middle brother, younger brother, and so forth (each of which has a separate name, with social distinctions to match, in certain Asian languages). According to no less an authority on Japan than humorist Dave Barry, as described in his meticulously documented sociological work, *Dave Barry Does Japan*, the most popular karaoke number in the entire country is a song made popular by Frank Sinatra, "I did it my way."

Of course, this could be a novel idea to someone with single eyelids. But if, like Sinatra, you have double eyelids, the concept of doing things your way hasn't been trained out of you much since the age of two. Not do it your way, how come? And what, pray tell, would be the inducement to do things anyone else's way?

Think of the hit song made popular by Frank's daughter, Nancy: "These boots were made for walking. And that's just what they'll do. One of these days these boots are going to walk all over you."

There we go. Ah, the refreshing independence of double eyelid folk. Sometimes, yes, we can carry this too far, with or without the boots. As East meets West, and double eyelid intermarries with single, let's see if we can create a world where we value both styles, individual spunk and collective kindness.

Eyelid thickness

Marching merrily into eyelid territory, yes, there's more! When you've found an eyelid with a double structure, you can observe one more

EYELID THICKNESS

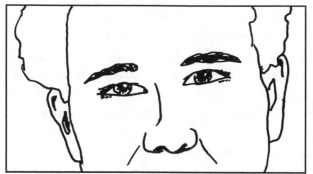

None

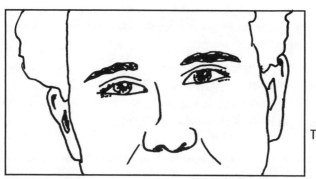

Thin

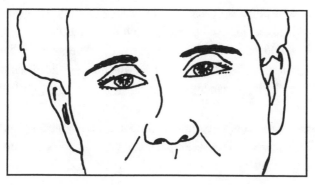

Full

interesting category: **eyelid thickness**. Notice the fold of skin directly above the eyelashes. (Usually eyelids with a single fold do not have eyelid thickness, but never say "never.")

Anatomists have a cute name for the stuff on the inside of eyelid thickness: *tarsal plate*. Yes, the previously-mentioned kid trick of turning eyelids inside out involves playing with the plate—an expression which was not designed to be used in the same conversation as "eyes like saucers."

We adults have very adult reasons to explore eyelid thickness. To recognize it, cosmetics can help. As you stare in the mirror, imagine that you have decided to slather your eyelids with a gaudy blue shade of eye shadow. How much will show when you open your eyes?

- To get your money's worth from the paint, you need **full** eyelid thickness.
- Cosmetically, what happens to your investment when you have **thin** eyelid thickness? Not much.
- If you have **none**, don't even bother with the eye shadow. The glop is only going to show when you blink.

Q. Hey, are you talking about bedroom eyes? The thick eyelids are bedroom eyes, right?

A. Show me a person whose eyelids are so large that they contain room for an actual bed (even sideways) and you're showing me a person with a major physical problem. But speaking metaphorically, as if a person could enlarge his eyelids enough to hold furniture, yes, some of our eyelids would have enough room for beds. Others would barely manage to fit in a clock radio. Let your imagination go wild. Then look at yourself (on the level, remember) and see what you physically have.

Eyelid thickness could be the most important face category to read if you're single and seriously seeking a mate. It shows how a person defines intimacy.

Look at that cute-faced single on the other side of the room. Sure he's attractive but, if you were to dance together through life, how tight would he hold on? Or to put it in the universal language of love (which is food, obviously) will he stick to you like peanut butter or barely hold on, like spaghetti cooked *al dente* and flung against a wall?

Every couple has some degree of attachment, but it can range from one extreme to another. Some pairs are so pairfectly fused they live in a state of perpetual closeness. Other pairs are nearly sepairate: they do an adult-sized version of parallel play. Lucky you, the physiognomist! To find out if a new date will want to share his castle, you don't have to take him to the sandbox to watch how he plays. Eyelid thickness will tell you any time, anywhere.

Full eyelids are rightly nicknamed *bedroom eyes*, assuming you re-alize that sex has nothing to do with this kind of bedroom. The trait means that relationship-wise, you'll be expected to *live* in the bedroom. No escape for you to the formal living room or the private bathroom. Forget it! You'll dwell close in, up front and personal.

Having full eyelids, yourself, means that you both give and demand closeness. Depending on your partner's needs, closeness could create a glorious relationship—or a nightmare. Emotional generosity of this order enables you to learn profound lessons about compassion and kindness. The trap to avoid is co-dependence.

Remember the O.J. Simpson trial? His photo, the morning after his wife's murder, showed a fascinating change to his left eyelid. It bal-looned out to humongous proportions, suggesting an inflamed need for closeness. His right eyelid stayed its normal size. When Simpson al-leged that he couldn't have wanted to kill his ex-wife, I thought about the statement made by his puffed-out, mate-related eyelid, "My rela-tionship with a significant other is severely inflamed." Coincidence that his wife had just been murdered? Alas, probably not.

Long-term full eyelids, with intimacy style to match, show in the face of the president who held America together, even if it took a Civil War to do so. My favorite story about Abe Lincoln concerns when the

Confederacy finally surrendered and he was asked what music he'd like the band to play. Lincoln asked for "Dixie." If that didn't sufficiently show his intent to stay close, what more could he have done?

Full eyelids also have reflected the personal style of civil rights leader Martin Luther King, Jr. The Rev. Robert Abernathy, once King's best friend, has them, too. As does Donna Shalala, Secretary of Health and Human Services under President Clinton. All these advocates for social justice have treated people with the tenderness expected from large right eyelids. In politics, I especially relish a story about Patsy Mink, a Hawaiian congresswoman with VERY large eyelids. She financed her campaign for office entirely through contributions and volunteer help. Her best volunteer? Her husband.

Speaking of husbands, Show Biz personalities Eva and Zsa Zsa Gabor have been well endowed with eyelids. Through the years, both have remained enthusiastic re-marriers.

In the arts, large eyelid thickness showed in the styles of novelist Boris Pasternak and composer Giacomo Puccini. By contrast, another operatic composer, Richard Wagner, had VERY small eyelid thickness. Fittingly he chose plots involving Norse gods in a slugfest rather than Puccini's typical tragic lovers. Having moderately full eyelids, especially during my teenage years, I survived high school by playing the first side of La Bohème on my record player. I'd listen to the love songs, have a good cry, and get on with my homework. (I still don't know precisely what happens in the remaining five sides of the opera, but I've heard rumors of death for poor Mimi.)

Q. So what are the thin eyelids about? I've been in suspense long enough considering these are MY eyelids you're talking about.

A. A me-first attitude shows in this trait. Replay your question for a clue.

What makes *thin* eyelids wonderful is independence. No matter how much you love, how deeply, how long, you remain your own person.

Tell your loved one, right from the start, that you always need plenty of emotional space—your own things, your own life, and probably your own room.

Follow the advice of women with VERY small eyelid thickness: Melody Beatty, author of *Co-dependent No More*, and Robin Norwood, author of *Women Who Love Too Much*. (What were their eyelids like before they got to the point where they wrote their bestsellers? I wouldn't be surprised if both of them had much fuller eyelids.)

Choosing a mate, or business associate, eyelid thickness can help you maintain the personal boundaries with which you feel comfortable. Perhaps to balance his Compassionate Conservatism*, President Bush has appointed a high proportion of individuals with little or no eyelid thickness: Vice-President Dick Cheney; Colin Powell, Secretary of State; Condoleezza Rice, National Security Adviser; Donald Rumsfield, Secretary of Defense; Tommy Thompson, Secretary of Health and Human Services; Karen Veneman, Secretary of Agriculture, and Laura Bush, wife. I'd agree that, if your heart overflows with compassion, it's wise to align yourself with people who have clear personal boundaries.

One more tip for those with small eyelid thickness: Even if you love Country Western music, don't believe in its worldview—according to which a true, feminine woman must be a sobbing, co-dependent wretch. Not all Country greats have eyelids as huge as Dolly Parton's. Many have teensy eyelid thickness, or none at all: Vince Gill, Faith Hill, Willie Nelson, George Strait, Shania Twain, and Trisha Yearwood.

The small-eyelid-thickness way of loving accentuates independence if you also have that built-in sign of clear boundaries, a double eyelid fold. If you have this combo, count your blessings: You can thrive as a loner. You can become a self-made success. If married, you can dearly love your spouse without a tad of co-dependence. And emotional self-sufficiency will help you take responsibility in all your relationships.

---

* Compassion shows in Dubya's speeches, not his face. Besides large eyelid thickness, he lacks either curved lower eyelids, down-angled eyes, large inner ear circles, curved eyebrows, harmonizer cheeks, or the Mark of Devotion. Oops!

Q. What do you mean, "take responsibility"? For what, having skinner eyelids?

A. Let's say you and your wife are going to a Halloween party. What will you wear? If your eyelids are large, you'll most likely wear something to please her. When she announces you'd look good as Mickey Mouse, you may inwardly cringe at wearing the ears but you're probably used to compromising a lot because your outlook is "Us" more than "Me."

So you go to the party as Mickey. Frankly, the results are disappointing. Although your wife, dressed as Minnie, receives compliments all night, people see you and move on, mumbling "Been there, done that."

What will you, the large-eyelidded person, then learn from this experience? You've pleased your wife, which may be what counts most. However, when it comes to choosing a costume, you haven't learned much because you weren't especially involved in choosing it in the first place. All the creativity, social calculation, and such, were done by someone else.

By contrast, what would you say as a thin-lidded husband if your wife sidled over and said, "Darling, please be Mickey"? Forget it. You're the one whose going to be sweating under the fake mouse fur. You're the one who'll be bumping into walls with your oversized ears.

So for you to say "Yes" will mean only one thing. You, personally, choose to be Mickey. Assuming that your costume flops, you'll have yourself alone to blame. Likewise with more serious situations and consequences, with small eyelid thickness you will weigh your lessons more objectively than if you were simply choosing to please someone else.

Q. My boss has large eyelids but VERY close-set eyes. He cares about us but the fault-finding ability you described is, also, right on. His motto around the office is, "Relax, everybody. I trust you to do things right." How can I sort out all these mixed messages without becoming utterly confused?

A. Balancing the complexity that shows in face traits is tricky, especially at first. Still, in the long run you'll be empowered rather than confused. More knowledge will bring you more choices.

Extra compassion is one of those choices. Maybe your boss says what he says precisely because he is trying to overcome the critical tendencies that show in his close-set eyes. A major conflict for him, I'll bet, is balancing the great closeness he feels to people with an equal, opposite tendency to watch everyone closely and critique the heck out of them.

Q. So he's not necessarily a hypocrite?

A. Don't label him a hypocrite unless you have no better choice. Seeing people as bad brings consequences which are the opposite from what happens when you are willing to see people as basically good. Besides, when someone with VERY close-set eyes learns the life lesson around being critical, he could become the most nonjudgmental person you've ever met.

Q. Does hypocrisy show anywhere, by the way?

A. One form of it does. Be wary of someone with VERY large eyelid fullness on one side and none on the other. For example, a large lid on the left and none on the right shows someone who is extremely attached to others in personal life yet has a business sense of self that is strictly "Me first."

Q. How about the opposite?

A. A VERY large right eyelid shows major (or, at least, apparent) closeness to people at work in contrast to a me-first outlook in personal life.

In either case, with this particular asymmetry I'd be wary. Neither type of eyelid fullness, in itself, proves hanky-panky. But the combination of both extremes in one face just might signal emotional trickery.

Detective work for face readers

What if you are hunting for truth? What if you want to use face reading to supplement all the other ways you test people for dishonesty?

Does any trait tell you for sure when someone is lying?

No, it's not that simple. But if you're willing to do a more complex form of face reading detective work, you can come up with highly useful information.

Lying shows when a person's expression dramatically contradicts a VERY strong trait. For example, if someone with the lowest possible score on lower eyelid curve comes across as excessively friendly, I'd wonder about an ulterior motive. Or if someone shows an extreme version of a mouth trait that we'll turn to later, reflecting that saying personal things is on a par with pulling teeth, yes, I'd be on my guard if he were to volunteer highly personal information or even (gasp!) gush.

Why? I would wonder. What could be the purpose behind all that emoting?

Several years ago a candidate for Governor of Virginia had a campaign photo that aroused this kind of curiosity. The man in question showed a tooth trait about killer instinct, the deepest level of competitiveness that can show in a face. (You'll read about this trait in the chapter on "Problem Solving.") This tooth trait showed clearly when the man smiled. Yet the expression projected in his smile was utterly opposite to the message of his teeth.

"Trust me to do whatever you say" proclaimed his boyish grin. "I'm meek and mild, your humble public servant."

With a different face, I might have believed it, but with those teeth, never. During that election, it happened that I was interviewed by a reporter with *The Washington Post*. Along with other face reading comments, I couldn't resist expressing my concerns about this candidate, who struck me as the proverbial wolf in sheep's clothing.The reporter laughed for a long time. "I have a friend who covers this guy and he makes it no secret that he loves campaigning. Just yesterday my friend heard him say, 'You know, I love the fight of the campaign more than anything else about it. I love a good fight.'"

Q. Do you recommend that we use face reading to sniff out dangerous people by looking for these contradictions?
A. Actually my answer is an emphatic NO. If you want warning bells to alert you of danger, you're better off with aura reading than any aspect of looking at either face traits, body language, or expression. *Aura Reading Through All Your Senses* contains three different lie detector tests, each of them easy to do and highly accurate.

The biggest danger to most Americans from crime doesn't come from criminals, though. Suspicion is a far worse enemy. One of the most common questions people ask, when they first learn about reading faces is, "Tell me how to spot a liar. Show me the crooks."

What a tragedy! I remember talking to Wendy, a prospective student who was really enthusiastic about finding the crooks. I countered by sharing the part that makes *me* enthusiastic: how face reading could help her plumb new depths of human nature, to gain compassion, to recognize her biggest talents. After I explained about this enchanting world of wisdom, she looked disgusted. "You mean it can't help show me the crooks?"

Had I sold burglar alarms, or fear, it would have been easy to please her. But since I'm striving for wisdom, this was a tough conversation.

Do you know the concept of self-fulfilling prophecy? What we expect from people is often borne out by reality. Therefore, if we're constantly looking for crooks, we'll find them. The best we'll notice in others is that they're non-crooks. Conversely, what happens if we choose to probe faces for wisdom or talent? We can find that, too.

In reality, the chance of your being attacked today by a criminal is relatively small. With a suspicious attitude, however, you're *guaranteed* to find evil lurking in every corner. To protect your quality of life, therefore, the best way to use face reading is NOT to go out of your way to look for lies. Look for life.

■■■

7. Noses

Pop quiz: Draw me a happy face. You know, the symbol for "Have a happy day." You'll find the cheery little things everywhere—handwritten notes, stationery, stickers, computer clip art, painted six feet high on the wall of your local Wal-Mart, wherever.

Whether you happen to feel perky or not, those insufferable little faces grin at you. So I'm sure that you know what I mean by a happy face. Go ahead, draw one.

Now, as an up-and-coming face reader, you can help me answer this:

What is wrong with this picture?

No **nose**, that's what wrong! Is nose-lessness a coincidence? I think not. Because what do noses represent?

All a happy face has is eyes and mouth. By now you know that eyes mean having an outlook. Although we haven't reached the mouth chapter yet, I'll bet you can guess what mouths represent... communication.

Symbolically a happy face has an attitude and can talk. No listening to others (ears), nary a thought (eyebrows) disturb the blissful experience. And possibly worst of all, from this face reader's point of view, is a very central omission: How about the face part that represents work and dealing with money? So we're just going to put that part off until tomorrow, are we?

Bah! Noses are central. They're serious face.

And you thought noses were just hard to draw.

After this chapter, you still may not want to draw them. But you're going to know much more about them than ever, including many reasons to be thrilled with your own nose, however it looks.

Nose length

Since we're already involved in a nose quiz, here's another question:

Which kind of **nose length** is supposed to be aristocratic, long or short?

Long, of course—but did you ever wonder why?

Are noses with generous length transmitted like a family name, along with write-ups in the Social Register and silver spoons. Can you tell an "old money" nose at a glance? Sorry, life isn't that simple. But at least seeing physical nose length is simple:

- **Short** noses are short.
- **Long** noses appear long, compared with the rest of the face.
- **Moderate** nose length is the label you'll give to a nose you squint at repeatedly, wondering why you can't decide whether it is short or long.

I look at the meaning of *nose length* this way: Breathing is a basic human job. Everyone must obtain the same amount of breath through the allotted equipment, enough to live. Some noses are designed to get this work done directly. These no-frills models are the short, get-down-to-business noses.

NOSE LENGTH

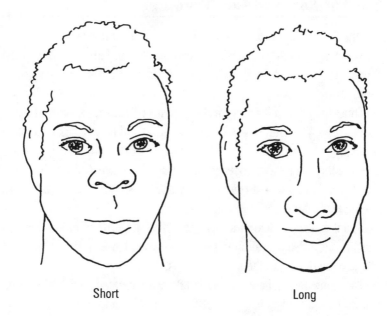

Short

Long

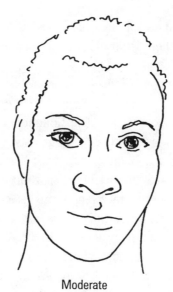

Moderate

Other breathing machines are designed to do the work more decoratively. Style counts. Accordingly, certain workers are set up with the longer, more ornamental variety. Work habits correspond: less rush, more style.

Thus, the gift you'll find with *short* noses is a talent for old-fashioned hard work. What Americans once praised as industriousness is looked on today with suspicion. It's called being a "workaholic." Whatever you call it, folks with short noses go into the workplace and produce like crazy. They can follow a routine. They don't just talk a good game, they get the work done.

I challenge you. Search any organization. Regardless of job title, social lineage, or pay scale, the ones who work hardest, day in and day out, are the ones with the shortest noses.

The potential challenge is being taken for granted. "Of course John will do it. That's his job." "No need to thank Sheila for all that overtime. She's a workhorse."

Should you be one of those hardworking short-nosed folks, here's my recommendation. Drop hints. Drop memos and requests for pay raises.

Many advocates for working-class people are notable for their short noses: Jacob Riis, author of *How the Other Half Lives*; William Jennings Bryan, known as "The Commoner"; attorney Clarence Darrow, who first won fame as a labor lawyer; and labor organizers Samuel Gompers and Mother Jones. Artist Norman Rockwell, the prolific artist, was also a member of the short-nose society. One of my favorites is Chief Justice Earl Warren, whose nose was as cute as a button. He said he wanted to be remembered as Justice of "the people's court."

As for the myth that short-nosed, hard workers are necessarily overworked and underpaid, think about "Gordo" Getty, son of legendary oilman Jean Paul Getty. Gordo has doubled the family fortune to $3 million. Joan Kroc, widow of entrepreneur Ray, works hard too, at philanthropy. She's so wealthy, she set up a $1 million scholarship fund—

nice work if you can get it. And how about Michael Jordan's. Whether the superstar athlete turns his short nose to a sport or to coaching, he's a go-getter.

The bottom line is that no face part, nose length included, predicts how much money you'll be paid. So forget expectations that long noses go with aristocratic trust funds. What is the real specialty of the long-nosed worker? Imagine a job where you punch in at 9:00 and out at 5:00. Your goal is to produce, produce, produce. Half the time, your boss never even tells you the big picture about what you're doing. The amount you get done in one day is fantastic. Sound good? Sure, if your nose is short. It's the story of your life. But for a long-nosed worker this is a description of job hell!

A *long* nose indicates a talent for planning and strategy. One example is a multi-million dollar real estate producer, Terri Murphy. Another is Janet Bodanan, the financial advisor also known as Dr. Tightwad. Neither one made her fortune in a jiffy. When you long-nosers work, you need time to display your full creativity.

Q. Wait a minute. Are you saying I can't work creatively with my cute short nose?

A. Everyone has creativity. Nose length relates to creativity with handling the scope of a project. The short-nosed version is to find ways to keep yourself efficient and motivated. You race against the clock. You race against yourself. The pile of widgets, customer invoices, and so forth that you produce become a justifiable source of pride.

By contrast, the long-nosed version of creativity is to envision the entire project, make sure it is one-of-a-kind, then follow it through from beginning to end. Your goals are a source of pride, with ingenuity running a close second.

Q. Yes, but what if you combine a long nose with starter eyebrows? My whole career, I've worked with someone who has that combo. (Me.)

A. Eyebrows predict how thoroughly you, personally, follow through on getting things done. Nose length shows how you define and envision your work. So your combination suggests that you prefer to plan an entire project, not just part of it. When you work at it, you have a big burst of creativity at the start. You're best off delegating the follow-up past that point, if you can, or finding a job that involves only the startup phase of a project.

With a VERY long nose, it's vital that you find work where you can strategize, regardless of how you personally handle the details. Examples of people who have done just that are bird man John James Audubon; Renaissance man Sir Francis Bacon; Chief Joseph, one of the greatest Native American strategists; and Walter Bagehot, the founder of British political sociology.

Because the typical long-nosed style is to enjoy the theoretical aspects of work at least as much as the practical side, it's no surprise that so many outstanding physicists have long noses, including Louis de Broglie, P.M.S. Blackett, and Nicolaas Bloembergen.

Q. Are you implying that my long-nosed ex-husband isn't the lazy bum I think he is?

A. Laziness is a matter of personal choice. Nothing in the face shows it, other than the glazed eyes of someone who would rather be elsewhere. Career counselor Marsha Simetar made a vital point about motivation in the title of her book, *Do What You Love, The Money Will Follow*. Money follows because you are willing to work.

It may well be that finding the kind of work that motivates you is especially important for someone with a long nose, like your former husband. When he can't connect with his overall goals for work, it's as though his way of working is like a slow-rising loaf of bread. When he can't keep on growing along with his job, it kills the vital spark, the yeast. His work falls flat.

You, by contrast, have a VERY short nose, suggesting that whatever job you happen to do, you'll make it meaningful by throwing yourself into it. That's a plus for you. So can't you afford to be charitable? Regardless of your ex-husband's shortcomings in other respects, his work style is different from yours—not necessarily lazy, but different.

When you have a VERY long or short nose, it's easy to misunderstand folks at the extreme other end. How about those blessed with a nose of *moderate* length? Their timing is flexible. Short-term projects, long-term projects—they'd do well at either. Think of Dr. Deepak Chopra: a prolific author, sought-after speaker, and practicing physician who masterfully juggles projects with all possible kinds of time constraint, somehow making all that he does seem easy.

Because scope of work isn't an issue for them, folks with moderate nose length may too readily judge their co-workers as bums and drudges. And speaking of judgments....

Noses in profile

I dedicate the next section of this book to America's 60 million *grumpy nose haters*. I consider it my personal mission to act as a sort of marriage counselor between your nose and the rest of you. Partly the reason we're such a nation of nose haters is our peculiar pop culture, with its assumption that the only good nose is straight and short. If you've been brought up on Disney cartoons, you've received the full treatment: Your subconscious knows that virtue and sexiness are inversely proportional to the size of a person's nose.

And how many movies, of all sorts, did you watch before you got the message from profile shots? Why do they almost always show nice straight noses? Obviously it must be because other nose shapes aren't attractive enough for a self-respecting movie star.

144 The Power of Face Reading

Bah, humbug! Let's at least reconsider this cultural conditioning. I invite you to summon up all necessary bravery, and straightforwardly (Hmm, side-forwardly) approach the delicate issue of **nose profiles**.

- If yours looks **straight**, this aspect of nosing around will be easy for you. Otherwise remember that the force of American culture, not to mention the nation's vanity surgeons, may be pulling against you. Keep reading until you find your own true nose!

By the way, is it a coincidence that the word *nosology* is a scientific word for classifying *diseases?* What's with all this negative nose stuff? Why can't we make up more positive words, like "nosetalgia," a longing for the times that make you feel really good, like the last time you saw the center of your face in the mirror.

Anyway, don't cringe at this very central part of your life. Honor it, by putting a couple of mirrors together to get a really good look.

- Maybe you'll find that your nose is a **scooped** shape that deviates from straightness by curving inward. The curve could be VERY or somewhat, and it counts wherever it occurs, which could be any part of your nose from the bridge to the tip.
- The third possibility for nose profiles is an **arched** shape. The curve could come anywhere between the bridge and the tip and still count as an arch.

Q. Is "an arch" what you call the bump in my poor nose?

A. Some of these outward-gliding shapes are more dramatic than others, but almost never are they really bumps. That's just typical bad-mouthing of nose parts.

A truly bumpy nose has a definite lump, like a pea on a plate. You'll only have one if your nose has been broken in a particular way.

Q. I was just about to ask how you can read a nose like mine, when it's been broken?

NOSE IN PROFILE

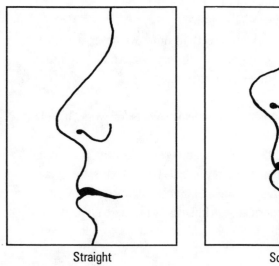

Straight

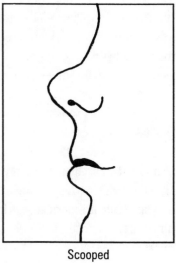

Scooped

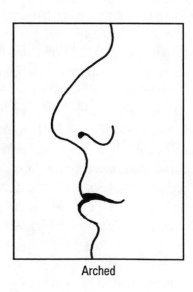

Arched

A. Read it just like any other nose.

Q. But it's not the original model, is it?

A. What matters is what you have right now. Whatever it took to make your face that way counts as your history—interesting as history but irrelevant to a reading of your current face.

Nose profile reveals your most distinctive talents for work. It's like carrying a business ID card.

A *straight* nose says, "Checklists done here." You work so systematically, you're in your element when you can start at Point #1 and continue down through your list, ticking off numbers as you go.

Lucky you! Typical American workplaces, with their emphasis on procedures, are designed by people with straight noses... for people with straight noses.

Consequently, your only challenge is that silly business of lack of tolerance for the rest of humanity. You know, "the slobs" who work with you—by comparison with you, nearly everyone works in a way that doesn't appear very systematic.

Especially if your nose is VERY straight and long (what I call *relentlessly straight*), your standards for rigorousness can be exceedingly high. Noses like yours are behind the work of these high flyers, for instance: Charles Lindbergh, whose nose may have been his compass during the first solo transatlantic flight; Francis Crick, reader of the genetic code; Ernest Hemingway, one of the most influential novelists in American literature; Sequoyah, the genius who developed a written alphabet for the Cherokee language; and Booker T. Washington, who institutionalized higher learning by creating the Tuskegee Institute.

Finally, guess what shape nose designed the relentlessly perpendicular, soaring skyscrapers known as the New York World Trade Center? You get one point if you guess "straight." Check off a couple of extra points if you named the architect, Minoru Yamasaki.

Scooped noses show talent for work as well, but don't expect it to run along the lines of the straight and narrow. These folks should design business cards that read, "Valentine at work. Feelings count here." In fact your greatest talent for work, if you belong to this nose club, involves checking in with your feelings. Rather than official coffee breaks, you need unofficial tune-in time:

"Hello, intuition. How is this job going? Does anything about it feel not quite right? If so, how should I fix it?"

Conversations like this may sound wacky, but what happens if you *don't* have them is probably even wackier. When you don't let yourself take intuition breaks, you'll procrastinate like crazy before finishing projects. I suspect your soul will stall you on purpose because it doesn't want you to end a job before you can show your real talent.

You'll also notice that whenever you simply follow procedures, instead of feeling revved up like a straight-nose worker, you become increasingly frustrated. Coincidence? Give yourself the benefit of an intuition break and watch the clouds of frustration blow away. Suddenly you're standing under blue skies, under the most refreshing of autumn breezes (or whatever your favorite weather-scape happens to be).

By the way, have you picked up an extra bit of poetic flair in my treatment of this particular nose shape? This may be due to recognizing yourself in the description. Or it may be due to your recognizing me, because my nose is a VERY for intuitive work.

Like the body itself, scooped-nosed workers need praise to function best; we're especially vulnerable to criticism. Our emotional involvement in work helps us, however, by making us powerful transmitters of feelings. Examples are actors Tom Hanks and Mary Tyler Moore, perennial puppeteer Shari Lewis, guitarist Andrés Segovia, and novelist Willa Cather. When the late scooped-nose singer John Denver was asked what made his work unique, he said he simply sang about how good it feels to be alive.

Norman Cousins owed his health, as well as his greatest fame, to the discovery that laughter can challenge the grim logic of disease. New Age healer Louise Hay, author of *Heal Your Body*, has helped millions *interpret* illness rather than simply diagnose it.

When it comes to interpreting work itself, there's a second way to diverge from strictly paying attention to the task at hand. It's creativity. And it shows in an *arched* nose. If you have one, your business card should read "Creative person reporting for work." That's right, the deeper the outward curve in your nose, the stronger your talent (and need) for working creatively.

Q. Hold on....

A. To your nose? It looks like it's staying on fine without any help from me.

Q. Let's start again. I have a VERY curved nose. I also happen to be a physicist. Do you mean to tell me that I need to start carrying around an accordion or some oil paints?

A. Creativity need not take such a conspicuous form. Creativity means finding a unique solution to a problem. You see the resources available. You know what you want to achieve. And your creativity involves finding one-of-a-kind ways to use what you've got. Economists might call it getting more bang for your buck. As a physicist, you might prefer to call it elegance.

Q. Are you implying that, with a not-curved nose shape, I'm doomed to never be creative?

A. Actually, each nose shape goes with a particular kind of creativity—and, remember, this category only applies to your behavior at work. Other aspects of creativity show in your eyebrows, your hairline, your lip proportions, and other places as well.

The reason I single out arched noses as involving special creativity is that, if you have this trait, you *need* to work creatively. This is not optional, not if you want to be happy on the job.

Q. So what kind of creativity goes with my "American workplace" straight nose?

A. You apply creativity to getting on a roll and staying on a roll. How can you whiz through that set of procedures? How many times can you do it in one day? Creativity is used to keep yourself motivated.

With scooped noses, creativity comes from finding ways to plug your intuition into reality.

By contrast, creativity with arched noses involves paying close attention to the resources available. What people, talents, materials, or concepts can be combined in an unusual way? How can you perform your task in a way that has never been done before? Musicians devote their creativity to ways of producing sound, choreographers to elements of movement, and so forth. Noses that move "out there" seem to go with a special sensitivity to whatever "out there" can contribute to the artist's medium.

Think of cellist Pablo Casals; composer Aaron Copland; choreographer Agnes de Mille, poet Pablo Neruda, novelist Mikhail Sholokhov, and singer/songwriter Aretha Franklin. One of the most famous noses in music belongs to Barbra Streisand. Another, that deserves equal fame, belongs to Gordon Parks, a versatile creator of beauty who has excelled not only as a musician but as a poet and photographer.

Q. What does it mean if your nose really does have a bump, not an arch?

A. Then your work flows in fits and starts. With each project you take on, you will have at least one burst of outrageous creativity.

The challenge is that you may come on too strong for others to accept easily. Of course, it's also possible you could become another Duke Ellington.

Q. As a salesman, would it be an advantage for me to have a nose job to make it look straight?

A. It might be. Commonly, other nose shapes are perceived as being undesirably "ethnic"—a curious attitude for a nation that owes its greatness to being a melting-pot, but prejudice sticks nonetheless. Of course, calling non-straight noses "Italian," "Polish," etc. is doubly silly because people from all ethnic groups can have arched or scooped noses—but whoever said that prejudice was rational?

Anyway, the social disadvantage of not having "the best" nose is common knowledge. Less obvious is another fact about how Americans are socialized about work. We're taught to value a work style that involves procedures (i.e., the personal style that corresponds to a straight nose profile).

Therefore, if you have the inner and outer attributes of straightness, your way of working may be judged by others as the "right" way. Work patterns symbolized by other nose shapes may take more thought to appreciate. Still, when their special excellence is understood, both arches and scoops signal highly individualistic work styles of great value.

So before you run off to the nearest plastic surgeon, I'd recommend you fall in love with the nose you already have. Appreciate your talents. When you truly use them, you will understand deeper than ever that God don't make no junk.

Nose padding

What's in a nose? There's flesh and blood and cartilage, plus the occasional boogers which you probably thought of first if you're a Dave Barry fan. Whatever popped into your mind, I'll bet it wasn't one of the most meaningful nose categories: **nose padding**. That refers to the amount of flesh around the nose, from bridge to right above the tip, as seen from a front view.

Q. You mean whether noses are broad or not?

A. I prefer not to use the term "broad" because it's so loaded with connotations related to ethnic stereotype. Besides, "broad" isn't specific enough. Is the nose equally padded at the bridge as at the tip? Does this extra nosiness, this padding, increase or decrease on the way down? That matters. Besides, the concept of broadness overlooks a subtlety of great interest to nose readers: Some noses show a narrow bone down the center. When a nose shows that bone, it has small nose padding, even if it is otherwise broad. Here are more specifics:

- **Small** nose padding means the nose bone is highly visible; you could call it relatively naked.
- **Big** nose padding means that you don't see the bone and, instead, see nose width.
- When a nose shows its bone narrow at the bridge, then widens on the way down, that's **triangular** nose padding. Sometimes this looks dramatic, sometimes less extreme. But by now you're practiced at seeing the VERYs, which can apply to this trait as well as the other kinds of padding in this category.

Q. I always thought having a wide nose was just a form of fatness that runs in families. You mean there's actually something meaningful to this "padding"?

A. If it's a human face part, it has meaning. When a trait "runs" in your family, pay attention to who has it. Who escapes that very same trait and evolves something different? Should a family member really share a face trait with you, you'll share a similar personal style related to that trait. But it's less common than people assume.

Q. So all these years when I said my Dad and I have exactly the same nose, I was just an impostor?

A. Often family members don't share as much physical common ground as they assume. Comparing your photos of him with how your own nose looks, can you see differences? I'd say he shares your nose profile but not the nose length. Your nose padding is different, too.

NOSE PADDING

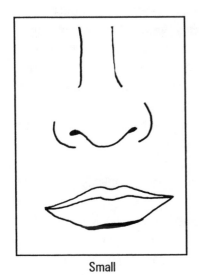

Small

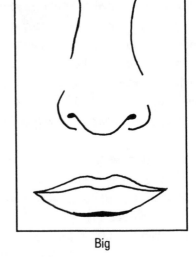

Big

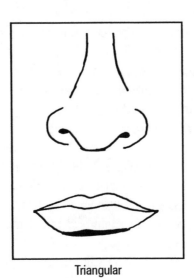

Triangular

Nose padding refers to your preferred number of people to share a project at work. What is your comfort zone?

If you prefer to start a project alone, continue it alone, even finish it alone, you probably have VERY *small* nose padding. It's a specialized form of independence related to work. And understanding this aspect of personal style can help you to take best advantage of a major talent. Just one catch though—how do you like it when a boss looks over your shoulder and starts in on you:

"Did you finish the job yet? When is this job going to be done? Are you doing it *my* way?"

Ugh! Narrow nose-wearers are allergic to bossy bosses. Tell this to anyone who tries to micromanage you:

"Once I commit to a project, I'm one of the most self-motivated people you've ever met. I push myself harder than you ever could. Leave me alone and I'll work best."

You might also want to mention that bossing you around is no more effective than flogging a dead horse, except that in your case, it's more like flogging a racing horse. Luckily Johann Gutenberg didn't have this problem in his career. Although internal business documents from 500 years ago aren't crystal clear, I think it's safe to assume that nobody looked over the great man's shoulder while he invented moveable type.

Actress Greta Garbo had the perfect nose to speak for people like you when she uttered her famous line," I want to be alone." In real life, Garbo died a recluse. Coincidence? No, but not to worry. Garbo had other face traits that contributed to her extreme aloofness. It's unlikely that, even with an equally VERY version of this trait, you have the rest of Garbo's face—a cinematic loss, perhaps, but your psychological gain.

At the opposite extreme comes *big* nose padding. To describe your version of "job hell" takes only two words: Solitary confinement.

However, on a good day at work, you do have contact with other human beings. How come you need this? People give you energy. Without them, work would drain you. One example is Jack Canfield, co-author of the bestselling *Chicken Soup for the Soul*—not a recipe, or even a book, so much as veritable publishing restaurant chain. Here's a guy who gets to work with people to his heart's content.

Should ample nose padding extend all the way to the top of your nose, you're one of the rare beings who actually prefers to start a project in a committee. One example is Maria von Trapp, on whose story "The Sound of Music" was based. She created her own committee of singers, the whole "Do-re-mi" crew.

As for *triangular* nose padding, you prefer to begin work projects independently. As the project gathers momentum, however, you feel more comfortable about sharing it through teamwork and delegation. Just how comfortable do you feel? Look at the relative width of nose. More dramatic triangling shows that you are especially attracted to working with large numbers of people.

Q. My nose does something really weird. That bone down the center stands out distinctly but there's also a great deal of fleshiness on either side. How can you interpret a nose that has both VERY small nose padding and a lot of it?

A. This relates to a difference between the impression you give others and a more private aspect of personal style. Here's what I think goes on: You make other people feel like you're a team player at work, and to some extent you are. However, in secret you prefer to do things your way. Inwardly this can lead to feelings of conflict but, if it's any consolation, the complexity could be advantageous. When people are looking, you're Mr. Team Player. In private, you do things your way. And nobody guesses you have this ruthless unsociable side, do they?

Q. No. I do sneak in my own personal additions but only when nobody else on the team is looking. Guess the secret is out now!

■■■

Nose tip angle

Sure, you've heard about the skill it takes to turn on a dime. Now we are about to try an even neater trick, to pivot on the tip of your nose.

The reason for this trick is that nose tips give information about two wildly different aspects of life. So first we'll view nose tips from the side; by considering nose tip angle, we'll read our final *work*-related nose news. Afterwards, with a deft swivel to full frontal face, we'll sniff out the *money* news lodged in that self-same tip. (Of course, you already knew that tips involved money, didn't you?)

To check out your **nose tip angle**, you'll need two mirrors. The **tip** is where your nose comes to a point. The **base** of your nose lies between the nostrils. To see nose tip angle, compare the height of the tip to the base.

- It the tip is higher, your nose tip angle turns **up**.
- If the tip is lower, either you're upside down or you have a genuine **down**-turned nose tip.
- And if you're scratching your head (or your nose), puzzling over the angle, it's probably **even**.

Nose tip angle relates to timing, especially related to your career moves. Remember the turned-*up* nose celebrated in the song, "Five Foot Two, Eyes of Blue"... you know, "Turned-up nose, turned-down hose" that's the way the silly song goes, "Has anybody seen my gal?" Where was I? Okay, the turned-up aspect goes with impetuous speech, impulsive career moves, and an all-around good time. Oops, I meant to say: potential difficulty keeping secrets. (Guess which angle of nose tip I've got.)

Once I was giving a book signing. A woman who identified herself as a librarian made a short and charming speech about how curiosity was the most important quality anyone could have in life. What made her speech doubly charming to me was her nose tip angle, the most VERY up-turned I've seen.

Q. I don't quite get how this could be related to impulsive career moves. Could you explain? We're talking about my nose tip here.

A. Let's bring in an example. Suppose that you work for a big-city department of public transportation. You're young, idealistic. Like all your co-workers, you consider cars to be loathsome engines of pollution. When nobody's looking, you spit on 'em.

One way you differ from others in your office, however, relates to your VERY up-turned nose tip. When it comes to curiosity, you're the champ. Co-workers have learned to put you at the top of the office gossip grapevine. Therefore, you're among the first to learn that your own boss has stopped riding his bike to work in favor of a car, and not just any old car, mind you, but a model that's notorious for being a gas guzzler. Multiple choice quiz:

What would you do, based on nose-tip angle alone:

a) Go outside and spit on more cars, to relieve your pent-up anguish?

b) Consider taking your car to work tomorrow, too, and parking it near your boss' automobile, all the better to buddy-buddy up to him

c) March straight into your boss's office, confront him, and quit.

If you chose b), your own nose tip probably angles downwards. Answer c) shows the up-turned attribute.

For another example of nose tips in action, return with me now to those thrilling days of yesteryear, if not all the way back to "The Lone Ranger," at least as far back as Doris Day and her movies of the "Lover Come Back" era, the late 1950's and early 1960's. In these films, a woman's career consisted of getting and keeping a man.

NOSE TIP SIZE

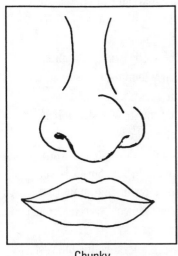

Chunky

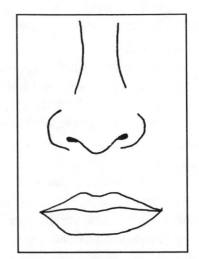

Tiny

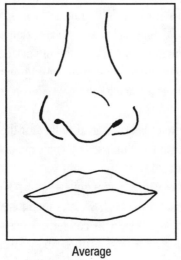

Average

You may well remember the style of the Day character in action: impetuous, independent, and possessing the enduring toughness of a well roasted marshmallow.

Day's short, narrow, up-turned nose was perfectly cast. By contrast, I find it intriguing that virtually every major early feminist's nose had a straightforward, *even* nose tip angle. This trait goes with more deliberate career decisions—not impetuous by any means. Risks will be taken, but not without full awareness of the potential cost.

So let's give all due acknowledgment to the crusading women whose nose tip angles suggest they knew what they were in for: Susan B. Anthony, Elizabeth Cady Stanton, Lucy Stone, Carrie Chapman Catt, Frances Perkins, Emmeline Parkhurst, and Mary Church Terrell. From our own era, we can include Betty Friedan.

Their only challenge with this trait was lack of tolerance for the rest of humanity, not so much with the guys who thought women's minds cutely inferior (despising *them* was appropriate), but how unfortunate to judge the mistakes related to up-turned or down-turned nose tips.

Down-turned nose tips show a deliberate style in making career moves. Once these people define their career plans, don't expect them to deviate. If you're among them, you know the importance of looking out for Number One. Regardless of your own nose tip angle, there's a related question you might enjoy asking the next person you meet who does have this trait:

"Most people either haven't heard of goal setting for their careers or they don't bother to do it. Do you think setting goals might be important for your career?"

If their eyes don't answer with a gleam, let me know.

For a great political leader, like Lech Walesa, the interest of a group of people may be treated as a personal concern. Richard Nixon, the only U.S. president ever forced to resign to escape impeachment, also displayed tenacity of career purpose. This was all the more extreme in his case when you consider another nose trait, the scoop, suggesting an emotional orientation to work. (Remember his short-lived retreat from politics, when he told the press they would not have Nixon "to kick around any more"?) For someone whose inner life was his strength as a worker to repeatedly lie about Watergate is hard to imagine, except for the personal tenacity that shows in Nixon's down-turned nose tip.

In general, this nose tip angle can involve shrewdness, even pursuing one's ambitions in a ruthless way. You could call it "The Machiavelli Advantage." (Yes, the scheming author of *The Prince* had it, too). The potential challenge with this trait is to guard against behavior that others would call selfish.

But self-interested advice can be more benign as well, witness the careers of David Chilton, who teaches strategy for financial independence, and Jim Jorgensen, editor of the financial newsletter "It's Your Money." And who'd grudge coach Vince Lombardi the oomph that shows in his nose tip angle?

Bernie Ebbers, chairman of an ever-expanding company called WorldCom Inc. negotiated a $37 million buyout of MCI. Having purchased more than 35 companies, Ebbers is described as someone who's unhappy if his company stays the same size for long.

As for a VERY down-turned tip that also is pointed in shape, self-interest in career choices is acute. Not an easy trait for others to live with, but such a nose came in handy for Basil Rathbone, the actor who had the perfect nose for his screen role as Sherlock Holmes, an intellectual bloodhound.

Remember the nose tip of the Wicked Witch of the West in "The Wizard of Oz" or that of the poisoned-apple-toting stepmother in Disney's "Snow White"? Long, pointed noses with drooping tips represent selfishness to our collective consciousness. For the rare real-life person who has such a nose, the challenge may not be wickedness so much as the need to constantly disprove this expectation of selfishness.

That's why my favorite example of this kind of nose belongs to author Ayn Rand, who unabashedly preached the virtue of selfishness. Dare I say it? She had a point.

Q. What if my nose is both up-turned and pointy? What does that mean?

A. A *pointed* nose tip, whatever the angle, shows a high degree of sensitivity to your work environment. You'll suffer more than others from any kind of grunginess in the workplace, from shabby furniture and bugs to dirty office politics. That's your potential challenge. But the good news is that pointy-tipped workers also uplift their work environment. Your high standards may even become contagious.

With a nose that's both *pointed and up-turned*, you've lucked out. You have the proverbial "nose for news." Makes sense, doesn't it? After all:

- You're curious.
- You're sensitive to what's going on around you.

Watch out, anyone with dirty secrets to hide! Ralph Nader has turned his nose to sniffing out consumer fraud. Authors Langston Hughes and Anne Morrow Lindbergh searched for truth. Where's the best place for you to hunt for this exotic nose tip? Try your local newspaper. Don't place an ad. Sneak into the newsroom and watch the reporters.

Nose tip size

In America at this turn of the century, we have funny ideas about **nose tip size**. Have any of your friends recently rushed off to the plastic surgeon because their nose tips seem too darned small?

No, large nose tips are the seeming problem, one more perfectly fine face attribute now considered undesirably "ethnic." The funny thing is, no matter what race box you check off on the census forms, people who check off that very same box can have any size of nose tip. Start looking!

NOSE TIP ANGLE

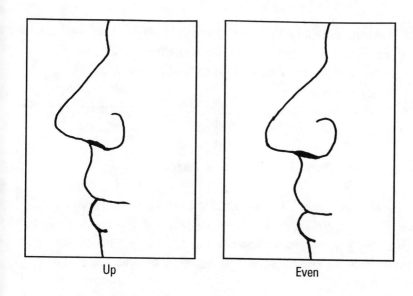

Up

Even

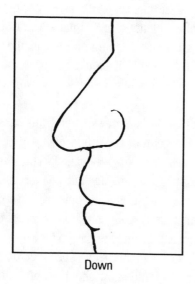

Down

- A **chunky** nose tip is the opposite of a **tiny** nose tip. Your point of reference is the person's face. How does the size of the tip compare to the rest of the nose, to the width of the mouth, to the length of the eyes?
- If the answer isn't immediately obvious, count it as an **average** nose tip.

Courage, now. Check your tip out in the mirror.

Nose tip size shows how you relate to financial security. *Chunky* nose tips reveal that saving for the future is a major concern. How much money is actually in the bank? Sorry, the nose tip won't tell. The desire for material security doesn't necessarily match the size of your subject's nest egg.

Ever see the TV commercials for American Express Travelers Checks with Karl Malden? Inspired casting! His VERY large nose tip said, "Don't leave home without money, plenty of it." Usually, you'll find *average* and chunky nose tips are more commonplace than the small ones. Bearing in mind that VERY = VERY, it should be apparent that the bigger the nose tip, the more often a person thinks (or worries or gloats) about personal savings.

When you browse through your newspaper's business section or watch "Newshour with Jim Lehrer" you'll find plenty of chunky tips—including Jim's. Back when the show was called "The MacNeil/Lehrer News Hour," you also got to see Robin MacNeil's on a regular basis.

Who thinks about savings most often? People who live in poverty—also people who are ambitious, greedy, philanthropic, art collectors—your answer can't be limited to any one category. When you read the Secrets, you'll find that savers come from every income bracket and ethnic heritage. TV's most colorful show about people who have accumulated wealth is hosted by a man with the perfect nose tip for his job.

That, of course, is Robin Leach, host of "Lifestyles of the Rich and Famous."

Q. Just yesterday I had a screaming fight with my parents about money. "You're almost 30" they said. "You're not married yet and your salary at that newspaper job is pitiful. When are you going to start planning for your future?" They were right. But you're also right when it comes to my tiny nose tip and my lack of interest in saving. What could I have told Mom and Dad in my defense?

A. Whenever people put you on the defensive for being different from them, it can help to consider the possibility that their personal styles are radically different from yours. This can take some of the sting away. Your nose tip is VERY *tiny*. What kind of nose tips do your parents have?

Q. They're huge, all right, especially my Dad's. But what they said did sting, and not just because I'm a mutant so far as my nose is concerned. You say that each face trait goes with a talent. What can possibly be good about the irresponsible attitude that goes with my tiny nose tip?

A. Apart from the social points you score for having such a nose tip, it has a wonderful meaning. Have you ever heard of **prosperity consciousness**? It means having a spiritual understanding of money as a symbol: for energy, for skill, for work, for appreciation. Money is a flow, rather than something to hoard, and it won't flow a bit more abundantly due to worry.

Although anyone can push herself to believe in abundance, you don't have to work at it, do you? Isn't it a given for you that there will always be enough? And don't you find that, somehow, you are always provided for?

Q. Absolutely, which is why I don't worry, even though my folks think I'm nuts.

A. See? You're a natural at prosperity consciousness. And the benefit is freedom in your own life plus the chance to teach other people this spiritual understanding of money. For other people, including your parents, you model an important kind of fearlessness. So feather your nest as best you can and don't be ashamed of yourself for not worrying.

Nostril size

Take a deep breath. Add a gulp, if necessary. We're about to delve into nostrils. I know, nostrils may seem like the ultimate in embarrassing face parts before you're a fully fledged physiognomist. Meaningwise, too, the subject is considered taboo. Even close friends may be reluctant to discuss what nostril size means.

But I can't wait to show you. Partly it's because anyone in sales has a critical need to know about nostrils. Partly, it's because nostrils on a physical level don't worry me with the usual fears about hygiene or manners. Instead they remind me of my son's keen intelligence.

When Matt was a toddler, one of his major hobbies was, to put it bluntly, picking his nose. Parental corrections didn't seem to discourage him, either. During one conversation between Matt and my husband, Mitch, this nose jazz had been going on entirely too long. So he said politely, "Your finger doesn't belong there, son. Please take it out right now."

And instantly Matt obeyed, taking that finger and sticking it directly into Daddy's nose.

Our face reading pursuits won't be quite that wild. But in our more reserved way, let's go forth boldly into nostrils.

How do you gauge **nostril size**? Don't worry. You won't need anything conspicuous, like a ruler. Simply look at the nostril from the front, at a level angle.

NOSTRIL SIZE

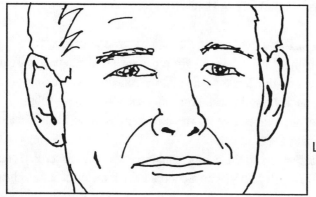

Large

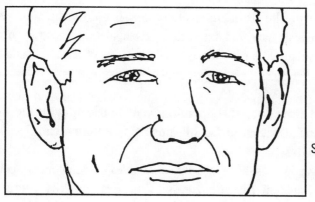

Small

■ When you can see the whole shape, count that as **large** nostrils.

■ Air holes you can barely see mean **small** nostrils.

■ No air holes? Either you're looking at a Barbie doll or else it's a person with VERY small nostrils.

Nostril size can be compared to the withdrawal capacity of a bank. Remember piggy banks? They have a narrow slit for depositing coins. Most of us toss our loose change into a container with easier access, such as a pocket. In physical terms, too, some of us have chosen a slot that makes the money easy to reach. Others have decided to make it harder to take the cash out.

And just when did this momentous decision take place? Personally, I believe that each soul sets up a contract about major face traits before undertaking a lifetime—see the section on "The Paradox of Talent" starting on Page 312. But if you prefer to think about it as some sort of cosmic gamble, you could always imagine that your nostrils came directly out of a slot machine!

Whatever the ultimate explanation, for thousands of years physiognomists have found a clear correlation: *Large* nostrils go with large spending, like easy access pockets. Those of us who spend less have *small* nostrils. People are walking piggy banks.

Q. Wow! How does this spending style stack up with the need for financial security? Do big nose tips automatically go with big nostrils?

A. Anything goes. Actually, some of America's leading money collectors have matched large nose tips with teeny nostrils. Alexander Hamilton, America's first secretary of the Treasury, had such a nose. The tradition continued with many famous captains of industry: entrepreneur Andrew Carnegie, banker J.P. Morgan, railway magnate James J. Hill. Today we have status accessories courtesy of the large nose suitcase and small breathing vents of entrepreneur Aldo Gucci.

But with spending style, as with physical face traits, you can't take anything for granted. John D. Rockefeller, perhaps the most famous rich guy in American history, was just the opposite of these other fellows. Rockefeller's nose tip was substantial. However, its proportions were rivaled by some of the largest nostrils I ever have seen. And wouldn't you know it, this steel tycoon wasn't just famous for bringing in the loot. He became a passionate philanthropist.

Fund-raisers and salespeople, before you start salivating over your large-nostrilled, large nose-tipped prospects, I'd better break it to you. The spending recipient isn't so simple to predict. Nostril size can't tell you whether rich folk might consider you or your company a worthy charity. Large nostrils only guarantee that a large proportion of a person's money is, somehow, going to be spent. Passionate spenders may prefer to spend on themselves.

Equally unpredictable is the Andrew Carnegie nose: a large nose tip plus small nostrils. As you may know, Carnegie was both frugal and philanthropic. More commonly, people with this kind of happy ending to their noses are generous mostly with their money *advice*. Ralph Nader has crusaded for consumers. So has makeup expert Paula Begoun, known as "The Ralph Nader of rouge." Arthur Frommer has guided travelers to see the world for less. Jane Bryant Quinn has shared her financial savvy with millions. *

Q. How about Gandhi? He had quite a nose tip didn't he?

A. For anyone who chooses the spiritual path of renunciation, your spending style takes the direction of helping others in the same way you would otherwise help yourself. Mahatma Gandhi, like Mother Teresa, became an advocate for the poor and dispossessed. So large nose tips and tiny nostrils can bring blessings to multitudes.

---

* Of readers and TV viewers, that is. It wouldn't be fair to represent Quinn as flinging her own bills, like so much confetti, to the multitudes.

Nostril shape

Now, if you aren't squeamish, let's continue to delve into nostrils. Four major patterns of **nostril shape** can be found—not all on the same nose, of course. Unmatched sets of two are quite common, however. So when you hold your own nose up to the mirror, see if you can highlight one nostril at a time. You may discover two different shapes in your own personal collection.

- **Round** nostrils show a circular shape. (Only the bottom-most part is round. Nobody's nostril is going to look precisely like a Cheerio.)
- **Rectangular** nostrils have a straight, longish shape. Often they are also small in size.
- **Flared** nostrils may be the hardest of the four shapes to recognize at first. But you'll have plenty of practice seeing them because this shape is the most common. Look for nostrils that start out straight, then curve as they move toward the ears.
- **Triangular** nostrils are the most unusual variety. It's like roaming across the desert sands of Egypt and bumping into a pyramid. Some day, you'll be amazed to behold a pair of nostrils like two miniature pyramids and you'll know that you've found a matched set of the triangular trait.

Doesn't that prospect bring new adventurousness to noses? Just think. Some day you may become a sort of nasal travel agent!

■■■

Although I've tried to make a case for adventure, you still may not be entirely convinced that nostril reading is a superb way to see the world. I, your teacher, can handle this. I know that once you learn the true meaning of nostril shape, you're going to go gaga over them.

NOSTRIL SHAPE

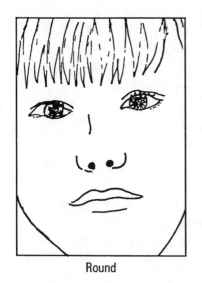

Round

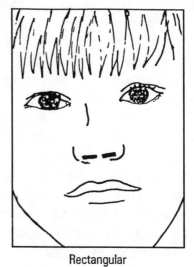

Rectangular

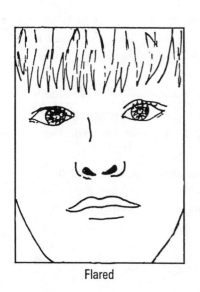

Flared

Triangular

Here's the deal: *nostril shape* informs you about spending style.

Salespeople, you may want to be extra nice to customers with *round* nostrils. If the Lord loves a cheerful giver, these folks must have front-row pews reserved in heaven. Their money style is resourceful, and they specialize in finding creative ways to manage their cash flow.

To put it bluntly, people with VERY large, round nostrils are the biggest spenders on earth. When a woman with this combination took one of my workshops, I told her so. I said her round nostrils also went with resourcefulness at juggling her debts. She laughed so hard, she fell off her chair. When she could talk again, she said:

"I have 22 credit cards, and they're all charged up to the limit."

Next time I gave this workshop, a woman with the identical nostrils sat in the very same chair. I made my same tactful assessment. She laughed hysterically too, but didn't fall off her chair.

"I also have 22 credit cards." she told the group. "But not every one of them is charged up to the limit."

The identities of these ladies shall remain anonymous. But Mary Hunt, with similar nostrils, has made it public that once she went into debt—to the tune of $100,000. Today she teaches financial resourcefulness as the editor of *Cheapskate Monthly*.

Rectangular nostrils go with analytical spending. Folks with these nostrils delight in budgeting. * I'll bet you can guess which shape of nostrils belongs to Carol Keefe, author of *How to Get What You Want in Life with the Money You Already Have*.

Flared nostrils go with a flair for adventurous spending. If you like it, you'll buy it, regardless of whether it's the practical sort of purchase that would appeal to your boss with the rectangular nostrils.

My favorite example of this adventurousness is Kenny Kramer, the man who inspired the fabulously freeloading character on "Seinfeld." The nostrils in question are flared and extremely small.

---

* Nostril alert: Folks with this trait who also are rich may take a special delight in concealing the extent of their wealth. And now you, as a face reader, can take an equal delight in guessing the truth. The beans will spill right out of their noses, as it were.

Triangular nostrils go with a highly developed awareness of just how much money can buy. The potential challenge is stinginess—from an outsider's point of view, anyway. A face reader's more compassionate insider's view is that this person's life has been marked by scarcity.

Wal-Mart CEO Lee Scott isn't hurting now for money, but I wouldn't be surprised to learn he has known financial pressure. I was shocked, shocked! to see his nostrils when perusing photos in a magazine article about a batch of up-and-coming CEOs. There he was, along with Jeffrey Immelt (of General Electric), Steve Ballmer (of Microsoft), Robert Nardelli (of Home Depot), and Craig Barrett (of Intel). All the others had the near-invisible nostrils I'd expect for stewards of major corporations. Scott's nostrils made me do a double take, being moderately large.

Then I took a closer look and saw that his had a triangular shape, especially the career-related right one. Aha! The instincts of a moderate spender would be tempered by a spending style about staying in tight control.

Q. I thought what you teach was supposed to be about improving self-esteem. Not only have I always hated my ugly triangular nostrils but now I find they have to do with stinginess. Great! What is this information supposed to do, build my character?

A. The trait of triangular nostrils is probably the most challenging thing you can find on a face. But think about what that means. We're here on The Learning Planet. As far as I'm concerned, your nostrils are the equivalent of a soldier's medal of honor. You've learned hard lessons about dealing with money, haven't you?

Q. Yes.

A. Don't underestimate the wisdom and compassion you've gained. Marie Antoinette is notorious for the lack of financial compassion she showed when, after being told that the peasants had no bread, she quipped, "Let them eat cake." You're not apt to make that kind of insensitive remark, no matter how financially secure you ultimately become. More than people with any other nostril shape, you have radar for finding the folks who, secretly or not, are financially strapped. Your compassion eases their pain; you may never know how much.

Q. When are you going to recommend the best kind of nostrils for single women like me to date? The suspense is killing me!

A. If money is a major concern, I do recommend that you carefully examine a prospective date's nostrils (Well, not so carefully that you lose the date by seeming like you have a thing about nose hair). Then think about what you want, short-term and long-term.

Maybe a wild, free-spending courtship appeals to your sense of fun... and your nostrils. Plunge into a dating relationship with someone who has large round nostrils; you'll have a great time. But should you choose that individual to marry? Factors that influence your decision might include your own spending style and the presence, or absence, of an enormous personal trust fund.

Dates with rectangular nostrils may not spend their way through courtship with so much abandon, but if your bank accounts get hitched, you'll appreciate how your mate budgets.

Secrets about work and money make noses a truly delightful part of the face. Whether choosing a date or a job, whether closing a big business deal or doing errands that are mind-numbingly dull, now you can stop along your path to smell the noses. They have so much to tell you, bringing more power to all your relationships. Next we'll turn to the face part that tells about power most directly of all.

■■■

8. Cheeks

Do your **cheeks** show you are powerful? Of course! It's a matter of HOW, not IF. Every human face shows at least one talent for getting your way with others.

About non-human faces, the news is not so good. Donuts, for instance, have a hole where the cheeks ought to be (also where eyes, nose, eyebrows, and mouth would be found, if any). Is it a coincidence that you've never heard of a donut running for president? I think not.

Fortunately, you're human, which means you can push for what you want. Is it political clout? High social status? Go for it! Hey, you can even joust, except that the required equipment is hard to come by these days. At least the cheek supplies you've been issued are totally up-to-date and Grade A.

You'll need them, too. If you work in sales or at relationships, power struggles can be discouraging. On a hard day it may feel as though you've done battle with a villainous knight whose armor is impenetrable; your self-esteem will need more mending than any shield.

On such a day, cozy up to this chapter and survey the splendor of your cheeks.

Cheek prominence

Cheek prominence means how much cheeks stick out.

- At one extreme are **prominent** cheeks, set like the sculptures atop Mt. Rushmore, eye-popping physical structures that grab your attention and make you say, "Wow!"
- At the other extreme, **recessed** cheeks don't make you say much at all, unless you're looking for them on purpose (as when applying yourself to a face reading book). If anything, your inability to find a part of the cheek that sticks out from the rest of the face will make you say, "Huh?" Well, consider that a victory cry, because it means you've identified recessed cheeks.

Q. But you promise there's still something good about having them, right?

A. Yes, and I dedicate this information to all my recessed-cheeked sisters who have had discouraging run-ins with blush. When you flip through the women's magazines and come to the inevitable makeup tips, you'll find depressing instructions for emphasizing the "apples" on your face. The article may tell you to locate these mysterious apples by sucking in your face, which some of us have to do with vacuum-cleaner force to notice much of anything.

Afterwards we daub makeup onto this not-much-there structure. And by the time we finally let out our cheeks and admire the final effect, what do we have to show for our labors? It's a cute little painting, with stripes and blobs, whose colorful streaks emphasize our interest in self-decoration, not the canvas beneath.

Unless you're working your way up to painting yourself as The Stars and Stripes, why bother? Eventually some of us realize that we can look pretty even without faking prominent cheeks. (Flatter cheeks mean less competition for your eyes and those winsome chompers.) Now you even have a name for your trait, recessed cheeks.

Since *cheek* prominence shows leadership style, you can probably guess that *prominent* cheeks go with a high profile style of leadership. The personality, not just the cheeks, can stick out in a crowd.

Why do so many performers have these prominent cheeks? Love of the limelight has helped them choose performing in the first place. For contrast, walk into a workplace where people are rewarded for less conspicuous power styles, your anonymous fellow travelers on the Internet for instance. You'll find folks with the incognito cheeks most people wear.

Performing takes courage. Lest you forget, I invite you to go into a roomful of strangers and try to bind them spellbound with your singing, dancing, or acting. Katherine Hepburn, notable for her VERY prominent cheeks, survived Dorothy Parker's scorching review that stated, "She runs the full gamut of emotion, from A to B." Hepburn also fought a courageous battle with a palsy condition. For years, she performed with a shaky voice and body, steadying them by force of will and letting go only when the trembling showed to dramatic effect.

Another notable set of courageous cheeks belongs to Katharine Graham who made a risky but historic decision when she chose to publish the first findings about the Watergate cover-up in *The Washington Post*.

Q. Speaking of politics, I haven't noticed too many elected officials with big cheeks. Weren't they supposed to be leaders? How do you explain it?

A. Remember, there's more than one way to have power. The high-profile style that goes with prominent cheeks can intimidate folks. In America, right from the days of the Founding Fathers, we've instituted government as a system of checks and balances. (Well, yes, I suppose you could call it cheeks and balances.)Ever since, the public

CHEEK PROMINENCE

Prominent

Recessed

has helped to spread electoral power around. Typically we'll vote for Democrats in the White House and Republicans in Congress, or vice versa.

Is this mere confusion and craziness? Or could it be a form of collective wisdom, a balancing act? Either way, noticing this national tendency will help you to understand the cheeks we Americans vote into office. Forget the Clara Bartons, the Harriet Tubmans, the Mother Teresas. We steer shy of folks who act outrageously courageously.

So is it a coincidence we've never elected Robert Redford? No, I sigh, like any red-blooded, frustrated American idealist. So far we've elected one—count 'em, one—president with prominent cheeks: Honest Abe. Runner-up in cheekiness is JFK, whose cheeks showed prominently just when he smiled, not the rest of the time.

Recessed cheeks go with a humbler version of power seeking. Should you have this trait, you haven't noticed a large chunk of cheek-flesh sticking out from your face, but I'll bet you have noticed that your style involves asking other folks for opinions and advice. Call it humility, call it democracy, it encourages people to trust you.

And the more closely you look into this highly social subject of cheeks, you'll notice that cheek prominence is often related to the dreaded subject of cheek padding.

Cheek padding

Even kids past the age of four hate it when Granny comes over, pinches a wad of cheek and says something like:

"Aren't you the sweetsiest-neetsiest, cutsie-wootsiest little love boffin?"

Well after your cheek pinching years, cheek flesh still poses a problem—at least if you are sensitive about America's most dreaded condition. Would that be tooth decay, moral decay, lack of fulfilling your potential in life, or an outright disease? Heck no. We're scared to be fat. And to many folks, flesh on the face means that the rest of you is fat.

But surprise! **Cheek padding** isn't necessarily related to obesity. When a figure grows fuller, the face may not, and vice versa. I've read skinny clients with big cheek padding and hefty clients with small cheek padding.

If you can calm down and face this emotional issue, you'll realize that even when faces pudge out they don't necessarily develop cheek padding. Look at Delta Burke, the actress who has developed a line of clothing for full-figured women. Look at reruns of "Roseanne." For both women, the fullness has gone right over their prominent cheeks, not beneath them. Even at her heaviest, Roseanne never had big cheek padding—and when you learn what it means, you'll appreciate why.

So how can you tell how you rate, cheek padding-wise? We've ruled out measuring the flab at your waist and other points south. Go directly to one of your upper cheeks (i.e., above your waist). Grab hold like a besotted grandma and pinch away.

Look at that chunk of flesh in the mirror.

- If it's a lot, yes you have **big** cheek padding.
- If the effort hurts and your knuckles jab rudely into your gums, admit it. Either you do a sadistic imitation of Granny or you have **small** cheek padding.

Now let's go on to consider what it's really about. You could call *cheek padding* "power cushions." The softer and fluffier your cushions, the less threatened others feel by your power plays. *Big* cheek padding corresponds to a power style that brings you lots of support: the more physical padding, the more support, so rejoice in it.

Padding marks a conciliatory leadership style, making everyone on the team feel important. Such padding has contributed to the success of

CHEEK PADDING

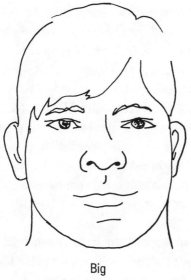

Big

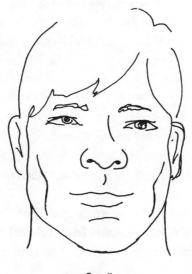

Small

Ken Burns, who has gathered immense support for his documentaries on Jazz, The Civil War, Baseball, and Lewis and Clark. Pioneering environmentalist Rachel Carson softened her leadership style with padding, as did Helen Keller, whose unthreatening approach helped to win recognition for all physically challenged persons.

Small cheek padding shows a completely different style with power. Here a person thrives on going it alone. You may have difficulty with delegation, probably because you believe deep down you can do a better job than anyone you might ask to help. Actually, you're probably right. So the challenge with this trait is not conceit so much as jealousy from others. Don't let it get to you.

Q. Delegation question here: I do have those hollow cheeks you're talking about but I also have the triangular kind of nose padding you call a delegator nose. So what gives?

A. Nose traits apply to work. Cheek traits apply to the rest of your life: the dates and roommates, the family relationships, the people with whom you spend holidays, buddies from church or the health club or the place where you go dancing. For example, when the time comes to fix your sock-chewing clothes dryer, what tone of voice will you use while speaking to the repairman? When you're dealing with the problem dryer at work, you'll have one tone of voice. If the repairman comes to your home, your tone will be very different.

You see, it's too simple to call a person a "good delegator." Face reading shows you the ins and outs, the when's and when not's.

Q. Isn't it a contradiction that a person could have small cheek padding (and thus VERY little support from others) along with something like a triangular nose (which you said goes along with a talent for teamwork)?

A. Noses show teamwork style when at work, while you're gainfully employed. Cheeks show your power style the rest of the time. Songwriter Woody Guthrie, for instance, involved people in his singing (triangular nose) but, deep down, was a loner (VERY small cheek padding). With combinations of face traits, believe me, anything's possible.

Q. So what are high cheekbones, already? You talked about Roseanne having them. Isn't that a kind of cheek padding?

A. Not necessarily—you're moving into the category of cheek set, which can be tricky to see at first. But I know you'll be up to it. Get ready, get set, get ....

Cheek set

"High cheekbones" is one of the garbage terms of unofficial face reading. People use "high cheekbones" to mean everything from prominent cheeks to unpadded cheeks to overall attractiveness. Bringing in ethnic stereotypes full force, people will say that someone has high cheekbones because of being Native American or Mongolian—but they might as well say being from Peoria or The Bronx or any other place under the sun.

To understand cheekbone traits, you need to develop an eye for **cheek set**. Where does the cheek stick out most?

- Does it happen right underneath the eye sockets, in which case the person has **high** cheekbones?
- Or does the greatest fullness come in the opposite direction? Some cheeks bulge out amazingly far down the face, closer to the mouth than the eyes. I call them **low**-slung cheeks.
- Another possibility is **far-set** cheeks, a trait that shows most commonly when the cheeks are also prominent and unpadded. Yes, these are the same traits that most folks who aren't yet face readers will mistakenly call "high cheekbones."
- Or you could be blessed with **close-set** cheeks, where the greatest fullness is near the nose.

If power is important to your career or relationships, you'll want to be able to see the truth about cheek set.

Q. Does cheek set show because the actual bones stick out or because padding sticks out?

A. Either bones or padding will count—whichever sticks out more from the physical face.

Cheek set informs you about the thrust of a person's power. Oomph shows in different directions, figuratively as well as literally.

High cheekbones may be sought after in popular lore, but don't be too eager to go for cheek implants. The trait can be hard to life with. It goes with using your social clout to fight for your values. You won't let anyone you're associated with do things you believe are wrong.

Q. You mean what just got me fired?

A. What happened?

Q. Some of the higher-ups in my company were doing something unethical. I was the only one who called them on it. They said, "What we're doing may be wrong, but it's legal. If you don't like it, you're out of here." I figured what happened was related to my being the only female executive in the company. But you're saying it wasn't just gender, it was related to my personal style?

A. For women and men alike, high ethical expectations of others go with high cheekbones. Other folks may be just as disturbed by wrong behavior around them, but they won't risk their jobs by speaking out. Who will dare to make a stink? Cheekbone height can tell you.

Q. I've gotten into trouble over my high cheekbones, too. And the funny part is that normally the last thing I'd do is pick a fight. I'm the kind of person who hates to swat a fly. But what is it about this cheek stuff?

CHEEK SET

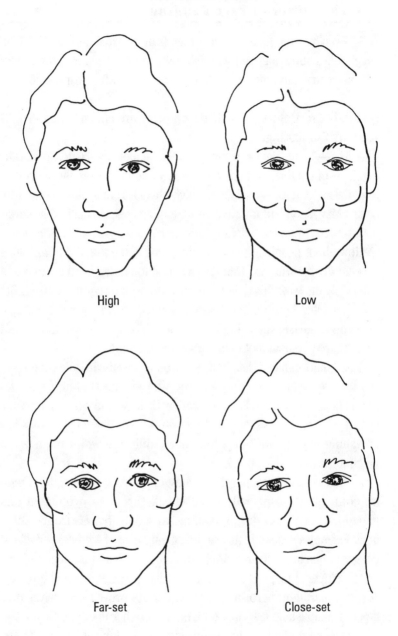

High

Low

Far-set

Close-set

A. Even if your face has no other traits related to conflict, high cheekbones show that you will fight over your values. And the bonier the cheek structure, the more bluntly your views will be expressed.

Q. Is all the fighting worth it? Look at my cheekbones. You'll see why I'm asking.

A. Hey—being right is a tough job but somebody has to do it. During times of conflict, perhaps you can draw comfort from the success of John Calvin, that awesomely bony, high-cheeked pillar of Protestantism. Louisa May Alcott had the cheek trait, too, and she specialized in novels that showed exemplary family values for *Little Women* and *Little Men.*

How about people at the opposite extreme, the folks with *low*-slung cheeks? People with this trait display great tolerance for the choices of others. By the way, this doesn't mean you have no morals yourself. But you figure that here on The Learning Planet, the whole point is learning. You'll advise, then let go. You believe, to the core, that moral choices are personal, not to be thrust upon anyone.

This could come in handy if, say, you're Elizabeth Dole, hoping to run for president, even vice-president, yet your husband insists on doing Viagra commercials.Or if you're Hillary Clinton during your husband's sex scandals. National Security Adviser Condoleezza Rice has low-slung cheeks, too; hopefully her public life won't require too much tolerance.

Far-set cheeks may offer the greatest opportunity for long-term public controversy, especially when cheeks are also prominent and unpadded. Expect enduring courage that only grows stronger over time. Examples are South African President Nelson Mandela; Geronimo, the great Apache warrior; Clara Barton, the loner who founded the Red Cross; singer and prejudice-eroder Marian Anderson; and Mother Teresa's marathon heroism. All these leaders proved themselves over time, accomplishing feats that took decades rather than years.

A lesser-known warrior with magnificent far-set cheeks is Dr. Elisabeth Kübler-Ross. Her pioneering studies on "death awareness" have helped millions, starting with the overcoming of denial—a fear-some task right there. And yes, let's not forget Roseanne. All comics have to be tough but she, and her cheeks, stand out among them as exceptionally spunky. Consider the hit show she brought to TV, a gritty but realistic comedy far ahead of its time.

Q. You're saying Roseanne's cheeks aren't padded?

A. That's right. Throughout the years when she taped her TV series, Roseanne's weight fluctuated a great deal. Even when she was at her heaviest, any extra weight that came to Roseanne's face distributed itself directly *over* those prominent, far-set cheeks, making them even more prominent. Weight on the rest of the body doesn't necessarily translate into cheek padding. It didn't for her.

Q. What can you say about close-set cheeks, that we have the opposite of courage? I don't like how my cheeks look particularly and now they're going to mean something crummy, too?

A. *Close-set* cheeks go with a knack for handling short-term crisis. Maybe you've never admired your physical cheeks but aren't you proud of how you perform well under pressure? When there's a crisis, *you* are the one who will come through every time.

What's the corresponding challenge? Avoid putting yourself in situations where you'll have to use this ability. Just because you come through every time doesn't mean that high-pressure work won't take its physical toll.

Q. I'm a manager. Would you advise me to take cheek set into account when setting deadlines?

A. Definitely. This would be especially smart to do with employees who have close-or far-set cheeks. Leave the 3-year or 30-year causes to your long-term runners. Give the 3-day assignments to the sprinters with close-set cheeks.

This gang of fabulous finishers includes a number of athletes: quarterback John Elway, linebacker Lawrence Taylor, basketball star Shaquille O'Neal, swimmer Mary T. Meagher, and golfer Sam Snead.

No doubt Thomas Gallaudet used the close-set power in his cheeks to leap over hurdles when he founded America's first free school for the deaf. And Wayne Huizenga applied his close-set timing to make a killing in short-term video rentals of Blockbuster caliber.

Cheek proportions

Have you found yourself in the cheek traits we've read so far? "Prominence-shominence" you may have muttered, as you stared at the mirror in vain, searching for the facial equivalent of mountain peaks. As for cheek padding and the set of your cheeks, they may be neither here nor there. But not to worry. You definitely have overall **cheek proportions**, the most vital of all cheek categories.

Ask this question as you stare at your reflection: "Mirror, mirror on the wall, where does my face width have its greatest width of all?"

If a voice from the mirror answers anything, you're trapped in a fairy tale. Make a run for it!

- But more likely, your own voice will answer. Perhaps it will say you have the trait of **cheeks widest**, where your face thins out below the cheekbones.
- By contrast, **under-cheeks widest** means the opposite. On the way down past the cheekbones, your face grows wider.
- **Forehead widest** is the relatively rare trait where cheeks don't look especially wide because the top of your head is even wider.
- And **even** width is the most common trait in this category. It means that the width of your face is pretty even from cheek to

jawline. For this to be the case, it doesn't matter whether the overall width is narrow or wide. Either way, the width stays constant.

Cheek proportions reveal how your leadership traits work in a crowd. *Cheeks widest* goes with a **"Leader-like" Power Style**—my quotes are meant to convey irony because there are many other effective ways of being a leader in addition to this one. But people tend to assume the only kind of leadership that counts must be highly visible. Other styles of leadership we'll consider in this chapter can be equally effective. They're just not as flashy.

Nonetheless, leader-like faces will always have an advantage when it comes to making a strong *first impression*. (They'll attract the most jealousy, too.) People who have this trait are considered natural leaders. And one funny aspect you may have noticed, if you're in this category, is that you don't have to say a word. People will find you anyway. There you'll be, hanging out at a meeting of your favorite club, when heads turn, fingers point. Oops, once more you've been nominated for president of the Optimists Club—or some other position of responsibility that you never even sought.

Some leader-like folks welcome their gift; others may spend years fighting it. But if you have VERY leader-like cheeks, nothing short of wearing a bag over your head will keep people from getting the message of your commanding presence. Even with the bag, I might add, your aura probably shows the same thing. However, a bag over your head will act as a pretty effective deterrent to unwanted presidencies.

And speaking of presidencies, remember how American politics is the grand exception to our usual preference for the leader-like power style? While it's true you won't find many presidents with prominent cheeks or leaderlike face width, their speechwriters and aides are another story. Consider, for instance, Peggy Noonan. She helped uncheeky Reagan and Bush with their images, coming forth with such

CHEEK PROPORTIONS

Cheeks widest

Under cheeks widest

Forehead widest

Even

memorable phrases as "a kinder, gentler nation." Noonan's face is VERY leader-like.

Under-cheeks widest shows an entirely different leadership strength, the **Pacifist Power Style**. If you have this trait, you've noticed: The longer people know you, the more they respect you. And they have the cutest way of showing it. They dump their problems on you. It's as though you have become an honorary mother. People come to you with their troubles, grousing and grumbling; they expect you to listen.

Remember, please, to take it as a compliment. People know you can handle their grumbling because, for any group you are in, you act like the rock. You'll make a wisecrack and extend a hug or simply a sympathetic ear. Eventually, the grumblers will leave. Radiant smiles will shine on their faces. Their hearts will be lighter and hold an ever deepening respect for you.

Leo Buscaglia, author of the self-help book *Love*, has your cheek proportions. His unofficial title is "Mr. Hug." Folks feel his love and love him back.

Unfortunately, there can be a problem with having the Pacifist power style. What happens when you are the one who needs to dump? Folks with your power style care most deeply about keeping harmony in relationships. Therefore, you may be assertiveness-challenged. Here's an example:

You sell chairs at a Bad Back Store. When your best customer slaps you on the back, not knowing that you have back problems, your first reaction is to say, "Lay off. That hurts." But that might mean hurt feelings, even hurt business. So you suffer in silence.

Next time this customer slaps you on the back, you grit your teeth a tad harder but still you say nothing. Why rock the boat?

This custom of your customer's may continue for years, with a growing annoyance on your part. Finally the day comes when you simply lose it. Pat! goes the customer. Pow! goes you.

Explosions like these are inevitable until you learn the life lesson about asserting yourself before a big emotional charge develops.

Two of my favorite exploders with this pacifist power style are Barbara Mikulski, my personal candidate for sainthood from the U.S. Senate, and Jackie Gleason, who exploded with comforting regularity in "The Honeymooners."

An even more intense style belongs to folks with *forehead widest*. Ideas are real for you, realer than obstacles that stop other people from reaching their goals. Thus, you accomplish more than others—and also risk burning them out if they work with you. I call it the **Passion Power Style**.

Even if you've learned, like Fred Astaire, to cultivate great charm, inwardly you're always intense. Ever see the dance number where Fred coaxed brilliant dancing out of a coat rack? His ability to make it all look easy took rehearsal after rehearsal to perfect, possible because his supply of mental energy was so great.

Another fellow whose career is a tribute to passion power is Bill Marriott, Jr., who built the Marriott enterprise from a $50-million-a-year operation to a $12-billion international giant. Harry Houdini, another passion power guy, had to settle for just plain magic.

At the opposite extreme come the faces that are, cheek-wise, a struggle to fathom. *Even* width relates to a **Polite Power Style** that is, similarly, inconspicuous. But don't sell it short. If you're in this group, you know how to work the system. Results matter more to you than calling attention to how great you are.

Your only challenge, with such a style, is fading into the woodwork. Remind your boss, occasionally, that you're the one who produced those magnificent results.

Cindy Villarreal, a former Dallas Cowboys Cheerleader, has spent much of her career making other people look good. Although it's not inconspicuous, being at the top of her profession, it's safe to guess that she could have been just as successful as a dancer in her own right, cheerleading for her own career.

Think, too, of the seemingly quiet impact of Sandra Day O'Connor, America's first female Supreme Court Justice (also one of its most powerful swing voters); or psychologist B.F. Skinner, less famous than he deserves to be for his influence as a behaviorist. Interior Designer Alexandra Stoddard has made her reputation as a decorous voice for improving quality of life. In the light of her cheeks, I applaud the title of one of her books: *The Art of the Possible*.

Which of the four power styles is best? Admittedly, the Leader-like style receives more than its share of recognition. Actor Michael Landon's career didn't really take off until after his cheek implants. That, by the way, is the cosmetic surgery to buy—not a nose job—when you want greater social clout. If, however, you want to earn your reputation just by doing worthwhile things, you'll be just as well off with one of the less conspicuous power styles.

Q. One of my major sales customers has that forehead widest shape. But I'm not sure you're right about the Passion Power idea. If you could only see his body language! This guy comes across as extremely laid back. Are you willing to admit you're wrong?

A. Not about your customer—I've done face readings for salespeople who work at the highest level of corporate sales. The Passion Power Style is disproportionately well represented here, and high-level salespeople have developed enormous skill at hiding their intensity. But how they love to be found out by an appreciative face reader! Here's something you can say, in a casual moment, to greatly enhance your personal relationship with such a person:

"I've been studying face reading and couldn't help but notice the proportions of your forehead. According to what I've studied, someone like you is secretly intense all the time and it never shuts off. This doesn't show in your body language but could it still be true?"

Be prepared to receive a shrewd and conspiratorial smile.

9. Mouths

Why do we stare so at eyes yet avert our glance when it comes to **mouths**? Usually we'll avoid lingering there unless a quick look shows a warm smile. It's like a storekeeper's sign that reads, "Open for business."

Smiles display that the establishment is available to the public, whereas other expressions show that the mouth owner has gone fishing or otherwise closed up shop. Everyday good manners demand that you avoid gawking at lips unless they greet you with a grin, a chunk of chat, or a kiss.

When was the last time you bumped into a friend who was walking alone, off in her private world? Remember what happened? The ringing tones of your "Hello" acted like a buzzer. She jumped to attention and re-arranged her face, most notably pushing her mouth into a public expression.

Ironically, mouths tell us a lot even when they make no attempt to communicate either verbally or non-verbally. As a face reader, you'll have great fun with how much mouths blab about their owner's styles of *self-expression*.

Lipfulness

Lipfulness means how full, even fat, lips are. To read it, you'll need to resist the temptation to see lips as simply big or small. You'll need to separate lipfulness from mouth length, which we'll consider separately.

- **Full** lips are at one extreme of lipfulness
- **Thin** lips at the other.

When you check out your own lip-quipment, please avoid the temptation to smile in the mirror. We know you like you (at least we hope so), but smiles change the way your mouth looks (or, at least, we hope so).

Q. Does it matter if you hate your mouth? I've always been ashamed of these skinny little lips.

A. All the more reason to throw inhibition to the wind and tell the world, "Read my lips." Look, your lips can't be skinnier than the ones on George H. Bush,* and he wasn't afraid to invite the whole country to stare at them. No doubt, Bush's handlers hoped he would be immortalized for creating a meaningful lip gesture universally understood to say: "No new taxes." And Bush probably meant folks to read the sincerity of his expression, as if his lips were pouting beseechingly or, perhaps, pointing.

Later, his tax promise turned out not to be true, which shows us not to trust when people use their lips for pointing. As for the lucky Americans who were physiognomists all along, we enjoyed the public prodding to go ahead and learn from the fellow's lips. Their message about personal style has never wavered; Bush's lips do show a special talent. To appreciate it, you'll need to educate yourself first about lipfulness, second about mouth length, and third how these categories combine. Then you'll delight in reading his Millionaire Mouth.

* Well, maybe President Calvin Coolidge's were—you remember "Silent Cal."

LIPFULNESS

Thin

Full

But first things first: *Lipfulness* is about self-disclosure. Does the person enjoy talking about personal stuff, like emotional secrets, psychological traumas (both mini- and maxi-sized), religious experiences, sexual preferences, ice cream preferences, why the socks he is wearing today don't match and what everyone else can learn from this experience.... You get the idea. There's a lot to divulge about me-me-me. And lipfulness shows your personal comfort zone in talking about, and listening to, these matters. In this regard, a stranger's amount of lipfulness is an even more reliable predictor of personal speech than asking if she comes from California.

Full lips are great for breaking a conversation wide open. The challenge is avoiding embarrassing others, especially in public. Remember the furor after full-lipped Jimmy Carter confessed to a reporter from *Playboy* that he had "lusted in his heart"?

People with relatively *thin* lips don't have to worry about creating a kiss-and-tell image. Their challenge is to talk about personal things at all. President Bush Sr., for instance—can you imagine him telling any reporter, let alone one from *Playboy*, about his lusts in any direction?

Fortunately, *talk* about sex bears no direct relationship to how often or well a person functions as a lover. Undeniably, *thin* lips are extremely helpful for politics, sales, and other aspects of business success. Maybe small lipfulness helped Bush Jr. to win Campaign 2000, his lips being far thinner than Gore's. And, based on lipfulness alone, guess which presidential candidate would be more comfortable planting a major kiss on his wife when being nominated at his party's convention, Bush or Gore. (Tipper's probably not the only person to remember that evidence of self-disclosure!)

Bill Clinton's fling with Monica Lewinski might not have reached media proportions if she didn't have the need to tell all to a friend—but then, consider her VERY large lipfulness. (Also that extra-full upper lip, related to outspokenness, as you'll read starting on Page 198.)

Back at the idea that small lipfulness could be advantageous for business pursuits, imagine yourself at a high-level executive's meeting. You feel absolutely no need to talk about personal things in order to come across as "authentic." Self-disclosure is not required for you to get close to people; your limited comfort with personal chat draws you into entirely different types of conversation.

Legally there's nothing wrong with making personal remarks at a meeting. It's a free country. But if even one major player at that meeting has thin lips, self-disclosing words could send shudders throughout the entire gathering.

Can you imagine Lee Iacocca, one of the nation's most famous executives, taking a break during a business meeting to talk up his longings for immortality? Reclusive author Don DeLillo, with his VERY thin lips, isn't likely to have this problem either. For 20 years, reports *The Washington Post*, he has carried cards printed with this message: "I don't want to talk about it."

Radio legend and author Garrison Keillor has joked about taking up the cause of "Shy Rights." When it comes to self-disclosure, with those VERY thin lips, he's certainly shy. But regarding talking to loads of people as a performer, he's obviously not, and we'll discuss this aspect of his communication style later in this chapter. The contrast between one kind of shyness and its exact opposite helps Keillor to be so funny when discussing shyness.

Q. What if your mouth is weird, and your top and bottom lips have entirely different amounts of fullness?

A. Almost everyone's mouth has that kind of "weirdness." Reading lipfulness involves making a general assessment of how full both lips, on average, appear. But now that you've mastered this category, you can leap forward—or lip forward—to the category of lip proportions.

■■■

Lip proportions

To read **lip proportions**, all you need do is compare the fullness of upper and lower lips.

- Most people have a lower lip that is somewhat fuller than the upper one, what I call a **moderately fuller lower lip**.
- Lips that differ from this norm are even more fun to read. An **extra-full lower lip** means that a lower lip that is two, three or more times fuller than the upper one.
- As for an **extra-full upper lip**, that means the upper lip is as full as the lower one.

Q. So the upper lip doesn't have to be two or three times fuller to count, like the lower one has to, in order to be a special trait?

A. That's right. Believe me, equally full or slightly fuller on top is plenty for a lip-wearer to handle.

Lip proportions contrast the relative amount of speech about objective, factual things (represented by the lower lip) versus the relative amount of speech about subjective, intuitive matters (represented by the upper lip).

Q. Hold on. Are you saying that a full upper lip is about talking in an emotional way?

A. No. Any lip proportions can utter speech that has great emotional intensity—or none. Upper lip fullness relates to speech that specializes in topics are that are inner, personal, even secret.

Most people, having a *moderately fuller lower lip*, talk more about the facts than the nuances.

LIP PROPORTIONS

Moderately fuller lower lip

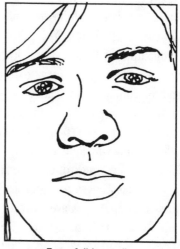

Extra-full lower lip

Extra-full upper lip

By contrast, an *extra-full lower lip* is a big deal. It's such a big deal to know about that the following information alone should be worth the full price of this book:

The meaning of these special lip proportions is persuasiveness. Lailan Young, the world's foremost practitioner of *Siang Mien* since the death of Timothy Mar, has coined the perfect term for it: **Blarney Lips**. Have you ever heard of kissing the Blarney Stone? According to Irish folklore, this is the rock to kiss because it conveys the gift of gab. From the instant you land that kiss, your speech will convince and charm the listener—regardless of what you're talking about.

Why is persuasiveness so important to read? As a consumer, you can put yourself on alert whenever someone with Blarney Lips tries to do a sales job on you, be it for designer ice needed by Eskimos, the neatest gadget since bread slicers, or a delightful job making new friends while you earn gobs of money... as a telemarketer.

Muster up your skepticism soon as you eyeball those lips. Not that the folks who have them are necessarily dishonest, they're just such darned good convincers. When *Washingtonian Magazine* ran a list of the nation's 50 most influential journalists, I spotted 46 of them with Blarney Lips, most of them VERYs. With average folks you'd find maybe one pair out of a group of 50, and a VERY pair for one in 500.

The following page lists a random assortment of people even more famous than those Blarney Lipped journalists. Some you may admire, others not. All they share is that special oomph in their lip proportions and, with that, a gift for persuasiveness.

If *you* are the one with Blarney Lips, congratulations. Your persuasiveness may come so easily that you haven't thought much about it. More than any other single face trait, it augurs success. Just remember to use it along with integrity.

As for having an *extra-full upper lip*, another name for your facial gift is **Outspoken Perceptiveness**.

This gift has three components:

VERY Persuasive Mouths

Elvis Presley	A singer of undying fame (and, some would say, undying body)
Pat Buchanan	Unsuccessful presidential candidate whose book, *A Republic, Not an Empire*, gave the most compelling revisionist argument you're likely to hear for going easy on Hitler
Margaret Thatcher	Longtime British prime minister
Keokuk	Tribal ruler
Bill Gates	Currently leads the nation's computer tribe
Andy Warhol	The Pop artist pops onto our list
Pablo Picasso	Expressive artist, even when painting only in blue
Marlon Brando	A convincing actor even when silent
Harrison Ford	The biggest box office draw in screen history
Russell Baker	One of the nation's greatest dry wits
Fran Liebowitz	An even drier wit, expressed with such persuasiveness that she causes readers to temporarily imagine they have dry wits, too
Dave Barry	Americans also think he's funny (We're not making this up.)
Rush Limbaugh	Radio host who has gone so far as to merchandize bumper stickers that read, "Rush is Right"
Roger Horchow	Who prefers selling catalogs
Larry King	A talk show king
Al Capone	A king of crime
Jerry Falwell	A one-time king among televangelists
P.T. Barnum	The circus impresario who claimed, "A sucker is born every minute."

1. You know what's really going on behind the scenes.
2. You're articulate. You can find the words to capture the nuances.
3. You want to tell all.

This last part is tricky because the person you're telling may not want to listen. Your challenge involves learning when to hold back, even if what you have to say is important. Otherwise, you'll be rewarded with defensiveness; even before you open your highly accurate mouth, people will be suspicious.

Nonetheless, courageous folks with outspoken perceptiveness sometimes are rewarded for speaking their truth. Chief Seattle is the only Native American to have had a major U.S. city named after him. Physicist Chen Ning Yang won the Nobel Prize; novelist Arundhati Roy won the coveted Booker Prize for *The God of Small Things*—small, yes, but Roy described them anyhow.

Marian Wright Edelman has dared to speak out on behalf of children, founding the Children's Defense Fund. Roberta Flack has sung with outspoken intensity. Gary Shandling's sitcom is arguably the funniest on cable; he says what's usually considered unsayable. Poet laureate Maya Angelou likewise specializes in telling outrageous truths. In *Even the Stars Look Lonesome* she shares a hilarious story about her mother's appetites and writes about herself: "I have reached the lovely age where I can admit that sensuality satisfies me as much as sexuality and sometimes more so." One more boundary smashed by Maya!

Q. What if, like me, you work in sales and you have those Outspoken Perceptiveness Lips? Should I get a lip operation to turn them into Blarneys?

A. You can be successful with any face trait. That's the underlying message of face reading, along with a reminder to make whatever you have work for you.

Q. But I do tend to speak my mind and say things that shake people up. It's the story of my life. How can that be an asset for sales?

A. Choose wisely what you sell, for starters. Services may be easier for you to sell than products, because you can draw out your customer's unspoken needs.

In addition, salespeople of all types need to look customers straight in the mouth. Full lips on your client mean you'll score points by volunteering some personal experiences. Your client will open up, knowing that self-disclosing to you is safe. But thin lips on your client mean "Don't open that mouth too wide or you'll blow the sale."

Mouth length

Now that you've graduated from lipfulness, with all its variations, you're ready to consider **mouth length**.

- Be sure to learn to read **short** lips.
- Admire the relatively rare **long** lips.
- And pay attention when people have **medium**-length lips.

Why not check out your own mouth length right now? When you do, please take the precaution of *not* smiling. A mouth should be in repose for an accurate reading of this trait.

Mouth length tells you about a person's most comfortable audience size. Maybe you've read that, according to surveys, the Number One Fear for Americans is public speaking. Go figure! It ranks even higher than death.

I can relate. Like the majority of people, I have *short* lips, which go with a preference for communicating one-on-one. Learning public speaking can be a great challenge for folks like us. I bumped smack into this problem when studying to become a meditation teacher. It was required that I give public lectures. After months of agonizing practice,

MOUTH LENGTH

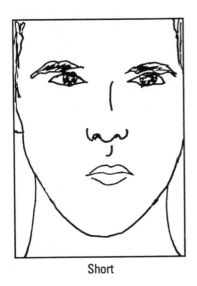

Short

Long

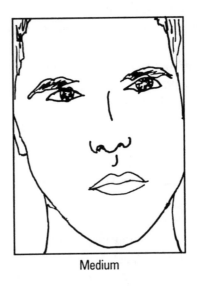

Medium

I delivered my first speech. Even though everyone in the audience was also studying to be a meditation teacher and had pretty much memorized that same speech, I didn't dare to look at a soul. Instead I read my notes straight from the page.

Afterwards I looked up and finally dared to make eye contact with my audience. Fifteen people had heard me. Every one of them was shaking—physically shaking. (Hmm, turns out I had communicated my terror pretty effectively.) It took years before I learned to use my power as a speaker on purpose. Having overcome the challenge, I can benefit from the gifts that go with short lips: sincerity and truthfulness.

Two short-lipped speakers have made supreme use of these gifts. I'm thinking of Supreme Court Justices Thurgood Marshall and Ruth Bader Ginsburg. Attorney General Janet Reno has displayed unwavering integrity, even when barraged with criticism. In the world of entertainment, Barbara Walters may owe her success to the sincere style that helps her coax out answers to outrageously personal questions. She charms her interviewees into thinking they're talking one on one, not in front of millions. Oops.

Long lips are more the norm in broadcasting. They go with the ability to talk with anyone. TV talk show hosts benefit from this gift, right from the pioneering work of Phil Donahue. Today you can see a huge assortment of long-lipped hosts, including: David Letterman, Joan Rivers, Charlie Rose, and Maury Povich.

Friendliness is another name for this gift. The potential challenge is being a social chameleon, saying things to go along with the group and, afterwards, rationalizing that what you said is what you really believed. What did you really believe, anyway?

When actress Julia Roberts married singer Lyle Lovett, it was a great match of VERY long lips. Even though their marital conversations didn't work out, apparently, their longstanding popularity as performers attests to the appeal of lips that, figuratively, reach out to the widest possible audience.

Q. How about mediocre lips like mine? What are medium-sized lips good for?

A. Please don't underestimate the value of traits in the average range. With *medium* mouth length, your range of communication is flexible. You feel equally comfortable talking one-on-one and addressing crowds (especially if you've had the chance to practice speechifying a half dozen times or more). Truthfulness is your strongest mode of self-expression but you are better at lying than short-mouthed folks, who are usually terrible at it. Being the life of the party is a role you can take, like the long-mouthed tribe, but you'll find it easier to share the verbal spotlight.

In general, an adaptable speech style makes life easier for you. The only challenge is a mere lack of tolerance for the rest of humanity. Adaptability is nothing to sneeze at, meanwhile. Medium-length-and-width lips helped TV's longest-running, most influential talk show host Johnny Carson. Newsman Walter Cronkite hasn't done badly with moderate lips, nor has Dustin Hoffman, revered as an actor's actor.

Special lip gifts

And you just believed in the tooth fairy.... There's a mouth fairy, too. She has bestowed certain gifts for communication on special people with extreme lips. You might be one.

Here are the mouth gifts we haven't discussed yet:

- VERY long lips that are thin
- VERY long lips that are full
- VERY short lips that are thin
- VERY short lips that are full

VERY long, thin lips signify that the owner has **Millionaire Mouth**. George Bush has it. Chrysler bail-out man Lee Iacocca has it. So does Garrison Keillor, which explains my previous comment that his mouth doesn't count as truly shy.

Millionaire Mouth is great for politics, business or wry humor, because it means you can talk to anyone about anything (so long as it isn't personal stuff about you). The words need not be, strictly speaking, true. But they will reach out to everyone in the group, no matter how large the gathering.

By not embarrassing potential clients with self-disclosure, Millionaire Mouths can discretely amass their fortunes, as has candyman Forrest Mars, Sr. or Sam Walton, founder of Wal-Mart and, at the time of his death, the richest man in America. Cordell Hull used his diplomatic speech in service to humanity, as the father of the United Nations.

The most exuberant way with words goes with **VERY long, full lips**, which I call the **Born Talker Mouth**. Think of bestselling author Amy Tan, whose idea of a relaxing hobby is to perform in a rock band. Feminist fitness guru Susan Powter has lost an awesome number of pounds but not an ounce of it, glad to say, off her lips.

It's hard to find someone with this trait who doesn't have a wacky sense of humor, just as it would be unimaginable for a short, thin mouth to belong to an Eddie Murphy.

But **VERY short, thin lips** have their special excellence, too. I call them **Privacy Lips**. Yes, their owners may hold in feelings, replay old insults, and frustrate friends by being taciturn. But the words that come out can carry such power, they shake people right to the core. Examples are songwriter Bob Dylan, cosmetics magnate Mary Kay Ash, and designer Giorgio Armani, designer of understatedly oomphy fashions.

Let's not leave out another extremely interesting kind of mouth. **VERY short and full lips** are **Best Friend Lips**. They suggest a willingness to tell the truth, the whole truth, without restriction. Just one catch, though—the juicy stuff will mostly be shared one-on-one. The tantalizing promise of these intense lips may help explain the popularity of actors Richard Gere and Michael Keaton.

Q. Confession time, all right? I still hate my lips, all right? I've never liked how they look and after all you've said about them I still don't. What do you have to say to that?

A. Nobody can force you to love your face. For most people, it's enough to understand the meaning of whichever traits you don't like, which puts a whole new spin, as it were, on that feature. In the case of you and your mouth, however, it sounds like we're going to have to recommend something more drastic—an operation.

Q. Cosmetic surgery, you mean?

A. No, the name for this procedure comes from cosmetic surgery, but this is a quickie operation that won't shed a drop of blood. And it's strictly do-it-yourself. Call it **lip-oh-suction**. For this version you won't need anesthesia or someone to extract anything out of your thighs. The only equipment you'll need is a mirror. Hold one in your hand now. Ready?

Suck in your lips as hard as you can. Press them against your teeth and slurp mightily, as if getting rid of your lips forever. Freeze.

Take a good look. Do you like your face any better this way? If so, you can always resort to this method whenever you look in a mirror. Otherwise, admit it. Your regular lips are just fine. So relax. Enjoy them.

■■■

10. Jaws and chins

Okay, **jaws** and **chins** may not seem as soulful as eyes. But they are the face's bottom line, revealing vital matters about principles, ethics, choices, and *handling conflict*.

By now you wouldn't be surprised to learn that chins and jaws are highly important, right? By now, you're so used to face parts taking on a life of their own that you could meet Mr. Potato Head walking down the street and not bat an eyelash— except perhaps to think he was on the short side for a grownup human. And if he flung you an extra ear or nose, you'd probably pocket it cheerfully, thinking how it might come in handy some day.

Such is the wisdom of a face reader. You know there is no such thing as a throwaway, or insignificant, face part. All of it counts. That includes chins, even though they're not generally loved or respected nearly enough.

In fact, it is my special pleasure in this chapter to restore the good name of what is commonly, and insultingly, known as a "weak" chin. Weak at what?

You'll be surprised, but first let's jaw your attention outwards from the chin. Let's explore the fascinating bony structure that comes complete with its own built-in hinge.

Jaw width

Just when you thought it was safe to go back in the water, Uh oh! It's time for **jaw width**.

- Exactly how wide are **wide** jaws, anyway? Let's put it this way. You can stash away several wads of chewing gum and still not have them show. One time, at least, in your face reading career, please give yourself the benefit of trying the gumless way to identify wide jaws: Find someone whose jaws look wide from the front (someone with a short haircut) and watch that person from the back. See how the ends of the jaws stick right out? Wow that's wide!
- **Narrow** jaws are harder to recognize, even from the front. They don't catch your eye the way wide jaws, too. You're more apt to overlook them. But as a face reader, don't.
- **Average** jaw width is what most people have. When you look at the overall face width, jaws fit nicely in proportion, sticking out neither more nor less than the area right under the cheeks.

Jaws symbolize two related aspects of life, *physical stamina* and non-physical *tenacity*.

With few exceptions, *wide* jaws are a job requirement for a professional he-man—common among professional football players, for instance. The jaws are endearing on long-running rock star, Mick Jagger, whose concert performances are aerobic feats of endurance. Professional he-men who lack huge jaws will have to make up for it with other facial signs of strength or sexiness.

Take Supermen, for instance. The original cartoon character has huge jaws, and so has Christopher Reeve, the big screen's most successful Superman yet. Since the accident that left him paralyzed, Reeve

JAW WIDTH

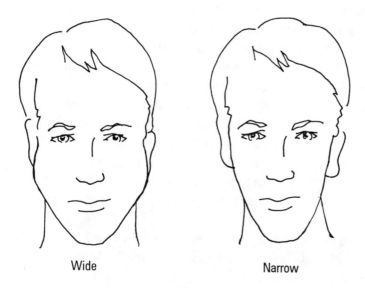

Wide   Narrow

Average

has relied on the non-physical talent that shows in his jaws. Tenacity helps him to keep stretching his limits.

TV Superman Dean Cain makes up for jaws of average width with his left cheek peekaboo dimple (see the chapter on Sex)—not to mention a body that ripples with a convincing array of muscles.

Rocky, Rambo-like Sylvester Stallone keeps finding new roles to flex his rippling jaws. Arnold Schwarzenegger is the opposite—his jaws are surprisingly narrow. Actually they are proportionally smaller than those belonging to his wife, Maria Schriver. But the next time you see his face, notice that VERY wide forehead (read it as the Passion Power style—intense psychic energy) plus VERY full eyebrows, suggesting a massive intellect.

It is, in fact, true that the strength of people with *narrow* jaws is early detection of conflict, rather than endurance for handling a protracted battle. Recognize yourself here? Then, when you land in a tough situations, initiate the difficult conversation. Resolve the problem fast or get out.

Author Terry McMillan's characters do that, helped no doubt by her own strengths in the narrow-jaw department. Jaws of country singers Randy Travis and Martina McBride show the same gift for quick recognition, and dispatch, of conflict.

By contrast, people with wide jaws revel at hanging on, despite the most difficult circumstances. World War II heroes Sir Winston Churchill and President Eisenhower fulfilled the promise of their VERY wide jaws. The place where you live might now be a Nazi suburb if Churchill didn't have the attitude he once spelled out this way:

"Never give in. Never give in. Never never never never—in nothing, great or small, large or petty—never give in except to convictions of honor and good sense."

Of course, men aren't the only ones whose careers can benefit from the toughness that shows in wide jaws. Outstanding specimens belong to Sally Ride, America's first female astronaut; choreographer Paula Abdul; yoga teacher Lilias Folan; and Sally Field, an actress whose popularity has shown enormous staying power. Kay Shirley is a wide-jawed financial commentator who advocates getting rich *slowly*.

Q. Funny you should talk about jaws in terms of staying power, rather than starting power. Although I've been married 12 years, my husband still teases me about how long it took me to commit to the relationship. Any comment?

A. Commitment is a major deal for someone with wide jaws like yours. Yes, the challenge is to agonize over making a commitment. You know why? Deep down you know what you're in for... if *you* decide to commit, you will stay in that relationship, or job, 'till death (or other catastrophe) do you part.

On the lighter side, I had to chuckle when I saw the face of author Carl Sewell. His specialty involves turning one-time buyers into *Customers for Life*. Wide jaws do tend to go with self-imposed life sentences. Even if you heal the challenge about agonizing, you're going to keep that magnificent loyalty. And others will value it in you....

Except, of course, for the lucky ones with *average* jaw width—by now you know the story of mid-range traits. If you have these jaws, you don't agonize over commitments. Your stick-to-itiveness works just fine, and your only potential challenge is questioning the strange behavior around you. Why not just handle a conflict, whatever it is, for a reasonable amount of time, then move on? But defining "reasonable" isn't easy to do on behalf of others, any more than recognizing one's own sneaky problem, a lack of tolerance for the rest of humanity.

Chin thrust

How do you read **chin thrust**? Watch the face in profile, of course. Then look at the overall sweep of face, not just the chin. You can draw

CHIN THRUST

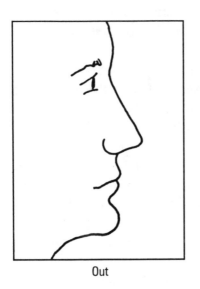

Out

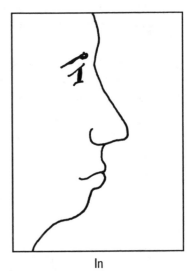

In

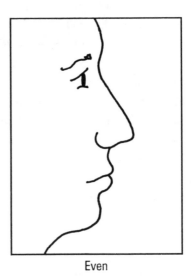

Even

an imaginary line, starting at the forehead, skipping over the nose, continuing at the overlip and going down to the neck. What is the angle of that line?

- When chins look **out**-angled, as most do, the person shows a lot of chin thrust.
- Some chins are **in**-angled, which is sometimes called a "receding" chin. I'm not fond of that expression because it implies that the chin is moving out from shore, much like a "receding" hairline. But chins and foreheads are not beaches with their inevitable tides. Their contours have meaning. Chin thrust has so much meaning, in fact, that it is one of the few face traits that seldom changes. Sometimes in-angled chin thrust is called "weak" as well as "receding" And sometimes small chin size is called "weak" too. Neither chin trait deserves contempt—on the contrary, as we'll see later.
- **Even** chins are rarest of all.

What do you have?

Q. But what happens to the thrust factor when people stick out their chins?

A. It counts. Thrusting the lower part of the face forward is a well-known act of defiance. Seems to me, anyone who is willing to spend day and night poking out her chin has earned honorary status as having an out-angled chin.

It's common knowledge that a VERY *out-angled chin* relates to competitiveness. During presidential campaigns, it's always fun to watch the contenders... and their spouses. So far, I've yet to see anyone beat Jacqueline Kennedy Onassis.

Outside of politics, feisty chin angles show in the faces of social work pioneer Jane Addams, and General John Pershing. If you're a fan of yacht racing, you can appreciate how Dennis Conner's style of aggression has made him a winner. Or if racecars are more your speed, how about the way Cale Yarborough has made his impression in the Daytona 500!

Marianne Williamson has many face traits that show sensitivity and gentleness. Her VERY large chin thrust balances it, however, and the grit in that chin has helped her to take the relatively unknown spiritual text, *A Course in Miracles*, and give it (and herself) a national following.

Actress Drew Barrymore didn't consider herself spunky enough for for her role in "Charlie's Angels" so offscreen she forced herself to jump off a waterfall. No doubt her chin led the way.

But the most VERY out-angled chin I've seen in show biz (or anywhere else, actually) belongs to Jay Leno. His rapid-fire, nonstop delivery as a comic perfectly expresses this aggressive style. The man does not pause until he has made his audience laugh so hard and long, everyone's breathless.

The potential challenge with out-angled chins is unnecessary aggression. Guess which people best appreciate this drawback? It's the crew with in-angled chins.

What a mistake it would be to call these chins "weak." After all, was First Lady Eleanor Roosevelt weak? She has been admired as the equal, at least, of her extraordinary husband. The terminology is revealing, however. It demonstrates how people can undervalue an honorable trait. *In-angled chins* show community spirit. Rather than tear apart relationships through conflict, people with these chins choose to conciliate and compromise. They'll take on extra work more readily than grabbing credit for what they may not deserve.

What's the challenge? It's obtaining respect, from others and self, in a society that undervalues community and overvalues aggression. Joseph Lieberman, America's first Jewish candidate for vice-president, has won respect in the Senate for his gently inclusive style, yet many commentators considered him an ineffective debater against out-chinned Cheney.

Once you start reading this facet of chins, you'll find that folks with the in-angled variety tend to be gentle souls. Philosopher Henri Bergson had such a chin, as does angelologist Rev. Jane Howard. Joni Mitchell and Aaron Copland have composed music with very different styles, both very intense yet balanced with their chin's trademark gentle, in-angled sensitivity.

As for *even-angled chins*, they go with a natural perspective about compromise and aggression. These folks will neither take advantage, nor let themselves be trampled upon. Lucky souls, their only challenge is the usual lack of tolerance for the rest of humanity. Examples are Laura D'Andrea Tyson, topnotch communicator as well as chair of Clinton's Council of Economic Advisors; U.N. Secretary General Boutros Boutros-Ghali; and ballerina Gelsey Kirkland.

Q. How about those who play a defensive game? Offensive attack isn't the only way to win, any more than conciliation.

A. Exactly right. To see who specializes in staying power, look at a chin head-on. As with mouths, there are two main sets of traits, vertical and horizontal.

Chin length

The simplest way to read **chin length** is to look at a chin from your usual straight, face-reader's angle. Make a quick decision about length, relative to the rest of the person's face.

- Does the chin look **long?**
- Or **short?**

Chin length relates to risk taking, also to bouncing back from adversity.

A *long* chin marks a person who is likely to take physical risks. It also suggests that, when misfortunes arise, the person can "take it on the chin." Literally, there's plenty of chin to take "it" on.

One example of such a chin is pilot Amelia Earhart. Another is May Kunin, who struggled to survive despite Nazi persecution. She became so astute, she beat the odds to join one of the most exclusive clubs in America: Governors Who Are Women. (Okay, I made up the name, but doesn't the acronym, GWAW, sound like a mighty growl?)

Patricia Neal's immense prestige as an actress has been rivaled by admiration for her courage in recovering from a stroke that left her unable to speak, read, or walk. And singer Ray Charles has fought even longer, with magnificent courage, against physical blindness, emotional instability, and the tough world of professional entertainment.

What about a *short* chin? Does it deserve to be called weak? Yes, if you mainly value taking *physical* risks. But short chins go with taking *emotional* risks.

Ethical strength is another factor. If you have a short chin, you know that you walk your talk. Sunday ethics aren't only for church. In fact, you may give yourself an awfully hard time over those personal ethics.

Let's say you absent-mindedly pick up a pen at the bank. You find it after you get home. What happens? With a long chin, you'd think, "Too bad. Well, the thing couldn't have cost more than a quarter. Anyway, they've got plenty." But with that blazing conscience of a short chin, you're more apt to worry, "Abe Lincoln would have walked all the way back to the bank to return that pen, even if it was 15 miles. I've just got to return that pen."

Another way to describe the loud Jiminy Cricket voice inside you is to say that you're *wired for guilt.* Not only sins of omission, like accidental pen thievery, can set off the alarm. So can criticism from other people. Consider yourself forewarned. Just because you have all those guilt circuits in place, you don't have to switch them on. Why torture

CHIN LENGTH

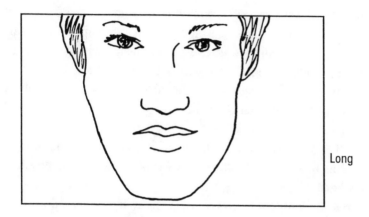

Long

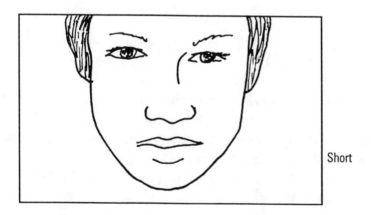

Short

yourself? In the words of Sigmund Freud, who supplemented his own chin length with a fine chunk of beard, "Sometimes a cigar is just a cigar."

However, a challenge with criticism doesn't necessarily make short chin-owners wimpy. Think of women who have competed in highly prestigious, male-dominated fields like Dr. Chien-shiung Wu. Diminutive chin notwithstanding, she has earned a reputation as "the queen of nuclear physics." Then there's astronaut Mae C. Jemison. Do you think the horde of male astronaut wannabes ever teased her at all?

Q. What if you grow a beard? Does that count as lengthening your chin to the point where you become more of a physical risk taker?

A. Yes, the longer you grow that beard, the more physically daring you'll become—just avoid the temptation to use the thing as a rope for bungee jumping.

Chin width

Having learned to see chin length as a separate category, you're ready to go horizontal and appreciate **chin width**. To develop an eye for this category, it may be helpful to bring a slang term to mind: mug. You've heard of mug shots, right? Well, with a face reader's sophisticated eye, you'll find the shapes at the bottom of faces can remind you of mugs and other types of crockery.

■ Some chins are small from the sideways direction, however long they may be. These chins can look like little teacups or serving pieces for demitasse. Call them **narrow** chins. Narrow, too, are

CHIN WIDTH

Narrow

Broad

the longer versions that look more like fully formed mugs (except that they have no handles).

■ **Wide** chins are built firmly into the jaw, like pottery that you would put underneath other serving pieces. Sometimes they're short and broad, like thick saucers; the longer, hefty ones are shaped more like the plates to go under your soup bowl in a fancy restaurant, or even a bowl to go under your bowl, which is too fancy for any restaurant I've ever been to but works just fine for some chins—and I'm not even talking about double chins. Incidentally, if what you see at the bottom of a face makes you think of a *flying saucer*, you've transcended the face altogether.

Q. This discussion of chins is making me realize that normally I overlook this part of the face. All I ever notice usually is the nice long chins. But short ones, wide ones, narrow ones—it's like a new world. Do many people start off ignoring the wide world of chins?

A. You bet, and it's wasteful. What if people said the only eyes worth looking at had to be a rare shade of gray? Take a good look at your own chin right now and see what you have. It's too revealing to pass up. Especially if you're marrying someone, you'll want to know which personal styles show in your chin widths.

Let's see if you can figure out the meaning of *chin width*. Here are some hints:

■ Width on a *nose*, the padding, is about being willing to work with people.
■ Width on *lips*, mouth length, is about the number of people in your ideal audience.
■ Given that *chins*, from the front, are about handling adversity, can you guess the meaning of chin width?

Q. Gee, could it be about having people around to cheer yourself up?

A. Bravo, that's it! *Narrow* chins suggest that when faced with adversity, your instinct is to go it alone, or with just one significant other. Think of how convincingly narrow-chinned actor Humphrey Bogart sent off Ingrid Bergman at the end of "Casablanca." Note the words of narrow-chinned songwriter Marvin Hamlisch, who has called composing "such a lonely life."

Wide chins suggest you have a support group. They tell the world that you expect (and, therefore, manifest) plenty of help in responding to challenges. Examples are Betty Ford, founder of the famous rehabilitation center, and Warren Burger, the exceptionally influential Supreme Court Justice.

Long, broad chins are an amazing natural defense against adversity. The challenge is putting oneself in a position where this defense must be used. Just look at the varied kinds of risk-taking involved in the careers of comedian Victor Borge, dancer (and Soviet defector) Mikhail Baryshnikov, and Tony Brown—he's the host of the longest-running national public affairs program for African-Americans. These are people who can "take it on the chin." As far as chin is concerned, they're well endowed.

Q. As a manager, I'm keenly aware of how people on my sales staff handle rejection. Can you give me any tips, based on chins, to help me keep my people motivated?

A. Glad you asked. Mouth traits have already clued you in to how much people will tell you about what they're going through (remember, the folks with full lips will share, the thin-lipped ones won't). Chins clue you in to the unspoken aspects of handling rejection or other adversity.

To keep motivation up, periodically honor your staff with wide chins by throwing them parties. Celebrations help them plug into group support.

But give folks with narrow chins private time to recover from adversity. Don't expect a rah! rah! attitude to cheer them up. Compared to wide chinners, their strength comes from a different direction.

Chin bottom shape

Might it ever be helpful if you could predict how a man makes decisions? If the answer is yes, you'll want to read his **chin bottom**. When you are wise to the Secrets about what motivates decisions, you can appeal to decision-makers on their own wavelength.

First, though, you'll need to know what to look for on the physical face. Start with your own chin and look at the shape it makes right at the bottom.

- **Curved** chins are most common by far.
- You'll also find **straight** chins—writing their signature on a face with an underline beneath.
- Hardest of all to find (and also to physically recognize), are the **angled** chins. These tend to be narrow in width, and when you look carefully you'll notice a tapering of the entire chin.

A *curved* chin shows that decisions are based on people: how they will feel, how their lives will be affected by your choice. Round-chinners tend to be humanitarians. Tipper Gore risked ridicule by taking on the unpopular cause of *Raising PG Kids in an X-Rated Society*. Other curved chins belong to children's songwriters Tom Chapin, Dennis Hysom, and Tom Paxton. One of America's greatest legislators of all time, Supreme Court Justice Thurgood Marshall, had a supremely curved chin.

CHIN BOTTOM

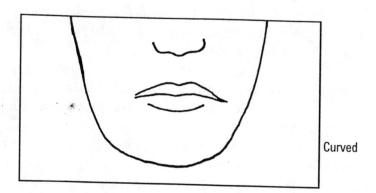

Curved

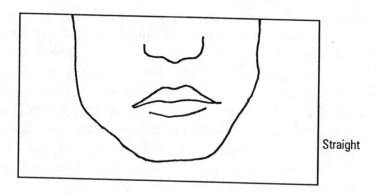

Straight

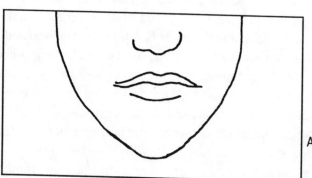

Angled

Curved chins also involve something very practical: hospitality. If you're going to crash a party, go to one given by a VERY curved chin. You'll be glad you came, food-wise.

One of my favorite images of hospitality is the photo of Laurel Robertson in the cookbook she inspired, *Laurel's Kitchen*. In keeping with her narrow but VERY curved chin, the book inspires the reader with friendliness and kindheartedness.

People with *straight* chins are more likely to show their mettle by hosting political rallies and other cause-related events. This style specializes in making choices based on ideals and ideas.

Does it sound abstract to imagine someone caring passionately about an idea? Just think of straight-chinner George Washington, hardly an armchair philosopher. Ballplayer Jackie Robinson's reliance on principle may have helped him break through the color barrier that had kept African-American players out of major league baseball. One of the most controversial idea-principled figures in America today has a VERY straight chin. It belongs to Dr. Jack Kevorkian, who has championed the cause of physician-assisted suicide. Attorney General John Ashcroft's extreme chin bottom is accentuated by a unique ridge of protruding flesh. He, too, pushes uncompromisingly for his beliefs.

Every chin bottom comes with its challenge. Curved chin people can be hopeless mushballs when they make their decisions, giving in to sentimentality rather than thinking "straight" about long-term consequences. We who have straight chins face an equally important challenge, however—thinking in black and white. To us, it's always the principle of the thing, either good or bad, with no middle-ground. Dr. Laura Schlessinger, in her hit talk radio show and bestselling books, promotes something admirable: the value of character (commitment, too, in keeping with her VERY wide jaws). Some listeners, however, feel that Dr. Laura's advice is a bit heavy on the judgments concerning right and wrong (not to mention her views about innate sexual preference).

Having a straight chin, too, I know how easy it can be to turn harshly judgmental. Witness an unfortunate incident from my own life (and chin) that clearly illustrates this challenge. One morning when Matt was five, we set out in the car. Although rushed, I was also determined to gulp down my breakfast as we raced through town. So I asked Matt to hold in his lap a plastic container filled with dry cereal. This container was shallow and flat, and I could imagine how stopping short would scatter crunchy little O's of goodness all over the car. I told Matt I needed him to hold onto my breakfast box with at least one hand until I was done. Then I gave him a little pep talk to inspire obedience:

"Remember the fairy tales?" I said. "The hero is given a difficult task to perform. And if he's successful, he gets to marry the King's daughter. If he fails, they chop off his head. It's like that. If you let go of my cereal box, I'm afraid it's going to be a big problem."

"But Mom" protested my kid. "Aren't there any shades of gray about this?"

It affords me some consolation to think of the things that must slip out of the mouths of parents who have *angled* chins (wish I could eavesdrop in their cars!) because of their need to stay in control. Control is their blessing and curse all rolled up into one chin-sized package.

No doubt such an angled chin helped Jim Bakker work the crowds as a televangelist. Then again, you could look at Alexander Haig, Jr., the controversial hawk who rose to power as White House Chief of Staff under Nixon. My favorite activist with an angled chin is the Duke of Wellington, famous for taking control of Napoleon (at the battle of Waterloo). He also was good at conquering excessive weather (thanks to Wellington boots).

Astute angled-chin tennis player Jimmy Connors has harnessed his urge for control to become a champion, if not always a perfect good sport. A similar chin bottom helped the career of the legendary female athlete Babe Didrikson Zaharias.

Folks with VERY angled, short chins may have the sneakiest face bottoms of all. Admit this little secret, if you have one of these rare chins: VERY angled chin folk (nearly always women) may appear delicate and

BEARD BOTTOM

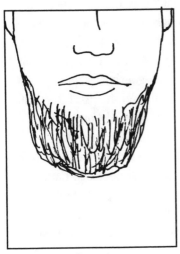

Curved

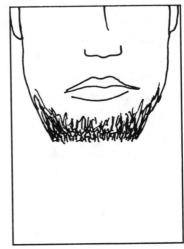

Straight

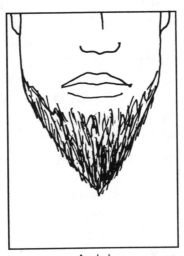

Angled

vulnerable, but it masks a will of iron. Your potential challenge is making choices just to show others, "Nobody's going to tell me what to do."

Think about Elizabeth Taylor, who has shown the mettle of her chin by insisting on frequent marriages, some of them to unlikely candidates—but that's her decision, thank you! In recent years, her chin has broadened out to a curve. Her choices have broadened, too, in a humanitarian direction, as she has become increasingly outspoken as an A.I.D.S. activist. Who knows what will happen with the lives (and chins, and clothing choices), of angled-chinned young stars like Jennifer Lopez, Toni Braxton, and Charlize Theron.

Control has its advantages, certainly. Another show biz legend is Mary Pickford, the silent screen star who won fame with her winsome manner and golden curls. Among financial experts, she is recognized as one of the shrewdest businesswomen ever to have come out of Hollywood.

Q. I think I can read all three chin bottoms okay except how am I going to find the real chin bottom underneath a beard?

A. Good news here—you don't have to play archeologist, unearthing one layer of chin under another. The topmost civilization counts: beard bottom *is* chin bottom.

Q. But what if a man disguises his real chin with his beard? Goatees are probably a heck of a lot more common than angled chins.

A. When you change your face on the outside, you also change your personal style on the inside. To rephrase a popular saying, "Be careful what you wish to disguise yourself as. You will surely become it."

Think, too, about the physical similarity between chin bottoms and **beard bottoms**. They can be **curved**, **straight**, or **angled**. One difference: with beards, whatever the shape, it counts as a VERY.

A *curved* shape is most famous as a **Santa Claus Beard**. Don't you associate it with a kindly humanitarian? A contemporary version is worn by holistic health guru, Dr. Andrew Weil.

The *straight* shape I call **Mountain Man Beard**. It speaks of independence and cerebral choices, as on the face of author/philosopher Leo Tolstoy.

As for the *angled* beard bottom, it is well known as a **goatee**. The Marquis de Sade may have had the scariest one ever. Revolutionary Leon Trotsky wasn't exactly Mr. Rogers, either. And in a class by himself is Orson Welles, the film great who accidentally (one hopes) brought panic to the country with his radio broadcast, "War of the Worlds," about the invasion of men from Mars.

Q. I'm confused. Chins and beards tell us about choices, but didn't eyebrows tell us about how people think? And don't choices hopefully involve thinking?

A. Don't let the distinction confuse you when it can sharpen your wits instead. A man will think and talk in a manner symbolized by eyebrows; he'll decide and act in a manner symbolized by chin/beard bottom. And have you noticed yet that the shapes are the same? Well, yes, the chin one is turned upside down, but otherwise the facial symbols are identical:

- Curved for people-oriented
- Straight for idea-oriented
- Angled for control-oriented.

Q. Can you give some specific examples of the various combinations?

A. Here's a summary of the nine possible combos, with three examples for each:

- Curved Eyebrows + a Curved Chin
Puts people first, in principle, practice, and performance
President Franklin Delano Roosevelt
First Lady Pat Nixon
Singer Marian Anderson

- Curved Eyebrows + a Straight Chin
Notices feelings but focuses efforts on abstract ideas and principles
President Abraham Lincoln
First Lady Rosalynn Carter
Makeup magnate Charles Revson

- Curved Eyebrows + an Angled Chin
Stages events to profit from sensitivity to people's feelings
President Franklin Pierce
First Lady Helen Taft
Novelist specializing in social irony, Jane Austen

- Straight Eyebrows + a Curved Chin
Fascinated by abstract ideas, but accomplishes goals by appealing to people's feelings
President Harry Truman
First Lady Martha Washington
Singer Johnny Cash

- Straight Eyebrows + a Straight Chin
Uses concepts to flesh out principles
President George Bush
First Lady Frances Cleveland
Movie mogul Samuel Goldwyn

- Straight Eyebrows + an Angled Chin
Intellectually captivated by ideas; uses them as part of the need to dominate
President William Taft
First Lady Louisa Adams
Billy the Kid, outlaw

■ Angled Eyebrows + a Curved Chin
*Needs to shape details into a pattern; managerial detachment
    with a harmonious ending*
President Martin Van Buren
First Lady Betty Ford
Composer Johann Sebastian Bach

■ Angled Eyebrows + a Straight Chin
*Finds the angles needed to create the desired result (which
    involves a concept)*
President Woodrow Wilson
First Lady Nancy Reagan
Pioneering baseball player Jackie Robinson

■ Angled Eyebrows + an Angled Chin
*Detached from feelings, can be ruthless—or deftly charming—
    in pursuit of the need to stay in control*
President John Quincy Adams
First Lady Jacqueline Kennedy Onassis
The Marquis de Sade

**Q. Thank you, Rose, on behalf of my chin. I never thought
much of it before. Before face reading, it was just a blob on my
face. All I ever really liked was my eyes. Is that common?**

A. Funnily enough, it is. When the point of watching a face is expression, of course eyes will come out on top. Mouths will rank next. And chins won't seem much use at all. The main way they emote is that, when you're about to cry, chins can crumple up like a paper bag.

Considering that, it's amazing how much chins express (to a face reader) about ethics, risk taking, and style of handling conflict. I hope this chapter will inspire you to greet the lowest part of your face with a new chin-thusiasm.

11. Sex

"What do you look for in a new date?" I asked a group of singles who had invited me as a speaker.

"Attractiveness," said the majority, seconded by "A pleasing smile." Last came, "Someone who seems friendly."

"Have mercy!" I wanted to shout. "Don't you think someone who takes the trouble to go out on a Friday night will be able to dress up and squeeze out a smile? All a friendly look shows you is **mating signals**. Don't you want to know how that stranger will act six months later—assuming that you're still speaking to each other? Don't you care about character?"

Politely, though, I settled for a simpler question: "What do you wish a new date would look for in *you*?"

This time the answer was unanimous: "I want a new date to see The Real Me."

"Hey," I reminded my audience. "You're not looking for the real them. How can you expect them to look for the real you?"

Sexiness in people does relate to "The Real Me." Isn't that who you want your lover to embrace, rather than some stereotype straight from the movies? What you'll investigate in this chapter will be R-rated—for "Real." You'll learn to look for traits related to thrill, closeness, completing your soul, traits that range from initial sex appeal to long-term compatibility. Face readers know some pretty unexpected places to look for **sexiness**, like overlips and earlobes.

Beyond social sexiness

Face readers also develop discernment between genuine sexiness and **social sexiness**, which is a matter of image and attitude. Depending on the social circles where you move, sexiness could mean someone with multiple body piercings, large Texas-style hair, the sleek look of a professional swimmer, bulked-up muscles, a great deal of makeup, or none at all.

Currently, a major craze of social sexiness is full lips. Now, if you're kissing someone who couldn't hit the broad side of a barn, perhaps it may help if a date's lips form a large target. (This is the dartboard school of kissing: the best lips are big and colorful and not too far away.) Otherwise, the sexual meaning of lips is purely social. As you've read in the chapter on "Mouths," full lips tell you about self-disclosure, not sexiness. The mysteries of sex-in-the-face lie elsewhere.

Vicky, one of my students, once had an embarrassing experience that illustrates this point. It was a close encounter with Kevin Kline, the versatile Oscar-winning actor. Kline has VERY thin lips, so the large-lip school of sexiness would give him VERY small points. Boy oh boy, would they be wrong!

Vicky was working in a school where the actor came in for tutoring. Her job was to check his skills, and the procedure was so routine that Vicky could do it in her sleep, except for an unexpected problem:

"This man's aura of sexuality was so strong, I didn't know what to do with myself. It filled the room. You could feel it all the way down the hall."

Just being in the room with Kline turned the normally articulate Vicky into a blithering idiot. Not only couldn't she talk, she found herself shaking down to her knees. While her heart pounded, Vicky's bewildered mind was asking, "What's going on here?"

Outrageous, off-the-chart sex appeal, that's what!

No wonder so many movie stars marry each other! Put together a couple of super-sexy people and maybe they'll find each other so normal they can even count to ten in each other's presence.

Phoebe Cates, Kline's wife, is also an actor with a deliciously large and alluring aura on screen. Happily married to Kline, she shares the same face trait, the one that really does show sex appeal, which we'll turn to next. Then we'll go on to embrace other traits that are even more important for finding and keeping a compatible mate.

Overlips

Movie stars don't look like you and me, or at least me. **Overlips** are an emphatic example. Stars of the stage and screen have something very interesting that goes on with their overlip sculpting.

Q. I hate to seem sexually ignorant, but what the heck does "overlip" mean, anyway?

A. Overlip is NOT the upper lip. An overlip lies *above* the upper lip, forming the area between the nose tip and mouth. One friend of mine calls it "the vital link," which comforts him because he often nicks it when shaving. If you're going to get medical about your nomenclature, you could call this part of your body the **philtrum**. All you're looking for is a vertical groove in the center of your upper lip.

Look for it now in the mirror. Do you see two more-or-less parallel raised ridges with a groove in-between? Or don't you see much of anything? How much you see will depend on the degree of **overlip sculpting.**

- A **defined** overlip has the two chiseled ridges.
- If you can't find much in the way of ridge, chiseled or not, you have a **low-profile** overlip.

Here's an interesting secret about this part of your anatomy. Under your overlip (to be precise, on the gums directly above your front teeth), you can feel a string-like structure called the **frenum**. Explore it—either with your tongue or your fingers. You'll find its length and position corresponds to the ridges you show to the world as your overlip.

At least, I'm told this is the case. From personal experience, I wouldn't know a frenum if it hit me in the gums like a strand of spaghetti. Like other folks with a low-profile overlip, my soul chose the model of body without much of a frenum. No frenum inside means no major ridges outside. So, as it turns out, this equipment is optional.

Q. Optional? You're saying I'm doomed to a life with no sex? While I was an innocent babe in heaven I thought "Who needs this" so now I'll have to pay for my mistake the whole rest of my life?

A. Hardly. Calm down and keep listening.

The meaning of *overlip sculpting* is sex appeal. Do you make heads swivel, even if you haven't just come from the hairdresser's? With a *defined* overlip, chances are the answer is "Yes!"

Understand, you could be grumpy, unsociable, sweaty, exhausted, dressed to the noughts. Who cares? You could be fatter than you'd prefer, or thinner. You could be old enough to be the mother or father of the ones who are looking at you with undisguised lust.

Probably, though, you and your defined overlip have dressed in a way that emphasizes your sexiness. Folks with this trait tend to be very

OVERLIP SCULPTING

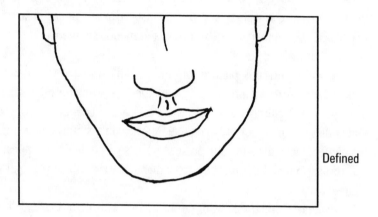

Defined

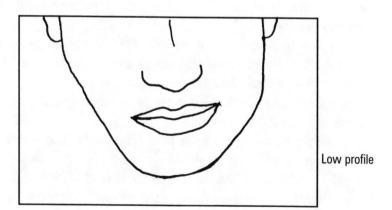

Low profile

aware of their magnetism—after all, people have been responding to it ever since those hot hormonal teenage years.

What explains this? Where is the justice? One of my students has astutely referred to a woman's well defined overlip as "upper cleavage." Regardless of whether or not you're in the mood, people who are with you will think about sex.

Free will enters this picture, of course. What use are you going to make of this form of power, if you're the one with the high-voltage overlip? Sexual energy is, simply, energy. You can channel the interest that comes to you in any way you like. Maybe you'll simply enjoy having people feel more alive in your presence. Sales or politics may appeal to you professionally because they are influential ways to use your sexual charisma.

Presidents Kennedy, Reagan, and Clinton, with their VERY defined overlips, have been among our most charismatic political leaders. My student Claudia is a Washingtonian who has hobnobbed with politicians since her childhood days. Here's how she reacted to being in Bill Clinton's presence:

"The man is so sexy, it's unbelievable. When he's in the room, you feel it. And I wasn't even physically close to him. I've got to tell you, I've never met any political figure with that kind of energy."

Now here comes a trick question. Would *you* really want to have that degree of magnetism?

Would you truly enjoy being like Kevin Kline, fated to have otherwise normal people stammer and drool in your presence? Even if your overlip is well defined without being at the level of VERY, your challenge with this trait involves handling the attention. Few people, deep down, yearn to be treated as sex objects. So the question becomes, once you get the attention, what will you do with it?

"Become a movie star!" is one answer. Did you know that VERY defined overlips are practically a job requirement if you want to play the love interest roles? Here are some examples.

Leading Man Overlips

Pierce Brosnan	Sean Connery
Harrison Ford	Morgan Freeman
Mel Gibson	Michael Keaton
Val Kilmer	Bruce Lee
Brad Pitt	Jimmy Smits
Patrick Stewart	Denzel Washington
Bruce Willis	Chow Yun-Fat

Leading Lady Overlips

Halle Berry	Cameron Diaz
Jodie Foster	Salma Hayek
Helen Hunt	Bette Midler
Julianne Moore	Gwyneth Paltrow
Julia Roberts	Meg Ryan
Susan Sarandon	Sharon Stone
Kate Winslet	Catherine Zeta-Jones

As for a *low-profile* overlip, the lack of animal magnetism doesn't mean you have no other kind of sexiness. You're set up, from the soul level, to impress people first with other aspects of who you are, such as your intellect, your kindness, your athletic prowess. When people read your aura, the part of it that's about sex may not reach out and grab attention—except for times like when you fall in love. But your aura can show gifts for charisma in many other ways. And there's something to be said for having people fall in love with you first for these gifts, then discover your sexiness as a delicious afterthought.

Whoopi Goldberg enjoys great success in her career in movies, on stage, and as a talk show host. But she doesn't come across as a sex symbol. Neither do Billy Crystal or Robin Williams. Their overlip sculpting don't grab you, but all have extraordinary auras that reveal kinds of charisma unrelated to sex.

Outside the entertainment world, you'll find people with low-profile overlips whose work far transcends the topic of sex: psychiatrist Jean Bolen, healer Ilana Rubenfeld; bestselling author about near-death experience, Betty Eadie. And advertising legend David Ogilvy has proven, in a highly lucrative manner, that sex isn't the only thing that sells.

Q. Forget about sex appeal. Which part of the face tells you who is sexy, really sexy?

A. You want to know the truth? Everyone can be sexy—or not. Each of us has our moments.

The most direct approach to gauging all-around sexiness comes from ancient Chinese face reading. According to the masters of *Siang Mien*, the sexiest people on earth are those with **short, wide chins**. (Exactly how did these face readers do their research? I have no idea, but I hope they enjoyed themselves.)

Logically their interpretation makes sense. After all, chins reveal how a person bounces back from adversity. A *short* chin goes with sensitivity to criticism; a *wide* chin reveals the need to console oneself with others. Put one and one together and, well, it's like putting together a person who often needs consolation with a significant other—and wouldn't it be fun if that other person could be you!

Certainly some women with short, broad chins have been outspoken about sex. Think of sexologist Dr. Ruth Westheimer; or the professional sexpots Jean Harlow and Mae West. Remember Sydney Biddle Barrows, the Mayflower Madam? Actor Charles Bronson has also profited by his apparent sexiness. Yes, men can have this trait, too.

Q. Isn't there anything else besides chins?

A. Novelist Josephine Tey has made an interesting observation about sexiness. In *The Franchise Affair* she had several characters comment on a particular eye color. **Slate-blue eyes**, they agreed, reveal that a person is "over-sexed." Maybe Tey's onto something. Think of the eye color of certain celebrities with a large and enthusiastic following: Paul Newman and Frank Sinatra.

Ordinarily I avoid commenting on people based on coloring, and obviously the vivid blue theory leaves out legions of non-blue-eyed people who may be equally fascinated by sex, but maybe this concept will help you—especially if you already have eyes of this color. So think about people you have known with this attribute and see if you find there's something to it.

Q. I've been disappointed in date material countless times. One thing that could help me eliminate dates who will never work out is getting a quick read on their sexual preference. Does any face trait tell you whether a person is straight or gay?

A. No. If you want to make it your business, you could always ask (unless you're in the military). Otherwise you can read sexuality straight from the date-material's aura. If you must stick to face reading, the closest you can come to learning about sexual preference is our next trait.

■■■

Macho knobs

Some chins, mostly male, include a raised, circular wad of flesh that looks like a doorknob so I call it a **macho knob**. Do NOT ignore it, especially the VERY version, which is punctuated by a dimple. (For illustration of the more common variety, *sans* dimple, look at the chin on the man who models Life Priority Proportions later in this chapter.)

Macho knobs relate to pride. When that knob decorates a male face, the pride has to do with being a man, where "man" is defined the old-fashioned way as an authority figure. He deserves to rule the roost. His word is law. And when gentler means fail, the macho man will pound directly with his fists or whatever weapon is handy.

You won't want to mess with this man. And some of us will be too intimidated to want to cuddle with him, either... unless you're a woman with a macho knob of your own.

If you *are* a woman with a macho knob, you have your own ways of intimidating foes. Because of your pride, when someone treats you disrespectfully you may react with an intensity of rage that surprises everyone concerned.

Q. Come on. Isn't it human nature to hate being dissed? You don't need a knob for that, do you?

A. Anyone can get mad. You're right. But people with macho knobs get madder. Take a survey among your friends and acquaintances.

The trick to making a macho knob work in your life in a positive way is to use the pride without going overboard on the pushiness. There's no harm in aggressively making your way through the world, but you don't want to act like the stuff that nightmares are made of. Who's got the most VERY knob in public life right now? Saddam Hussein—his knob takes up about 20 percent of his face.

Smaller, cuter versions have empowered generals John M. Shalikashvili and Colin Powell. Civilian knobs have undoubtedly contributed to the careers of football great Joe Montana, actor Edward James Olmos, legendary tenor heartthrob Enrico Caruso.

And let's not leave out Christopher Columbus. Or a different kind of explorer, Ted Turner, owner of the Atlanta Braves and Hawks and, of course, Turner Broadcasting. Turner isn't physically as famous as the empire he's built, but if you have a chance, read a biography of him complete with photos of his macho knob, enormous by comparison with anyone but Saddam Hussein's. Turner is a walking advertisement for testosterone.

Q. Does the meaning of the knob change for people who are gay or lesbian?

A. The trait under discussion may be a knob but it isn't a peg. It doesn't mean you automatically belong to any particular sexual orientation. Each of us responds to certain qualities as masculine or feminine. And macho knobs go with being VERY masculine, whatever that means to you.

Q. What if you're a guy without the knob? Can't you still be very masculine?

A. Sure, considering that you live on the free will planet—but the difference is this: Men who have macho knobs wouldn't be caught dead at a unisex barber shop. They prefer a traditional view of what it means to be a real man. Guys like you, without the knob, may be equally manly —even devastatingly sexy—but you won't be so concerned with defending your manhood. You may be so confident that you dare to eat quiche, to let your sensitivity show in public, and even to experiment with the sexual message broadcast by your mustache.

■■■

Mustaches

Mustaches aren't just hair, by gum. They're *symbols of masculinity.* You need not be a face reader to know this.

Given this symbolism, female mustaches aren't going to win prizes for daintiness. I suppose it's just a matter of time before teenage girls try wearing them. These days they must content themselves with such boring ways to impress their elders, like shoulder tatoos and navel piercings. Even so, it's a brave young lassie who will deliberately accentuate facial hair, rather than get rid of it with drugstore products like bleaches and depilatories.

More common sense about mustaches: you need not be a physiognomist to realize the sexual meaning of how a man grooms his mustache. When he fusses over it, trims it immaculately, curls it, twirls it, tweaks it, or tugs at it, you can tell that he is someone with sexiness very much on his mind—his own. As for the fellow who lets his mustache run amok over his face, like an irrepressible smile, here is somebody equally fascinated with his own sexual prowess. Either that or he's just a slob.

Grooming considerations aside, face readers will find mustaches most informative if you will pay attention to whether or not the hair covers a man's upper lip.

- A mustache that **reveals the upper lip** may be so short it dramatically frames his upper lip from a great distance. Or the hair may deliciously flirt with the edge of his mouth, as if to say, "Shall I touch you or not? Perhaps not, just for today. But ask me tomorrow."

- When choosing a mustache that **hides the upper lip**, a man may give himself the VERY version, which is a big, slipcover-like creation that upholsters the guy from overlip to beard, leaving any bare mouth to a minimum. At the opposite extreme, the hair may hang just low enough to cover part of his upper lip.

MUSTACHE

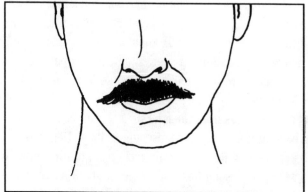

Hides
upper lip

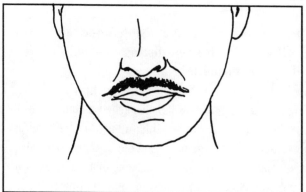

Frames
upper lip

Q. The suspense is killing me. I have trimming scissors ready. What do these mustache sizes mean?

A. Let's start with the more common version. If you have a mustache that *reveals the upper lip*, it symbolizes your willingness to divulge deeply personal feelings. Basketball great Kareem Abdul-Jabbar has shown an inspiring willingness to talk about his life. Influential pediatrician Benjamin Spock has stopped short at advising parents about mustache trimming but his own example has been to let his upper lip hang out. Bobby McFerrin doesn't just let his upper lip show, he uninhibitedly lets his voice express itself when he sings, octave after octave.

Looking backward to England's most famous king, Henry VIII, he is portrayed as having had this sort of mustache, and history shows a parade of his wives, suggesting he wasn't reticent about showing at least his matrimonial preferences. * Today, you'll most often find upper-lip-revealing mustaches on "sensitive men," the sort who'll admit to taking growth seminars or (gosh!) being face readers. Use your imagination to translate the sensitive style of masculinity into bedroom behavior.

Q. What if a guy doesn't have a visible upper lip—so he has what you call a dislike for self-disclosure—but then he wears this tell-all type of mustache?

A. Either he's making a heroically extreme effort to become more self-revealing or else he just trims his mustache way too much. Realistically though, how often do you see this? Men who don't self-disclose comfortably seldom portray themselves at the opposite extreme.

They're far more likely to grow a mustache that *hides the upper lip*. Here's a man who chooses to define his masculinity ruggedly, even outrageously. President Teddy Roosevelt coined the perfect slogan to express his style of mustache sculpting: "Speak softly and carry a big stick."

* As you may know, Henry VIII was un-shy to the extent of also killing his rejects, but happily this has nothing to do with mustaches one way or the other.

Charlie Chaplin and Groucho Marx created on-screen personas that involved their trademark mustaches. With Chaplin, the mustachioed masculinity presented a sharp contrast to his waif-like, tentative body language. Marx clowned about his great interest in sex, drawing much of his humor from his contrasting shyness. I wonder. Did Groucho's swaggering persona hide his off-screen character even more effectively than Harpo's cinematic shyness hid his real identity? Was it a coincidence that these shy guys in disguise were *brothers*? Film buffs, help me out here.

Back at mustaches, one of today's greatest storytellers is Robert Fulghum. His bestselling books inspire a wide readership. You'll note, however, that they don't reveal much about him personally. And should you see him in person, or through a photo, you'll notice that his mustache does an effective job of hiding his upper lip before melting into a copious curved beard.

Jim Henson, the soft-spoken genius behind the Muppets, once said, "Puppetry is a good way of hiding." He might have been talking about his mustache, the kind that hides the upper lip. Since this is a distinctive style of living, it's also going to play out as a distinctive kind of loving.

Earlobes

Earlobes—now that's a sexy face part. Even if you don't kiss them or caress them, earlobes can teach you an intimate kind of sexual lore. Check out the size. The easiest method involves earrings. How many pieces of imaginary jewelry could you fit on the earlobe whose size you're gauging?

- **Large** earlobes can hold a sizable collection. Picture studs, hoops, dangles, enormous gemstones in rainbow hues. (Not to worry, you're only imagining them. You don't have to pay for them.)
- **Small** earlobes have room for one or two, well maybe three, depending on how you feel about crowding your jewelry.

Now feel free to erase the jewelry. As if by magic, you're left with beautifully sized earlobes. Quite a trick, huh?

Q. But this is serious stuff. Weren't you implying that on top of all the rest of the sexual competition, now we've got to worry about the size of our earlobes?

A. I hope not, since every size of earlobe is a winner, with a winning kind of sexual style. By the way, I hope you'll consider it safe now to take your hands off your ears.

Earlobe size matters because it reveals unconscious grounding. Does she have it or doesn't she? Don't ask her hairdresser; ask her ears.

Q. Well I must flunk completely, because I've never even heard of grounding. What the heck does that mean?

A. **Grounding** means paying attention to the physical aspects of life. And it relates to sexiness because people vary in their needs for grounding with a partner. Often opposites attract. Sex is one of the most enjoyable ways to remind yourself that you live in a physical body— something I'll bet you've noticed, even if you never heard the term "grounding" before.

Here are the specifics: Someone with *large* earlobes is grounded. With this trait you have keen powers of observation. For instance, you won't just notice how a date dresses. You'll notice how her dress fits. If she leaves for the powder room and comes back wearing a different shade of lipstick, you'll notice that too. You could be a detective, you're so observant.

The potential challenge involves sometimes being a bit too literal. For instance, your buddy Jerry says, "Meet you at the Cheap But Good Restaurant, right under the small green sign at the front of the building." When you get there, you see that the sign is blue and no less than twelve feet wide. As someone with large earlobes, you'll never respect Jerry again. It's that silly lack of tolerance for the rest of humanity!

Undeniably, though, chunky earlobes remain a great asset. Director Alfred Hitchcock scared people silly, in true grounded fashion, by including plenty of convincing details. Ethologist Konrad Lorenz exemplifies large-earlobed folk who have made their reputations by paying attention to what is going on around them.

You need not be a rocket scientist—or brilliant observer of how ducks bond with their mothers—to appreciate how important grounding could be for sex. People with large earlobes are going to differ in the quality and quantity of sex they prefer, compared with those of us who use sex as a chance to come in for a landing.

Yes, *small* earlobes suggest that a person's interests are more metaphysical than physical. Please understand, if you're in this group, I'm not saying you can't be sexy in that highly satisfying, body-parts way, just that it's a shift for you to pay attention to physical stuff. With sex, as with the rest of life, you're mostly attracted to the soul within the body.

Judging by ear proportions, I suspect that bestselling author M. Scott Peck fits into this category. Huge inner ear circles suggest that his style of relating to others emphasizes spiritual subtext. Small wonder that he wrote *The Road Less Traveled*! Who would expect someone with ears like his to be enthralled with a big superhighway?

Vice-president Al Gore has gone on record with his enthusiasm over superhighways but they're electronic, not physical. With his very small earlobes, that figures. Gore's earlobes are also **straight**—very unusual because you'll look far and wide to find earlobes that aren't curved. This unusual trait suggests an abstract, intellectual style of relating to the beauties of physical life. (By contrast, **curved** earlobes relate to a heartfelt enthusiasm over life's sensuous joys.)

Do Gore's rare earlobes help to explain his efforts on behalf of the environment? Gee, does an ocean have water? His earlobes suggest that he enjoys the outdoors with appreciation that is metaphysical, not simply physical. And his intellectual grounding style causes him to reflect on what he enjoys, including how to preserve it.

Back to the subject of sex, is someone like Gore, with those small earlobes, sexy? He'd definitely appeal to someone on that metaphysical wavelength. This is the key to *"Real Me" sexiness.* Its deepest definition transcends sheer physical attraction. It means that a person's presence has something that calls to you as a soul. Even more than the "everybody gets the message" form of sex appeal that shows in a defined overlip, "Real Me" sexiness shows in a variety of traits. You'll respond to people who are opposite enough to arouse your interest, similar enough to bond with.

So I chalk it up to my VERY small earlobes that I reacted as I did to the sight of Al Gore on TV, dancing at his first inaugural ball. Honest to God, I thought, "What a wonderful dancer." Only later did I hear that pundits (and, who else, the nation's foremost ballroom dance authorities?) had the opposite reaction, calling him "wooden." Gore came across like an enormous intellect and spirit, pushing around a body. To me, that's mighty attractive.

Coincidence #101: While writing this chapter I received an excited phone call from one of my best friends, someone who, like me, has VERY small earlobes. "I just got to meet Al Gore at a teacher's reception. I got to shake his hand. Rose, you were right. He's so sexy!"

■■■

Priority areas

Much about "Real Me" sexiness is a matter of life priorities. If you're looking for long-term relationships, you'd be wise to pay attention to the face's three **life priority areas**.

- **Priority Area I** reaches from the hairline to the highest part of the eyebrows—basically, foreheads. (If hair has been ebbing away from somebody's hairline, imagine where the hair used to be at high tide.)
- **Priority Area II** stretches from the highest point of the eyebrows to the lowest part of the nose (either between the nostrils or at the nose tip, depending on nose tip angle)—basically, eyes plus nose.
- **Priority Area III** stretches from below the nose down to the bottom of the chin (Hey, that's the *first* chin)—basically, everything from the mouth down.

Q. How on earth am I going to measure this stuff?

A. I recommend the Two-finger Method.

Span the distance from hairline to eyebrow with your thumb and forefinger. That's Priority Area I, remember. Keeping these two fingers in place, freeze! There's your measuring stick.

Now move the same two fingers down to Priority Area II. Is it bigger or smaller? How about Priority Area III? If either is bigger than Area I, expand the distance between thumb and forefinger to set a new standard for size. What you're looking for is the largest area.

Q. Isn't everybody like me, with Priority Area II much bigger than the others?

A. Priority Areas vary much more than you'd assume. Pick 20 people at random. Read them for this category; you'll find every Priority Area can be the biggest or smallest. And these differences are highly meaningful.

Q. Won't all older people have biggest Area III, then, because of our double chins?

A. Please, stop at the first chin. Similarly, on folks with receding hairlines, imagine where the hair would normally be.

You've brought up an interesting point, though. According to stereotypes, it's inevitable that as you age you'll develop a receding hairline. You're also warned that you'll gain multiple chins. But think about this: When was the last time you saw both on the same person? Not often, I'll bet. To learn more about why, and what these changing traits mean, turn to my follow-up book about faces, *Wrinkles Are God's Makeup.*

Meanwhile you'll surely want to read Priority Areas right this minute, especially if you're seeking a mate. These face proportions (which can definitely change during your lifetime) reveal life priorities.

People with *largest Priority Area I* are into thinking. They revel in abstract ideas, imagination, theories, and such. Expect them to excel at occupations like theoretical science, philosophy, teaching at the college level, and writing.

Some famous Thinkers are Pope John Paul II, composer Walter Piston, physicist Enrico Fermi, linguist Noam Chomsky, and psychologist Carl Rogers. Malcolm Forbes has chronicled the exploits of America's wealthiest achievers—not done them—though he is clearly no slouch. Writing is a natural for people in this category, including thriller writer John Grisham and cartoonist Charles Schultz.

Q. Maybe because this is the shortest of my three Priority Areas, I don't get it. What does a relatively long forehead have to do with sex?

A. People in this group adore long words and unusual sentence constructions. They find ideas sexy. A challenge for them—especially strong when they're in the company of people like you—is seeming

LIFE PRIORITY PROPORTIONS

Thinking
(#1 biggest)

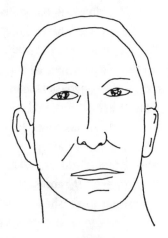

Ambition
(#2 biggest)

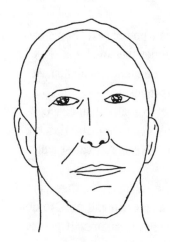

Earthiness
(#3 biggest)

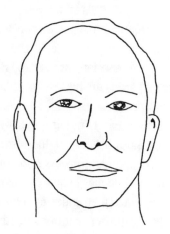

Balanced
(all three equal)

overly theoretical, be it pedantic or airy-fairy. Or, as in the case of one of my favorite entertainers, Robin Williams, having VERY *large Priority Area I* may make him seem beyond the laws of this planet altogether.

Folks like you, with *small Priority Area I* may have the opposite problem. You won't be criticized for excessive subtlety. In fact, your strength is to go like gangbusters after what you want. Filmmaker Spike Lee and political activist Cesar Chavez have made this style work for them. In a more decorous ways, Judith Martin and Marianne Neifert have risen to the tops of their professions. (They're more commonly known as Miss Manners and Dr. Mom.)

Large Priority Area II represents a leaning toward ambition. With this trait, you're an unabashed go-getter, caring passionately about money, status, prestige, and *owning* the best. (By contrast, Area III people care more about *enjoying* the best, savoring creature comforts.)

Is it a coincidence that high-level political player Henry Kissinger, with his VERY large Area II, uttered the famous words, "Power is the great aphrodisiac"? Let's take a vote.

Both George and Martha Washington found power sexy, hopefully, since both were large in Area II. Ditto Alexander the Great and Napoleon Bonaparte. And let's not forget "Blonde ambition," Madonna. Actor Harrison Ford is the biggest box office star in history.

A large Area II doesn't hurt one's ability to make financial conquests, either. Ask Tom Hopkins, who has been described as the nation's top sales trainer, or Joe Girard, the "World's Greatest Salesman" according to the *Guiness Book of World Records*.

Ambition people may be just as smart as the Thinkers, but they differ in emphasis. Once they understand an idea, they yearn and burn to do something with it. Not notorious for their mellowness, Area II people must be reminded to schedule play time. Potential lovers, beware. Early in the relationship, you'll be impressed. Later on, you may be ignored.

By contrast, those with *small Priority Area II* work hard at everything, relationships included. And the push comes from commitment rather than ambition. Their potential challenge is being taken for granted, a problem presumably overcome by Nobel prize-winners Aleksandr Solzhenitsyn and Ilya Prigogine.

What gives with a *large Priority Area III*? If you have this trait, sexiness is probably on your mind, so let's start with that. Yes, you're probably pretty secure about your sexiness. American pop culture reinforces this confidence because so many sports figures and models have the same face proportions. For instance, a lot of cover girls and guys have what you have. (And this face proportion isn't common, either, except in the Midwest.)

As if all that popular adoration weren't enough, you've got something else going for you. How many times have you been told you're "the salt of the earth"? How many times have you been told you have a "salty sense of humor"? Being so salty—oops, I mean "earthy"—you have great credibility with others. You don't talk about pie in the sky. So when you say something will work, you've already checked to make sure that it will. Maybe groundedness helps explain Magic Johnson's credibility when crusading for AIDS prevention (and it didn't hurt his basketball skills, either).

Hugh Hefner made his fortune out of appealing to earthier instincts. In different ways, so have playwright Tennessee Williams and outrageous film star Mae West. Exercise gurus Jane Fonda and Richard Simmons have used their earthiness to rehabilitate countless couch potatoes. No-nonsense advice columnist Ann Landers is famous for urging her readers to "wake up and smell the coffee."

Yes, given their street smarts and eagerness to dwell on physical matters, it seems obvious that Earthy faces come across as sexy. But before you run out and grab one for a mate, remember this. For a relationship to last longer than a quick fling, you may need to share similar Priority Area proportions. Otherwise your relationship could be done in by this trait's potential challenge, a lack of respect for other life priorities. You don't want that to mean *yours*!

As for faces with a *small Priority Area III*, their challenge is lack of interest in physicality. Compensating for this can become part of their life work, as in the case of Mary Baker Eddy, founder of Christian Science.

Generations of English students have read William Wordsworth's "Lines composed a few miles above Tintern Abbey." Given his lack of Area III, I'm surprised Wordsworth was only "a few miles" above. Congrats that he found it at all! Definitely Wordsworth was a great poet, but I wouldn't have trusted him to follow a map.

Jules Feiffer, the great cartoonist, has also written something that sheds light on what it is like to live with a VERY small Area III. In describing his own life he quipped, "One of my great desires to grow up was that, as I understood it, adults did not have to take gym."

Q. Both I and my current crush are tied for first place between Priority Areas I and II. Does that put us in sexual limbo?

A. All combinations of Areas can be compatible. Partners will just find it easier if your proportions are similar. Let's consider all the possibilities for two Priority Areas tied for first place.

When *Areas I and II are largest*, expect you and your crush to fall in love with ideas, then add a creative, practical spin.

Sexual performance may not be in the reference books, at least those I've been privy to, but you will find that the annals of business show perpetual success stories about people with this innovative combination. Examples are Harvey Firestone, who set up the Firestone Tire & Rubber Co.; investment strategist Kirk Kerkorian; and Ned Johnson, among the nation's top marketers of financial services. Harold Geneen, as president of the International Telephone and Telegraph Company, kept expanding the scope of operations while he increased financial profits—a neat trick indeed.

When *Areas I and III are largest*, expect a down-to-earth personality that is strong on imagination (and I'll leave the sexual translation of that to *your* imagination).

James Underwood Crockett has grounded his ideas, quite literally, as a gardener. Ulysses S. Grant helped hold his country together, first as a Civil War General, later as President. (His nemesis, General Robert E. Lee, used similar Priority Areas as he tried to maintain the Confederacy.)

When *Areas II and III are largest*, expect a go-getter who cares as much about physical pleasures as life's more monetary forms of success. Consider Julia Child, who single-spoonedly transformed American cooking for those who liked French elegance but lacked servants, French or otherwise. First Lady Dolley Madison had servants aplenty but used them more creatively than her predecessors in the White House, thus winning fame for her version of American hospitality.

Q. You've left me out. What if all three Priority Areas are equal in length?

A. Lucky you! *Equal Priority Areas* are relatively rare. They show that, more than the rest of us living in this frenzied age, you tend to keep your life balanced.

Some cultural leaders whose faces show this gift are psychologist Erik Erikson; social forecaster John Naisbitt; Richard Scarry, illustrator and author of beloved picture books so detailed they are in themselves, practically scary; and Dr. Benjamin Spock, the child-care expert whose views on balanced upbringing have affected the lives of millions of baby-boomers.

Aside from personal balance, folks with Equal Priority Areas have another advantage over the rest of us. Intuitively they understand people of every Priority dominance, making friends with them all. As a woman with this attribute, you might simultaneously date an exercise freak, an ambitious workaholic, and the most ivory-towerish of intellectuals. And, other factors being equal, you could be happy with any one of them.... Or you could represent them all in Congress, becoming a Senator, like Dianne Feinstein.

The rest of us, in the long run, will find life easier when our life partner has similar Priority Areas. Certainly if you have one Area that's especially small, look twice before making long-term commitments to a partner for whom that Area is by far the largest.

Q. What if you've already married one?

A. Your best recourse may be dimples. If you don't have any, grow some. Failing that, hold onto your sense of humor for dear life, because you and your mate are in for a wild ride.

Dimples

Everybody loves **dimples**. Why? It makes sense when you know what they mean. But before we delve into these tiny face caverns, let's make sure we can distinguish the major types.

- **Peekaboo** dimples are the circular shapes that pop out with a smile, disappearing afterwards.
- **Permanent** dimples pop out regardless of whether or not you happen to be smiling. These dimples work full-time.
- **Powerline** dimples look more like a crease than a circle. When you smile they pop out like vertical accordion pleats. Some faces even have a couple of parallel dimples on either cheek. Even one of these line-like dimples counts.

Q. Since you're being so persnickety about the nuances of dimples, what do you call chin dimples like mine?

A. **Chin dimples** are the equivalent of permanent dimples—placed on your chin, however, instead of your cheeks. Unlike cheek dimples which can come in sets of either one or two, dimples attached to your

DIMPLES

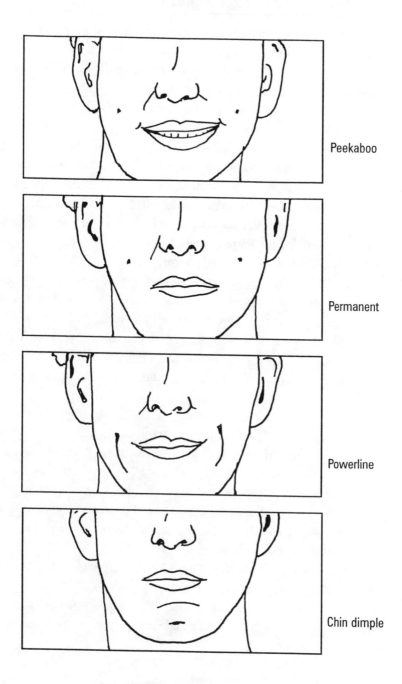

Peekaboo

Permanent

Powerline

Chin dimple

chin are most likely singular, and that's regardless of how many extra chins you may develop.

If your chin dimple shows only when you smile, like a peekaboo dimple, send me a video, please. I'll cherish it along with my memory of another rare skill—how my son as a toddler, could play the kazoo with his nose.

Dimples are about playfulness. *Peekaboo* dimples symbolize talent for helping others to laugh. When situations grow tense, you see the funny side and make the wisecrack or joke that breaks the tension.

Deservedly, this sweet disposition will win you popularity. What's the catch? People with dimples, women especially, may not be taken as seriously as their sterner-cheeked co-workers.

This challenge is especially galling—and ironic—when the dimples are of the more permanent variety. Your willingness to charm others hardly ever goes away, enduring beyond all reasonable expectation, much like the smile of the Cheshire Cat in *Alice in Wonderland*. Your personality prognosis with *permanent* dimples is this: you will win love more easily than others but have more trouble being taken seriously.

Maybe that's why you're more apt to see dimples on entertainers than business moguls or politicians. Some captivating dimpled performers are singer Bonnie Raitt; today's screen sensations Jim Carrey, Minnie Driver, and Laura Linney; yesterday's icons Clark Gable and Vivian Leigh; and TV perennial, Betty White. Finally, let's not forget the child star who owned most the famous set of dimples in the history of show biz, Shirley Temple. They lasted into adulthood, no doubt helping with her later role as ambassador.

The *powerline* dimple shows graciousness, especially when you're in a position of power. Instead of flaunting your one-up position, you help your social inferiors to feel good. The challenge (to the dimple flasher as well as the flashee) is that this easygoing appearance may not be genuine.

Yet the suave charm of powerline dimples has inestimably helped performers, including Frank Sinatra, Spencer Tracy, Sean Connery and Ricardo Montalban; also Babatunde Olatunji (not as well known as the others simply because not too many movies are made about drummers). President Lyndon Johnson had the most VERY version of powerline dimples I've ever seen. Another outstanding wearer of powerline dimples is New Age leader Shakti Gawain, who has perhaps created them directly through her expertise at creative visualization.

Another affable powerline dimple (left cheek) belongs to Alan Cohen, the spiritual writer who has been called "the most eloquent spokesman of the heart." Eloquence and charm haven't hurt the career of Howard Schultz, either. He's the brains and charm, and for all I know, also the caffeine behind Starbucks coffee.

How about *chin dimples*? They suggest playfulness at the game of life, including making decisions. Diamonds may be forever but the engagement may not. And don't expect the dimpled one to stay at any job long enough to collect a gold watch.

For people whose chins show a dimple, fickleness is a potential challenge. Still, your incontestable advantage is that love is true—or else it's over. No pretense allowed.

Q. Are chin dimples the same as clefts, the way you interpret them?

A. No. **Clefts** show as a vertical line that crosses the bottom of the chin. *Clefts* signify conflict over major life choices. The advantage, for the one with the cleft, is personal growth gained by mulling over the conflict.

Q. The big lesson I've been learning from this discussion of sexiness is that I may have been dating all wrong. Could it make sense to choose dates based more on what faces show about character than what I've been considering sexy all these years?

A. What do you have to lose? In fact you can go one further and purposely seek out partners whose face traits relate to the qualities that matter most to you. Maybe the woman of your dreams has a short broad chin, a huge Area II, and monumental earlobes... whatever! While I don't suggest you sketch out her face in detail, like a sketch artist for the local police department, it couldn't hurt you to keep a wish list of a few favorite traits.

■■■

12. Problem solving in relationships

Here on The Learning Planet, life is either bliss or lessons. Relationships exemplify this. Since we devoted the last chapter to the more blissful aspects of togetherness, it's only fair (or, at least, realistic) to turn to the problem side. Intimacy teaches us, but so can distance.

Relationship experts like John Gray, author of *Men are from Mars, Women are From Venus*, and Deborah Tannen, author of *You Just Don't Understand*, have helped countless couples to reinterpret everyday problems by understanding gender differences.

In a similar way, understanding differences related to personal style can help us to communicate better, to feel more compassion, and to recognize that our point of view is only one out of many possible points of view. When faces show you a person's comfort zone with a particular aspect of life, that knowledge can help you avoid some conflicts and resolve others.

Q. Could we please start with avoidance first? Personally, I'm a big fan of The Fight or Flight Response. Only I prefer to put the Flight part first, if you catch my drift.

A. So you'd rather run than fight? Well, preventing conflict can be a wise choice. In the cause of prevention, do you realize how much more help face reading can give you than the more common practice of reading expression?

By the time you register a red glare behind Igor's eyeballs, it may be too late to politely excuse yourself from his tea party. Soon he's gonna be screaming and you're going to be screaming back, dripping saltwater tears into your teacup, or flinging the crockery right back at him.

It's not that I advocate insensitivity. By all means, pick up emotional signals. Respond to someone's rage, and preferably do it before it's boiling so hard you could drop a teabag into it.

But face reading can warn you *in advance* about sensitive areas. You wouldn't wave a red scarf in front of a bull to signal your interest in having a quiet chat. By the same token, you may remember from the chapter on "Sex" that you'd be a fool to joke that a guy with a Macho Knob wears pink underwear.

Apart from gender and speech patterns, such as those pinpointed by Gray and Tanner, everyone has idiosyncrasies. By all means, by all honorable face means, let's learn preventative strategies so we can avoid having to choose between fight or flight.

The top 10 temper traits

Here's my personal warning system. The facing page lists the 10 most important traits to notice as a preventative measure. All have been discussed previously excpet Items 2, 8, and 10. (Check Index II, Face Data, to find them again.)

Q. Forehead furrows? Are these made by some kind of a lawnmower?

A. **Vertical forehead furrow** is my name for a certain type of wrinkle, and it's made by the soul, not by any lawnmower. Mostly I'm

The Top 10 Temper Traits

	Face Trait	Potential Problem	How to Avoid Conflict
1.	Puffs over eyes	Irritability over small things	Make concessions early in the argument—otherwise the peevishness will only escalate
2.	Vertical forehead furrow	Stored-up frustration	When the volcano erupts, move away from the lava.
3.	VERY full, VERY angled eyebrow	Confrontational style	Hold your ground if necessary, but don't resist unless you want to fight.
4.	Macho knob	Pride in being a man (or having a macho partner).	Love the blustering, if you can.
5.	Goatee or VERY angled chin	Control freak alert	Laugh, but don't let it show.
6.	Close-set eyes	Criticism	Though annoying, the person is probably right. Consider the possibility.
7.	VERY thin lips	Intolerant of sentimental speech	Respect this person's emotional limitations. When biting comments come, don't let them leave teethmarks.
8.	Large front teeth	Strong, even unbending, sense of self	Stroke that ego. Humor helps, too.
9.	Fine eyelashes	Hair-trigger temper	Validate the person's sensitive reactions.
10.	Prominent canine teeth	Determination to win	This is killer instinct. Stay out of the way.

saving discussion of wrinkles for the companion volume to this book, *Wrinkles Are God's Makeup*. But you'll want to know right now about vertical forehead furrows. To recognize them physically, look for lines that rise upward from one or both eyebrows. Be sure not to mix them up with the vertical line that can be located in the center of the forehead, near the third eye. That's the Mark of Devotion.

A *vertical forehead furrow* represents stored-up anger. If you have one, you know how hard you work NOT to show a bad temper. No doubt, too, you have good reason for your anger. Each vertical line shows your frustration savings account is large and has, in fact, been collecting interest. If you can, find some ways to make withdrawals from this anger account—milder ways than the explosions that are, otherwise, inevitable. And consider active attempts at finding forgiveness, for your own sake.

Lines like these take time to develop and time to heal.

Q. Does it matter whether the line is on the right or the left?

A. You bet. A vertical forehead furrow over the *right* eyebrow shows stored-up anger related to work. A furrow that originates from the *left* eyebrow shows stored-up rage about relationships, often a spouse or child.

Q. What about the Mark of Devotion?

A. Physically, it shows as a vertical line directly over the third eye area, between the eyebrows and above them. Symbolically, the *Mark of Devotion* means a spiritual vocation. With this trait, you have a life contract whereby you're on the escalator. Other people take the stairs, evolving at a slower pace.

Sounds enviable, doesn't it? Here on The Learning Planet, your soul has made education a priority. But, yes, there's a challenge. It involves what happens if you'd like to slow down for a while. You can't. Other folks can get away with numbing themselves spiritually, using denial, or blundering forwards in a direction they know, inside, is wrong. You, however, can't get away with this stuff. Sometimes you may even be called upon to make sacrifices for the sake of your spiritual life.

With this trait, you may go public with your commitment to religion. Examples of people who have done this are Mother Teresa, a Catholic nun with The Missionaries of Charity in Calcutta; the Dalai Lama, the Buddhist leader driven from his native Tibet; Pir Vilayat Inayat Khan, head of the International Sufi Order; religion scholar Huston Smith; and Thomas Moore, a former monk who helps people cultivate sacredness in everyday life.

The devoted one may go incognito with his religious affiliation, like the Reverend Fred Rogers—the same Mr. Rogers who puts on a sweater to visit with children over Public Television. But public or private, religious or not formally religious, you can be sure that a person with the Mark is highly spiritual.

About one in four U.S. presidents has worn this mark: Washington; Monroe; Lincoln; Grant; Roosevelt (Teddy); Harding; Coolidge; Ford; Nixon (like it or not); and most VERY of all, Carter, whose public service has blossomed since leaving office. Ben Franklin, perhaps America's greatest patriot yet, had the mark as well.

Q. Tell me about eyelashes, please. Why would fine lashes be related to temper?

A. **Eyelashes** tip you off to how intensely a person is going to react to immediate situations. When a nervous system has been put together with *thick eyelashes*, you'll find a relatively easygoing temperament. But *fine eyelashes* imply extreme neurophysiological sensitivity. Beware of a hair-trigger temper!

■■■

Looking a gift friend in the teeth

Q. Okay, what's the deal with the tooth traits in your Temper list? I haven't thought much about teeth since the braces came off, thank God.

A. **Teeth**, in general, symbolize the ability to break down life experiences, analyze them, and make choices. Despite the old saying about what bad manners it is to look a gift horse in the mouth, it's perfectly good manners to size up a new friend's teeth, particularly if that person shows them voluntarily with a smile.

Teeth are fascinating to read because they represent the deepest level that face traits can show: How does that personality learn life lessons? What major patterns can be found?

Fittingly, newborns rarely deal with lessons involving choice and free will. They're busy enough with basics like finding their feet. So they don't have to deal with teeth, either literally or symbolically.

Early childhood learning styles, symbolized by *baby teeth*, emerge, then are outgrown. Parents, have you noticed how those cute baby ways, and the teeth that go with them, begin by fitting nicely with the rest of your child? But by first grade, they start looking too small for comfort. The child's reality has, likewise, expanded. And when the "grown-up" teeth first come in, they look overwhelmingly big in a little kid's mouth. The very sight would be enough to start a Mom's milk flowing, except probably she's not breastfeeding any more. Those big, oversized teeth can remind you how overwhelming adult kinds of learning seem to an elementary school kid.

With *adult teeth*, individual patterns emerge that carry useful information about personal style.

Front teeth symbolize the size of a person's ego, when compared to other people in general. Usually these two teeth, top and center, are somewhat larger than the rest, symbolizing a serviceable sense of the self taking precedence over all else. That comes in handy, just like your physical teeth when you try to say "symbolizing a serviceable sense of the self."

Large front teeth are tricky to see at first, because *regular*-sized front teeth are somewhat large, too, compared to the rest of the teeth in a mouth. But large teeth look larger than the somewhat large ones; these chompers look downright chunky. And what they mean is a good chunk of ego. The potential challenge is a self-centered kind of stubbornness, which can definitely spark conflict. Baseball legend Joe DiMaggio may have depended on stubbornness for his staying power as a hitter. So, too, Stephen King, has demonstrated staying power as the author of hauntingly horrifying fiction.

The opposite trait, *small* front teeth, shows in chompers that are close in size to the neighboring teeth. This shows self-effacement. One example is Dr. Susan Love, the health activist and breast surgeon, who works tirelessly for her fellow woman. And speaking of tirelessness, consider Dr. Wayne Dyer, a bestselling author who has trudged through more than 5,000 TV and radio interviews. A man of his talent would sell plenty of books without them, and having been through many interviews myself, I can appreciate the selflessness involved. Interviews aren't just glamour. Even though I, personally, love them, experienced authors know how interviews mean hours attached to your phone during commercial breaks (complete with traffic and weather reports about cities you'll never visit), endless waiting in studio green rooms, and vague or even insulting questions from overworked interviewers who've never read a single word you wrote.

Q. Are you saying that people with small front teeth are so humble they never explode?

A. They explode all right. Anyone can. But when people with small front teeth explode, it's most likely out of concern for others rather than themselves. Mother Teresa didn't set up her operation in India without some forcefulness, I suspect. Senator Barbara Mikulski blusters delightfully when politically provoked; her anger explodes all the more because of her previously-mentioned cheek style.

Q. How about those canines you call Temper Trait #10? No, wait. First I need to ask this: What are canines, anyway?

A. You don't need to go to dental school to figure out this bite of tooth data. Give yourself a big tooth-baring smile in the mirror. Look at the upper set of chompers. Find the four in the center. On either side of these four, you'll see one pointy, fang-like tooth, a canine tooth. Bingo!

Q. So what does it mean that some people's canines are prominent?

A. **Prominent** canines hang down lower than the four teeth between them. For most people, canines are shorter, not longer, than the four teeth between them.

Canine teeth are about aggression, a.k.a. grit. So a prominent pair signify killer instinct.

Admit it. If you have this trait, you go after what you want tooth and nail. The method you take may not be obvious to others but the results will be: you'll do whatever it takes to win.

This is not a bad trait to have—just a scary one to find on someone else, especially a competitor. Ask Julie Krone's competitors. She's the top female jockey in the history of American horse racing. Or consult with Tony Robbins, one of the nation's most successful motivational speakers.

Madeleine Albright applies the oomph that shows in this trait to her work as Secretary of State. Her motto, I've read, is "Anything we're asked to do, we will do."

A beloved set of prominent canines belongs to actor Jimmy Stewart. For evidence of his well concealed but powerful drive to succeed, you could look at his war record or the screen roles where he had the chance to portray a menacing character. But my favorite example is the holiday classic "It's a Wonderful Life" where Stewart plays a lovable version of Everyman, George Bailey.

When you watch his performance carefully, you'll notice scenes where extraordinary hidden expressions flit across his face, from lethal-intensity rage through resignation to politeness. Admirably, Steward learned the life lesson of how to feel this trait's killer instinct, then set it aside.

Notorious spy Robert Hanssen also has displayed the strength of large canines, but not quite so admirably.

One final tooth trait should be mentioned in the context of conflict: the **bite**. When uppers meet lowers, how do they make contact?

Underbites occur when the lower teeth stick out further than the upper teeth. A noticeable *underbite* signals another kind of aggression, a type associated with grimness or bitterness rather than active rage.

Whatever the person's prevailing mood, it's the mark of an indefatigable fighter. Certainly it has well served General Norman Schwarzkopf, who commanded U.S. forces in the Persian Gulf War; Dennis Banks, founder of the American Indian Movement; and Vice President Dick Cheney, veteran political survivor.

For better or worse, people with **overbites** are far more common. Just as their upper teeth curve over the lower ones, people with *overbites* figuratively bend themselves out of shape to please others. They're eager, sometimes overeager, to please—at least unless they spend years retraining and restraining this impulse through orthodontia.

Even bites belong to people who can pronounce "s" with an enviable crispness. As if this wasn't advantage enough, from a face reading standpoint *even* bites go with a rare form of inner balance. Their social needs (as symbolized by upper teeth) mesh with their survival instincts (as shown in lower teeth). All the better for getting along with people.

Q. Enough, already! I'm turning green with envy. Can you give me one reason, just one reason, not to be jealous of people with those obnoxious picture-perfect bites?

A. No tooth trait, even the blessing of a perfectly matched bite, can spare a person from learning life lessons. And you can envy someone's seeming perfection all you like but the fact remains: Each person on this planet has something to learn. Otherwise that person wouldn't be here, teeth or no teeth.

10 tips to avoid tiffs

Give peace a chance. Lovely sentiment, isn't it? As a face reader, you have at least a fighting chance (as it were) to avoid tiffs. Remember the Face Reader's Golden Rule:

■ Consider that someone else's different personal style could be just as valid as your own.

Reading the Secrets can help you to accept people as they are, even when they react to situations in a way you wouldn't. This is not to discount the moral obligation a person has to speak out against actions that are genuinely wrong. Much of the behavior that gets on our nerves isn't wrong, just unexpected. This bears repeating. It's normal to expect other folks to have the same personal style as one's own. It's normal but unfair, because there are so many different valid styles. Here are ten tips to help you through the most common everyday conflicts arising from differences in personal style.

1. Don't stifle those noses

When you work with people, let them work their own way so long as they get the job done. Maybe you're breaking in a new salesman. Maybe you're trying to persuade your spouse to de-grime the shower stall. No matter what, you'll be rewarded if you read and honor the talents for work that show in nose profiles.

People with scooped noses need permission to rely on their feelings. People with arched noses demand the chance to work creatively. Be patient when people without straight noses deviate from customary ways of accomplishing things. They'll produce better results that way, with less inner friction.

Especially if your work style is different, be generous with your respect.

2. Thou shalt not take for granted

Save headaches all around by respecting the different productivity styles that show in nose length. Admire the high-volume productivity of a short-nosed worker. Just don't burn her out by taking her efforts for granted.

Similarly, accept the style of a long-nosed worker. Don't expect enthusiasm if you hand him just one part of a project to do over and over again. He needs to know context to feel he has purpose. When you ask his opinion on planning that project, he'll light up like a Christmas tree. All workers appreciate the chance to contribute ideas to management, but it's especially important for those who come to work with a long nose.

3. Let teamwork flow

Everybody has a preferred teamwork style. Don't isolate workers with generous nose padding. They need to work together. What seems to you like goofing around may be seriously productive.

Also, whenever possible, protect the unpadded worker from meeting-itis. Nose narrowness is most common at the bridge. When folks have narrow nose bridges, regardless of how much their noses widen out towards the tip, it's a form of torture for them to start a new project on a committee.

Also if your loved one brings home horror stories from work that strike you as unreasonable, consider that you might have a different nose narrowness. Probe into the experience. Maybe you're not being quite nosy enough.

4. Why squabble over details?

God is in the details, some say. But to those of us with starter brows, the more interesting aspects of God are NOT in the details.

The moral of this eyebrow story is to protect everyone from giving a starter type responsibility for too many details. Starters: team up with an ender if you can. Your second choice teammate is an even. If you're stuck with yourself, or a whole bunch of starters, hire a consultant. Otherwise make do by lowering your standards. Sometimes you don't have to cross every T and dot every I.

Starters have so much creativity for beginning new projects. Make use of that whenever possible. Everyone will be happier.

5. Know when to ignore asymmetry

Asymmetry shows a depth of experience that commands respect. But here's a word to the wise—if someone you work with has a great deal of facial asymmetry, avoid getting involved in that individual's personal life. Don't ask. Or, be warned, you're in for complications.

The worker's personality is bound to be significantly different outside the workplace. For your workplace relationship, focus on the traits that show on the right side of the face. Leave the left side alone.

One example is ear asymmetry. It's much more common, I've found, for people to have a right ear angled in and a left ear angled out than vice versa. Very convenient! During the work day, that person will toe the line; after 5:00 p.m., she'll kick up her heels. "Independent" puts it too mildly. Try "wild and crazy." * It's great fun to have a friend or spouse with wacky, non-conformist ways. But, again, think twice before you ask to hear the sad tale of life at work or you may be in for a rude shock.

6. Power cocktails: Know what you're mixing

With mate, date, co-workers, or family members, you're making a mixed drink: one part each of every person's power style, including your own. Now that you know what your strengths are, consider the mix.

For instance, two leaderlike cheek styles may find themselves competing to be the center of attention. Two with a pacifist power style may mellow each other into a torpor; when a leaderlike buddy enters the group, the dynamics are going to shift. Enjoy the new mixture. Don't fight it.

When you mix with someone who has the passion power style, be prepared for intensity. Too many power breakfasts together could leave you feeling as though you've been for a ride in a cocktail shaker.

7. Ear today, gone tomorrow—or whenever

If you live with someone whose ears are VERY low or high, and yours are just the opposite, consider yourself forewarned about problems with patience—impatience *toward* the one with lower ears and *from* the one with higher ears.

---

* Less commonly, folks will have an out-angled left ear along with an in-angled right ear. Translation: expect pretty conventional standards for what it means to be a spouse, a parent, a friend. Also expect that person not to fit in easily with co-workers. This can be helpful for some professions where work depends on bringing the fresh perspective of an outsider, such as management consulting. The potential challenge is inner conflict over "selling out" or otherwise feeling alienated while at work.

8. Flexible chins? Forget it.

Chins lose when it comes to flexibility. Don't take my word for it. Pick up a mirror and compare how bendable your chin is compared to your eyebrows, eyes, mouth, or jaws. It's easier to wrinkle your nose or wiggle your ears than to scrunch up your chin.

How appropriate! The principles for making decisions don't readily alter, either. Disagreements between curved and straight chin bottoms can be worked out with patience, but the true wild card will be anyone who has a VERY angled chin bottom. Acknowledge that powerful need to stay in control. Reverse psychology may help, or else a long leash.

9. Eyelid fool-ness

Eyelid fullness can fool you, so don't take it for granted. Your mate's eyelid proportions (and with it, his need for intimacy) can change faster than you might expect. All it takes is one sleepless night or a good cry.

So check in on a daily basis, glancing lightly at eyelid fullness when you give a soulful greeting. Not that you will necessarily adjust to dia-metrically different needs for personal space (after all, you and your eyelids have needs, too), but you can use your awareness to understand better what your mate is going through. Also, possibly you'll protect yourself from guilt. You can only be who you are!

10. Cheekbone alert

Many a time I've seen it: a soft-hearted, curvy-featured face seems to show a loathing for confrontation. And then, you happen to notice his high cheekbones. They change everything.

Remember, this trait is about the use of personal power to stand up for ethics. Your bashful husband or co-worker may recoil at using harsh words, but if he and his high cheekbones catch you at living a lie, watch out. You're going to see facial expressions and hear words you might never have imagined.

Play it safe with those outspokenly ethical folks. Play it straight.

Eye angles

Some of the most unnecessary relationship problems happen because people cannot accept each other's eye angles. They won't know this consciously, of course, and eye angle hardly qualifies as legal grounds for divorce in any court. Nevertheless, when you find out what eye angles mean, you'll appreciate how important they are.

First let's get the physical concept. **Eye angles** mean the tilt of an eye, end to end, compared to the rest of the face. And it's not hard to spot once you know what to look for. Frankly, it's easiest to use *spots*, or dots, to get your bearings. Here's how:

Start with *one* eye since asymmetries are more common than you might assume. Imagine a dot on the inner corner of that eye, right at the tear duct. Imagine a second dot where the eye tapers off at the opposite side—and look carefully to see this place; it's often much higher on the face than a novice face reader expects.

Now that you have your two dots, connect them with an imaginary line. This line will have an angle. That, and that alone, shows what I mean by eye angle.

Q. Gee, does this angle have anything to do with almond-shaped eyes?

A. Have mercy. No! This almond business is one of the silliest face clichés around. I've mused over it many a time and have concluded

EYE ANGLES

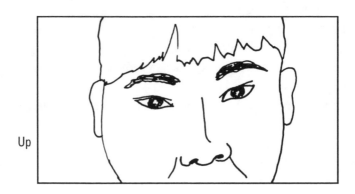

Up

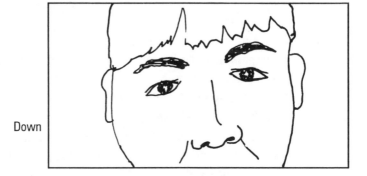

Down

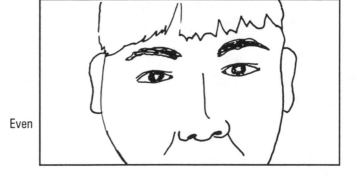

Even

that, as a way of distinguishing eye characteristics, it's absolutely nutty. What are you supposed to have, lacking the almond seal of approval, peepers that look like peanuts?

You've heard it before about reading the face, but some of us go so ga-ga over eyes, it bears repeating. To look for face categories, be discriminating. Look for one trait at a time. Look at a face on the level.

Look in the mirror now. Line up two dots per eye, follow the angle and see what you have.

Once you develop your eye for the angle of eyes, you'll notice three variations.

- Most eye angles go **up**.
- Others angle **down.**
- The rest, of course, are **even**.

Q. Honestly, you're claiming that your typical Caucasian person like me has eyes that slant up?

A. See for yourself. I do invite you to drop the "Caucasian" label and just see the human part. When you do, you'll discover that about 85 percent of human beings, from all over the world, have eyes that angle upwards to some extent.

The more pronounced the physical trait, the more likely that person's outlook will be optimistic, even idealistic. Yes, *up*-angled eyes come with high expectations for a spouse, child, parent, boss, or employee.

Plenty of conflict potential presents itself right from the start. Try a quick multiple choice quiz. Where might conflict arise?

   a) Between idealists and the people who must put up with their high
      expectations
   b) Between two idealists, with their differing high expectations
      about each other
   c) Within an idealist's own mind and heart, as reality sinks in.
   Give yourself a bonus point if you guessed the answer is:

d) All of the above.

And, not to be unduly discouraging, there's an even worse problem that goes with the territory, the kind of problem that optimists, by definition, hate to acknowledge: denial. Here's the most VERY example I've encountered yet in a client. One day John came home to his wife of 16 years and discovered that she was gone.

She had also taken the kids, the furniture, everything but a little mattress for her husband to sleep on. "This was a terrible shock," explained John and his VERY up-angled eyes. "As far as I was concerned, our marriage was perfect, no problems at all."

Admittedly John had some traits beyond his up-angled eyes, but you get the point.

Let's not deny, though, a wonderful tendency that goes with this eye trait. An idealistic outlook goes with adventurous risk taking. "Look before you leap" was probably coined by the despairing parents of a kid with VERY up-angled eyes. Disappointment is most likely when expectations are high, but does that discourage the world's native optimists? Of course not, and the world's a better place for it.

Q. How does this optimistic risk-taking fit with what you said about chin length and risks? Being in sales, it could help me a lot to know in advance who is more of a gambler.

A. Up-angled eyes accentuate the risk-taking styles that show in the chin. Good for you for putting these factors together! Customers with long chins take *physical* risks, like being attracted to the speed and deft handling of a new car. Customers with short chins avoid physical risks but will put themselves on the line over personal *ethics*. I'd sell them first on a new car's safety features, plus the convenience of the car for offering rides to passengers.

Of course, customers with VERY up-angled eyes plus VERY large round nostrils are any salesperson's dream. These are the biggest *financial* risk takers, because they believe in every glorious possibility.

Apart from profiting directly from an optimistic outlook, everyone in society benefits when a trailblazer looks past limitations to find possibilities. Helen Keller smashed the world's preconceptions about what a physically challenged person could accomplish. Rosa Parks defied segregation. Studs Terkel has given people self-worth by taking their oral histories. Decade after decade, Abigail Van Buren has offered advice to the lovelorn, the frustrated, and the downright peculiar.

What gift goes with eyes that tilt *down*? Not to worry, you've got your share of blessings. To summarize them, you're a problem finder and a problem solver.

Q. Aw, shucks. What if finding problems is just your job? With the kind of sales job I have, you've got to be able to handle problems.

A. It's not just your job. Most people, even if they had your job, wouldn't focus on problems the way you do. And they might be just as successful. Their styles would be different, that's all.

For example, if you have this eye trait, think back to the most recent family gathering you've attended. Weren't you one of the first to spot the impending divorce of Aunt Gail and Uncle Ferdinand? Weren't you the one to foresee potential difficulties when your Cousin Sylvia raved to everyone about her new job selling Happy Fat Cookies, the new brand whose goal is to make cholesterol "a more cheerful, chewy word"?

Admit it, you find problems where nobody else does, which makes you a fabulous problem solver. And one of the fringe benefits is your compassion. Because denial isn't an issue, you can handle hearing about people's problems. Think about the VERY down-angled eyes of John Gray and Deborah Tannen, those outstanding relationship experts. The world needs people willing to face up to problems.

Your only serious challenge is a little agreement you may have unconsciously made with the Universe. It goes like this:

"God, I'm so good at finding problems and solving them. Let's make sure I always have at least one really major one going on in my life."

If that has been your agreement, why not re-negotiate?

As for eyes with an *even* angle, you have a rare degree of realism. Not a pessimist, not an optimist, you can remind people that a glass of water can be simultaneously half full and half empty.

Emily Post has used this gift to help her generation walk the straight-and-narrow path of good manners and tact. Cartoonist Cathy Guisewite draws on realism, then allows her characters to agonize over tact. Another cartoonist, Gary Trudeau, writes "Doonesbury" satire that's not so much cynical as realistic.

Dr. Bernie Siegel has VERY even eye angles. Fittingly he has observed: "Pessimists hold a more accurate view of reality, but optimists live longer."

The only challenge for even-eyed people is a lack of tolerance for the rest of humanity, in all their moody extremes, from the contagious enthusiasm of "Touched by an Angel" stars Della Reese and Roma Downey to the down-angled gloom of William Golding, author of *Lord of the Flies*.

Mouth Angles

Words have a special importance when it comes to problem solving. Often it's not the deeds that rile us but chance comments that slip out of a mouth. If you've ever been a parent, I'll bet you still remember the strange way babies have of eating their first solid food: now it's in, now it's out, and the infant seems blissfully unaware of the difference. This turns out to be a perennial human problem, not with food but with words.

By the time your kid learns to talk, it becomes time to teach which remarks would be better not to spit out. People of any age need to be reminded periodically of this saying: "Make your words soft and sweet because some day you may have to eat them."

MOUTH ANGLES

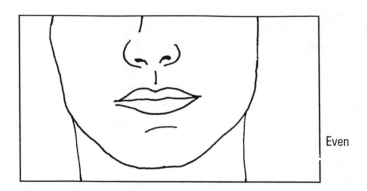

Even

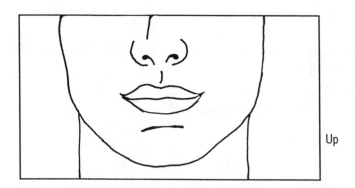

Up

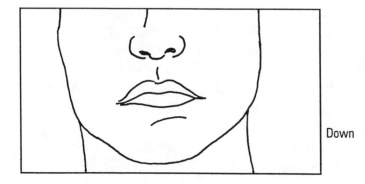

Down

Well, here's good news for all of us who have to contend with everyday life's sitcom situations caused by words that slip out unexpectedly. As a physiognomist, forewarn and forearm yourself by looking at **mouth angle**.

To do this, examine a mouth when it is in repose (unless you're delving into the personal style of someone who always smiles, a rare being indeed—in fact a being so rare he probably could stand some more cooking).

Imagine dots again, just as you did with eye angle. This time, place one imaginary dot at each mouth corner and one at the center of the mouth, where the lips meet. Connect these dots to form two lines, one for each side of the face. Usually, but not always, the same mouth angle will prevail on both sides. Now read each side separately.

- Does the angle march **straight** across the face? Then it counts as straight.
- Do you see lifting at the corner? Reckon the angle as **up**.
- Does the mouth steer downward? Count that mouth angle as **down**.

Here's the meaning of *mouth angle*: how a person interprets what other people say. It's one thing to be an idealist, problem-finder or sage about life when you're the one who's talking. You may well have a different reaction when other people talk to you. It's a deep down way of receiving what life brings to you and, fittingly, it shows all the way down the face, at the lowest moveable feature.

Let me give you an example to illustrate how this trait works. Let's say you're considering dating a woman named Jane. One afternoon you see her as she's leaving a restaurant and you're racing in to meet some business clients. You're running late so you blurt out: "I'm in a terrible rush. Can't stop to talk. Sorry."

If Jane's mouth angle is *straight*, she might react, "What's going on with him? Wonder why he's in such a rush?

If Jane's mouth angle is *up*, she might react, "He's probably rushing to make one of his fabulous business deals. Nice of him to stop and acknowledge me, even when he was in such a hurry."

However, if Jane's mouth angles *down* (by far the most common trait in adults), she's more likely to brood, "There was such coldness in his voice. And to think, once we were friends. Reminds me of the time that Hubert did the same thing."

You see, the more *down*ward the mouth angle, the more the mouth wearer interprets comments to mean the worst. The challenge is obvious. Don't overlook the strength, though, if you are habitually down-in-the-mouth. Being highly sensitive to hurt feelings, yourself, you tend to be kind to others. When words that slip out could hurt feelings, aren't you quick to apologize?

The best sitcom on TV for featuring down-angled mouths at their funniest is, undoubtedly, "Frasier." The main character's mouth, in repose, incessantly struggles to moves from down-angled to even. His brother, Niles, shows a mouth with a VERY down angle. And their father, the sardonic ex-police officer, also has a mouth that cascades downward to an extreme degree. Dialogue on the show plays with everyone's quickness to interpret personal remarks in the worst possible light.

Mouths that angle *up*wards don't hold grudges about chance remarks. Left-handed compliments may be accepted at face value. Actually, the challenge with lips like these is too much teasing for more verbally-sensitive folks. How often has it happened that people took offense at remarks you've made that would never, even on a bad day, bother you? You've heard of having a bad hair day. Compared with you, most people are having a bad mouth day, and it happens day in and day out.

The rare beings with *even* mouth angles show an amazing instinctive behavior. You'll sort through a statement to fathom its actual intended meaning. Then you'll react.

286 The Power of Face Reading

Others may find this style weird. For once, with a moderate trait, your challenge isn't a lack of tolerance with the rest of humanity. It's the rest of humanity's lack of tolerance for you!

Perhaps that has been an asset to American presidents who needed to hold their ground despite controversial views: Abe Lincoln, Teddy Roosevelt, Woodrow Wilson, Gerald Ford and, of course, "Give 'em hell" Harry Truman.

Lucille Ball used the deadpan resilience of even mouth angles to create the classic sitcom, "I Love Lucy."

One fascinating face in terms of eye and mouth angles belonged to Dr. Norman Vincent Peale. His eyes and lips pointed down on the right side of this face, up on the left. My interpretation is that he had a major life challenge with transforming a negative attitude into a positive one. Mastering this life lesson prepared him to become the world's foremost positive thinker.

A dozen talents for problem solving

Many of the face traits we've seen in previous chapters reveal distinctive talents for problem solving. The list on the next page is, therefore, a cheer-up chart. If the person you're arguing with has any one of these traits, maybe it will help you to recognize it. Think about how that person's talent can be turned to your mutual advantage.

Imagination

Q. "Imagination's Peak"—is this some mountain range that sneaked into our discussion of problems? Have you decided that travel is the best revenge?

12 Talents for Problem Solving

	Face Data	How the Gift Works
1.	Far-set eyes	Broadening everyone's perspective, making a molehill look less like a mountain.
2.	Close-set eyes	Focusing on the problem, in minute detail, until it is fixed. Note: this style can drive people with other eye sets absolutely wild with frustration.
3.	Thin nose padding	Figuring out the solution alone. (Give this worker space!)
4.	Full nose padding	Including and valuing everyone on the team, helping to make the solution a group effort.
5.	Ender eyebrows	Tying up every loose end; pushing through to fix the details that hold up the rest of the project.
6.	Angled eyebrows	Refusing to waste another second on solutions that don't work; shaking everything up in pursuit of a new order that can work better.
7.	High ears	Dazzling people with quick, intuitive problem solving.
8.	Low ears	Showing the patience to wait until the problem can be solved fully.
9.	Close-set cheeks	Demonstrating grace under pressure. When a solution must be found now, somehow, this person will find a way.
10.	In-angled chin	Using co-operation to solve problems—selflessness and kindness toward others.
11.	Blarney lips	Persuading everyone that the problem is solved (whether it is or not—at least this temporarily takes care of all the folks who are angry about the non-solution of the problem).
12.	Imagination's peak hairline	Solving problems through the use of imagination; creative vision that may come years ahead of its time.

A. Well, I've changed the name of a physical trait because the old one was, frankly, a stinker. You've heard of a "widow's peak" haven't you? It's an angled shape at the hairline. I refuse to limit this wonderful trait by giving it a name associated with death.

Quite possibly it's the single most intense trait related to creativity. In honor of that, as well as its physical position as a high point of the face, I've renamed it the **Imagination's Peak Hairline**.

Q. Hold on. You're not really expecting us to believe that one little trait is supremely creative, are you?

A. No. Creativity shows in a wealth of face traits. For instance, each of the three major nose profile shapes (straight, scooped, and arched) suggests a different creative specialty when working (with procedures, intuition, and the resources of the work environment, respectively). These traits didn't make it to our list of talents for problem solving, but they could have.

In fact, just about every face trait shows a nuance of creativity that can be applied to problem solving. For the previous list of A Dozen Talents for Problem Solving, I selected forms of creativity that are especially distinctive, even quirky,.

Imagination's Peak Hairline earns its place on this list by relating, specifically, to creative imagination. All of us have it, and can strengthen it, but some folks have been issued a super-huge lifetime supply. It comes with only one challenge: dealing with the rest of the world, especially those who feel threatened by imagination.

But mathematician Dr. Andrew Wiles isn't complaining. His off-the-chart ingenuity enabled him to prove Fermat's last theorem. Big deal, you say? Who the heck is Fermat? Well, to some mathematicians he's at least as important as Elvis, and they've been trying to prove his theorem for more than 350 years.

Currently, the brilliant young mezzo-soprano Cecilia Bartoli hasn't been shy about showing the world that unusual hairline style. Good

IMAGINATION'S PEAK HAIRLINE

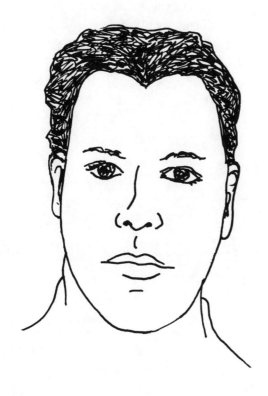

move! Nobody who has this trait should hide it. The problems of the world cry out for more imagination.

Other imagination experts are physicists Maria Goeppert Mayer and Rudolf L. Mössbauer. And let's not forget Mickey Mouse, America's most creative cartoon character. Did you know? When it comes to hair-line, Mickey looks a lot like his Dad, Walt Disney.

■■■

13. Sales strategies

Sales isn't for snails. Sometimes you have to make your move and make it fast. Your client's first impressions are lasting impressions.

Face reading can help you, unless you're a telemarketer.

Face reading can help you, not only if you work in a point-of-sale, big-or-small-ticket, merchandise-or-service moving operation, i.e., conventional sales. "Sales" also applies to you if you are persuading, teaching, managing, or trying to motivate anyone to do anything. And the tips in this chapter can help you do it more skillfully.

Helpful intent

Every day of her adult life, Oprah Winfrey has prayed for the same thing: to be of service to others. Amazing! She hasn't demanded big ratings, a fan club of millions, or even a career, let alone the chance to become America's wealthiest self-made woman. But, as it slipped out in an interview in *Redbook Magazine*, Oprah has asked, from the heart, to be of service.

Oprah's success has depended on many factors, but maybe this one matters most to people like you and me because it's one factor that we can duplicate at will, starting now.

The intent to help others pays. In practical terms, it pays because most folks have a well developed sense of smell when it comes to greed. We're like bloodhounds for sniffing out somebody who's using us to meet a sales quota.

And just as you feel repulsed when somebody looks at you with dollar signs in his eyes, don't you feel attracted by a truly helpful intent?

Like you, your clients can tell. So even for the most selfish of reasons, it pays to set a specific intention to care about your sales clients. Face reading can help those of us who cherish good intentions, especially when we grow weary. Even the freshest snow, the kind that takes your breath away with its pure white innocence, can't hold up to traffic. It turns into grimy, lumpy slush. So can our do-gooder wishes.

Face reading, however, is an amazing resource as a pick-me-up. When it's 3:00 o'clock on a Friday afternoon and, frankly, you've had it with humanity, give yourself the benefit of eyeballing a nose or a chin.

When a new nose walks into your showroom, take a few seconds to read it. Forget the expression. (At that time of the day or the week, neither the customer nor you is likely to win a prize for expression anyway.) Actively look for a talent or two and you will show forth what makes that customer an individual. Automatically, you can be in the sales equivalent of an exquisite snowscape. You can see that person new.

Admittedly, today's sales climate is harsh. Customers unabashedly shop for price. Frankly, they often look at *us* with dollar signs in their eyes—or don't look at us much at all until convinced that we can deliver what they want at the cheapest price, and while making it snappy.

Being treated by a customer as a sales object is akin to being treated as a sex object. (Hmm, if the customer is bad enough, you might be treated both ways.) So thank goodness for your free will, energized by your face reading prowess. When you choose to meet your client as an individual, it can be contagious. Insist on talking person to person, rather than object to object.

Humor yourself

Even when you have high intent and you do your best, success doesn't automatically follow. That's when a sense of humor can keep you from feeling discouraged.

At the end of my classes, each student is invited to fill out evaluation forms. Usually they inspire me. Sometimes they offer useful suggestions. But occasionally their comments make me groan over how tough the climate is out there. No matter how many pages of materials I give students along with their class, predictably some will howl at the lack of handouts. Some students have complained that I didn't know the subject well enough (an odd comment, considering that I invented it). Some students have even griped that the class wasn't held at the date or place advertised in the catalog. (Really? Then how did all of us chance to be there?) Oh well.

In a world where you can't please everyone, at least we face readers can always win the consolation prize. Whatever else happens, we can add to our face reading knowledge.

Thus, when your intent to be of service yields no apparent result, you can switch to Plan B: laugh and learn as much as you can. Sometimes people in service occupations spend so much time humoring others, we forget to be kind to ourselves. Face reading can add a delicious element of humor to business transactions.

My husband and I will long remember a party where I was hired to read faces. The hostess, Elvira, had booked a one-hour gig, insisting that she couldn't possibly afford my services for any longer, in view of the cost. Since she was so adamant, my husband drove me there, planning to wait in the car. Afterwards we would drive straight to a friend's birthday party.

Waving goodbye to Mitch, I sailed into the gig, where I read faces for a most enthusiastic group of guests. Elvira began to worry, and justifiably so. Her VERY curved chin suggested she was a generous hostess: nothing was too good for her guests. At the same time, she had VERY small, triangular nostrils, suggesting a major challenge with spending money. What was our conflicted hostess going to do?

Obviously her guests wanted me to stay longer, for which she would have to pay, and although her household suggested affluence, her nostrils pleaded poverty. As I packed up to leave, she asked what it would cost for me to stay longer. I quoted my hourly rate. Mindful of her nasal endowment, I emphasized that she could hire me by the quarter hour, if she preferred.

"Just 15 minutes longer," Elvira said.

So I stayed and read faces for another quarter hour. Then another. And another. And another. I felt a little like Scheherazade and her Thousand and One Nights. It seemed every minute would be my last.

By the time my engagement ended, I had worked nearly four hours. Back at the car lay Mitch, his legs propped up on the dashboard, his seat inclined backwards.

Yes, my incredibly sweet and good-natured husband was napping. I had never warned him that I would be gone all that time because I hadn't computed, right until the end, just how many 15-minute chunks were adding up. Together we laughed over the unintentional outcome: Four hours had passed while Mitch was a prisoner of Elvira's nostrils.

Over and over again, you'll watch people act out their faces. If you had to pay theater admission, you'd couldn't find a more entertaining show. When you feel like a prisoner of slow business, at least you can enjoy a face reader's show business.

■■■

Find the person with power

So much for attitude—it's time for specifics. And nothing is more specific for a salesperson than power.

When you sell to more than one person, you need to identify the decision maker. Otherwise going through your paces could be just a dress rehearsal. Depending on the type of sales you do, and the training you've received, you're probably wise in the ways of body language. You've learned to assess office hierarchies and politics so you can pick out the leader.

Whatever you're doing already, why not supplement it by looking at the face's power structures? This will be especially helpful if you're dealing with professional negotiators or others who have been trained to conceal their emotions. Other things being equal, the person who has the last word will be the one with the most of these attributes:

1. Cheek prominence

The one whose cheeks stick out most will go ahead with decisions, regardless of the presence or absence of approval from others.

2. Nose thrust

A nose that pushes out most in profile belongs to someone accustomed to having a great deal of impact on others.

3. Chin thrust

When situations turn competitive, the one with the most aggressive chin thrust expects to win—and probably will.

Q. What if the players are tied? What if it makes you dizzy, pitting the chins against their noses plus... what was the other face part?

A. To keep things simple, pick the person with the largest chin thrust.

Q. Once you've decided, what then?

A. Look first at that person every time you make an important statement and when you move toward closing your sale. Also, whenever somebody in the group presents an objection for you to answer, after you answer it, take a quick confirming look back at Numero Uno.

Setting priorities (based on theirs)

Of course, you'll want to be sensitive to what your client verbally states as priorities for the product you're selling. Yet, as you know, people don't always tell you the whole truth about what matters most to them. Sometimes they don't know themselves.

But sometimes their faces can tell you. One of the most basic things about any customer is life priorities, which show in Priority Areas. For best results, be sensitive to what customers tell you verbally but supplement that information with what their faces show.

Start by pitching your sale in terms of the most powerful person's Priority Areas. Reading that should take no longer than five seconds. (If the face proportions aren't clear enough to show at a quick glance, they're not VERY enough to bother considering.)

1. Area I largest

These people are fascinated by ideas. So be sure to present plenty of theoretical background for every one of the features of the product you're selling. For instance, if it's computer software, don't just explain what it can do. Explain why the software was designed that way. What were the objectives? How do they matter?

2. Area II largest

These people are driven by ambition. Emphasize results, the more personal the better. For selling that computer software, ask about what she will use it for and show how she can accomplish more with less effort or time.

3. Area III largest

Down-to-earth people won't feel comfortable with you unless you pace your presentation right. Build in frequent breaks for jokes, small talk, coffee. In terms of information, bring out every fact that can boost the product's credentials. For instance, if a particular kind of software is selling best right now, be sure to mention it.

Q. What if your client has a big Area III but also out-angled ears? Aren't these people nonconformists, even if down-to-earth?

A. Excellent! As a precaution with your Area III client, it wouldn't hurt to check ear angle. If your client has VERY out-angled ears, don't breathe a word about popularity. These folks, as you recall, pride themselves on not being one of the crowd. Just talk about practical features and any facts that prove they work well.

Q. Are you saying you can predict when an appeal to herd instinct will backfire?

A. Often you can. Even if you're selling to a teenager, at the time of life when peer pressure is strongest, read the face and don't brag that

"It's our most popular item" if you see either out-angled ears or a predominant Area I.

The people with Area I largest take an intellectual approach that can include contempt for the masses. If you say your product appeals to everyone, your would-be client may avoid buying it on principle.

Mental flexibility

Speaking of intelligence, one way that you can show yours is to appeal to more than one kind of logic. As a sales communicator you may deal with people who think altogether differently from you. If you can adapt to another person's way of thinking, you'll boost your sales.

This matters most if you are selling your services. As a realtor or a therapist, for instance, you're in a competitive field. It isn't enough to impress a potential client with how knowledgeable you are. When you demonstrate that what you know fits your client's mental compartments, you'll command more respect.

Probably you've heard the nonverbal tip that you can win friends and influence people by copying their body language. If your client crosses his legs or leans forward on his chair or cocks his head to the right, do the same. It works because body and mind are connected. By putting yourself in your client's position literally, you also reposition yourself figuratively.

Good as that tip is, you can do even better by copying mental styles. Nose and eyebrows can tell you what you need to know. Start with noses. Which kind of logic appeals to your client?

■ The straighter your client's nose, the greater her respect for a systematic presentation. Work from a checklist, or act as if you do.

■ If the nose scoops inward, be sure to appeal to feelings rather than giving a strictly factual argument.

■ As for an arched nose, put some appeal to beauty into your pitch. That's the "logic" surest to win such a client's sympathies.

Q. Hold on. You're advising me to say, "This blender is the loveliest shade of eggshell?" Maybe I've been working too long in small appliances, but I don't think beauty is that great a selling point.

A. You're right. Sometimes the product doesn't have much aesthetic appeal, unless you're an engineer. But you can make small talk about things that connect to your client's sense of beauty, like the color of his socks. And don't miss the chance to discuss how your product can help the client be more creative.

Talk to their eyebrows

Once you have gotten onto your client's wavelength, nose-wise and logic-wise, turn to eyebrows. Eyebrow shape can give you insight into how to shape your sales pitch.

1. Straight-browed folks are idea people.

Emphasize ideas. It might be ideas about logical benefits. It might be ideas about feelings. It might be ideas about beauty and creativity. Whatever the specifics, you'll want to go briskly through your argument. What won't help is for you to linger at any one point, waiting for a show of enthusiasm. Straight-browed clients enjoy when you jump through hoops, one idea (or hoop) at a time.

2. Curved-browed folks care about feelings.

Why not intersperse your selling points with anecdotes? Describe how what you're selling helped people feel better.* Use your emotional side to win your client over.

3. Angle-browed folks need to stay in control.

How can you cater to a client's need to stay in control? Early on, be sure to ask her, "What is most important to you about this product (or service)?" Giving your client a chance to shape the conversation in this way may help you to control her need to stay in control. And, whenever possible, follow your client's lead in a way that conveys the feeling that she's in control of the conversation.

Q. Won't any client, with or without angled eyebrows shape, want to stay in control?

A. You'd be surprised. If the feeling level of your conversation is right, someone with curved eyebrows can be charmed into talking with you for at least as long as you, personally, wish to continue the conversation. Someone with straight brows will be a good sport about following your ideas, especially if you can present them crisply. But folks with VERY angled brows care as much about being in control as about anything you might say.

Q. Won't any client tell you if he feels you've been wasting his time?

A. Many clients won't tell you until it's too late. They're already turned off. In particular, watch out for clients with deep-set eyes. They may go through the motions of politeness long after they've put up a great wall of China, or at least a great wall of skepticism.

* Hey, you can tell stories about just about anything, so long as they're upbeat, tasteful, and related to people's emotions.

Intuition can always alert you to someone's hidden withdrawal from your conversation. But you'll want to pay special attention to someone with VERY deep-set eyes and ask, as early and often as possible, "What do you think?"

Timing

Time is of the essence in today's mega-scheduled society. You don't want to rush your clients, but neither do you want them to feel like you're wasting their time. Or have a tire-kicker waste yours. Ear position can give you invaluable information. Especially be on the lookout for ears that are low or high.

1. Low-eared clients

They make decisions in a thoughtful, deliberate way. If you ask for the sale too early, you'll startle them. It's like what happens when you watch your favorite TV show. Without realizing it, you fall into a light trance. If someone says "Boo," you jump. Or, even worse from a sales perspective, you *grump*. When you're selling, let people with low ears gather all the information they need. Be as patient as you can afford to be before announcing that the show is over and now it's decision time.

2. High-eared clients

They make their minds up instantly. Don't insult their quick intelligence by repeating a word.

Q. What if I have a set bunch of sales points to make. You're not suggesting that I break the rules, are you?

A. Who, me? But a quick summary can do the trick when people have high ears. They decide extremely fast. Beyond that, they will gain nothing but disgust.

■■■

Money alert

Since spending style shows in the nose, you could do worse than to tie your time management to your client's nostrils.

- Lavish attention on any client with large round nostrils. These folks are the biggest spenders on earth.
- Curtail your investment on clients with triangular nostrils or VERY small nostrils. They may need a great deal of persuasion before buying.
- When a client has flared nostrils, emphasize the fun of the purchase.
- When a client's nostrils are rectangular, make the purchase appear as sensible an investment as possible—even if you are selling pet monkeys.

Q. How about nose tips? Wasn't that supposed to be important for spending style too?

A. Yes. When you find someone with a chunky nose tip, make the best case you can for security. Explain how what you're selling will help your client to save in the long run—like the discount store in my neighborhood that tells you, on your receipt, how much money you have "saved," as though that cancels out all the dollars you've actually spent.

Fishing for objections

Who wouldn't rather fish for compliments? Asking for objections isn't the most enjoyable part of the sales game, unless you have large chin thrust, or some other sign of a competitive spirit.

Sales is a tough business. Even if you hate risking rejection, it's worthwhile to ask for your client's objections. Face reading can make this task easier, or at least, funnier. Five face traits, in particular, show distinctive behaviors related to 'fessing up to objections.

1. Down-angled eyes

They belong to folks who thrive on problems. Thrive along with them by asking questions like, "Do you see any problem with what I've just said?" or "Can you see any situations where this wouldn't work?" Believe it or not, this is like asking an aerobics instructor to demonstrate a few fancy steps. You'll start your client doing what he does best. Above all, don't feel threatened when your client cuts loose naming problems. Work together to solve them, one by one, and your client will respect you as a kindred spirit.

2. The pacifist power style

When faces are widest under the cheeks, these are customers who hate to argue. Unless you make it safe to complain, they'll politely hide their objections until they leave the room. Once the door closes, out will pop all their unspoken complaints about everything you've said. Of course, the long-suffering spouse is hearing these valuable objections, not you. Therefore, I urge you to go out of your way with people who have this trait. Show that you are someone who loves hearing objections.

If you can manage it, act as though you have exceedingly high self-esteem and you're so used to being dumped on that, in a sense, you thrive on it. "That's okay, give me a hard time" is a safe thing to say with these people. Many of them are dying for a chance to complain to someone. They may buy from you out of sheer relief.

3. VERY thin lips

Remember how different people can be about self-disclosure? Forget about *your* comfort zone. Someone with thin lips prefers to talk in a businesslike manner. Don't make the mistake of initiating conversation about anything personal.

Being indirect won't hurt you, either, if you get the feeling you must handle certain objections. For instance, let's say your client makes a comment that suggests he's afraid the model of fax you're selling won't be dependable enough. He doesn't have the cash flow to buy a higher end product, and you're afraid he will race out the store without buying a thing. How can you handle objections that are too personal for him to comfortably tell you?

An indirect comment, bringing up *someone else's* experience, might get the problem out in the open—for instance, "Last week I had a customer like you who was buying a fax for the first time. He was afraid the pages would curl up to such an extent they'd be worthless but a plain paper fax wasn't in his budget. Yesterday he was in the store. He said that the inexpensive fax he bought from me has been a lifesaver. 'It didn't matter that the copies were on thin paper,' he told me. 'What mattered was that I got them at all. I'm already finding it hard to believe I used to do business without investing in a fax of my own.'"

4. VERY Short Lips

They go with a passion for truthfulness. If you share that passion, so much the better for your chances of selling to this individual. Otherwise, put yourself temporarily under oath. While you're talking with that client, make sure it's: "The truth, the whole truth, and nothing but the truth."

Please, avoid giveaway statements that make your integrity suspect, such as: "To tell you the truth" or "My honest opinion is...." You don't want your client's main objection to the sale to be *you*.

5. Lowbrows

As you may recall, the folks with this eyebrow trait have a need to blurt things out instantly. While they politely hold onto their thoughts, because you're rambling on, they'll turn off to you and your sale. Maybe your client's impulse to ask a skeptical question will strike early on, or mid-sentence. Quick: If you suspect this may be happening, instantly cut yourself off (even if it's mid-sentence) and ask, "Hey, what do you think about all this?"

Q. Aren't you afraid of appearing insecure? "Help! Did I do something wrong that last second? Ooh, I'm so scared of displeasing you. Do I have the right to live?"
A. Scoff at this strategy, if you must. But it's good advice for dealing with a lowbrow. You know, you can always show by your body language that your question reflects your security, rather than insecurity.

Q. How exactly, would you recommend finding out when these lightning flashes of skepticism appear?
A. Soon as you spot lowbrows, turn up your intuitive radio. Watch for any flicker of skepticism that crosses your client's face. Soon as you

see a smirk flash across her lips, ask: "What's your reaction to that?" If you can get an honest, spontaneous reaction you'll be well on the way to winning your client's confidence... and her sale.

Q. How can I look for all these face things without driving my-self nuts? I've already got my regular sales points to worry about, you know.

A. Luckily you don't have to work hard at using your face reading skills. Once you've gone through this book systematically, chapter by chapter, you'll be familiar with the basics about different face traits and what they mean.

Once you've finished this chapter don't try to do everything at once. Choose one face trait strategy that fascinates you, like something from nostril reading. Try out my strategies for a week. Then add a second strategy the following week.

After a while, you'll be consciously schooled. Your unconscious will then take over. You'll be having a normal conversation, not thinking about face parts at all, when boing! deep-set eyes or thin lips will jump out at you. Inwardly, you'll go "Aha!" And you'll know just what to do.

■■■

14. Self-esteem

Assuming that you've read this far, not just flipped to this chapter first (a smart move, actually—who couldn't use more self-esteem?), you've learned that your face is a perfect reflection of the inner you. Every trait on every feature means something about who you are inside. You are, in fact, loaded with talents that make you distinctive.

What I've found, however, is that self-esteem issues still come up for many of us, even after we become face readers. We may agonize over being pretty enough or looking too old and wrinkly. Some of us may struggle over looking "just like" relatives we hate, which brings lingering doubts about the concept of justice in faces... or in life.

Is life fair, when it comes to faces? The answer is a resounding "YES" when you combine Face Reading Secrets with knowledge from psychology and metaphysics—just what we're about to do in this chapter. [*]

---

[*] Skeptics, relax. You can be a first-rate physiognomist without agreeing with a thing in this chapter. Take the metaphysical side strictly à la carte.

Pretty or plain

The plain truth about **beauty** is that it's pretty deceptive. Socially, beauty gives you a clear advantage, particularly during those years of high school popularity contests—years that seemingly last forever to those of us who don't make the in-crowd. From the perspective of face reading, everyone can be a winner at what matters in life. Beauty carries one set of advantages; **plainness** confers another.

We'll consider both. Let's start with *beauty*. Did you know that it literally pays? Leave it to an economist to crunch the numbers. Daniel Hamermesh, co-author of *Beauty and the Labor Market*, has determined that attractive people earn about 5 percent more per hour than those with average looks. And, all other things being equal, they earn as much as 10 percent more than the truly homely.

Attractiveness may also cut down prison time. Two New York psychologists, from Iona College, devised an experiment* to test this idea. Wesley Kayson and Andrea DeSantis asked subjects to act as jurors in a fictitious burglary case. Sentencing varied according to beauty quotient, with mock jurors recommending that good-lookers spend, on average, 9.7 years in the slammer compared with 14.7 years for the less-attractive defendants.

Another psychologist, Karl Wuensch, of East Carolina University, has uncovered similar prejudice in his extensive research.** "Better-looking people are treated better in court. We've found this to be true not just in mock criminal trials but in civil trials as well."

As if this wasn't depressing enough, the reasoning behind this treatment is even worse. Wuensch has found that attractive people "are seen as being trustworthy, honest, reliable, bright, warm and friendly" whereas unattractive people "are seen as lazy, hard to get along with, untrustworthy, not honest."

*Morin, R. "Beauty and the Beast in the Courtroom." The Washington Post, November 30, 1997.
**Ibid.

Folks make the inference that "Good is good-looking." Wuensch says. This is a form of face watching, of course, not face reading.

Because most Americans haven't yet learned to look deeper into the physical face, we go loco over attractiveness. For example, we spend $18.5 billion a year just on cosmetics. Did you know they can be dangerous as well as costly? According to Jack Anderson, a columnist with *The Washington Post*, in 1987 alone, hospital emergency rooms reported 47,000 cases of injuries caused by soaps, hair straighteners, lotions, facial masks, and other products. Maybe you never thought of cosmetology as a high-risk profession. Well, it is. [*]

Nevertheless, the main factor in beauty isn't grooming. Beauty is widely acknowledged to lie primarily in the shapes and proportions of physical features. But what is it about these features? Psychologists at the University of Texas and University of Arkansas have made a shocking discovery. What we're really admiring when we gawk at handsome men and gorgeous women is how **average** they are. Or to describe the research done by Judith Langlois and Lori Roggman with appropriate scientific language, beauty means having features that approximate the mathematical average of all faces in a particular population. [**]

Here's how they figured this out. The researchers designed a study using head shots of 96 male and 96 female college students. The photos were scanned by a video lens hooked up to a computer that converted each picture into a matrix of tiny digital units with numerical values.

Each group of faces, female and male, was divided into three sets of 32 faces. From each set, the computer randomly chose two faces, mathematically averaged their values, then transformed these numbers into a composite face of the two individuals.

In a similar manner, composite faces were generated for 4, 8, 16, and 32 members of each set.

[*] Anderson, J. "Beauty and Beast of Makeup Chemicals." The Washington Post, December 12, 1988.
[**] Bower, B. "Average Attractions: Psychologists Break Down the Essence of Physical Beauty." Science News, vol. 137, No. 19, May 12, 1009, p. 298.

Then came the beauty part. As reported in *Science News*, 65 students were asked to be judges, rating each set of mug shots (individual faces plus composite faces all in the same batch). Which faces won? Overwhelmingly winners were the smoosheroos, the 16- and 32-face composites. Composites of 8 or fewer faces were not judged differently from the singleton faces of mere mortals.

As a face reader, you can appreciate what it means for a face to be average. In terms of the traits we've looked at, a beautiful face would have eyes that are mid-way between close- and far-set. The nose would be moderately long, the ears in average position, the eyebrows would have even fullness, and so forth.

Now remember what these traits mean. Average traits give the advantage of flexibility. Every time you have one, your personal style can go either way. Regarding perspective, you can take either a broad or narrow view. Regarding timing for work projects, you can work equally well on short- and long-term projects. When making decisions, you have no deep preference about making them slowly and thoroughly or with dazzling speed. Details are no issue, with your being equally comfortable with starting projects or finishing them. You just do the work.

Get the idea? If you had a perfectly average (and, therefore, "beautiful") face, your biggest challenge with any trait might be a lack of tolerance for the rest of humanity. But you also might have a hard time finding *distinctive* talents, other than the ability to turn heads.

Being drop-dead beautiful isn't easy, emotionally or socially. It is, of course, a talent in its own right—as is eye-popping ugliness. In either case, people stop, stare, and proceed to treat you like a symbol. They project onto you their hopes, fears, lusts, resentments... whatever has been stored up.

A student of mine, a Franciscan nun from Springfield, Illinois, had a habit of wearing the distinctive clothing of her order. She told me how strange it was to walk down the street and be treated like "a nun."

"Some people come up to me with open arms, as friendly as could be. Others, people I've never met before in all my life, come up to me and complain. Some even yell at me. It's interesting, to say the least. I never know how people are going to react."

Without going to the extreme of wearing a habit or taking vows, many of us have had the chance to become symbols temporarily. Did you ever wear a cast, walk on crutches, or ride in a wheelchair? How about being eight months pregnant, wearing a black eye, walking a very expensive pedigreed dog, being the only person of color in a roomful of whites or vice versa?

Whammo! come the reactions. Some folks love you, others hate you. None of these extreme reactions has anything to do with the truth about you, personally. Remembering this may help you to stay sane. Meanwhile reactions come flying thick and fast and crazy; it's as though you have become a human dart board.

That's routine for a beauty object like Tom Cruise, Kim Basinger, or any of the other glamour faces, famous or not.

To the extent these faces are NOT average, distinctive talents show. Otherwise, the beauty's outstanding talent consists in fitting in well anywhere—plus the life lesson involved with handling life as a human dart board.

In researching this book, I've given examples of hundreds of famous faces. They belong to people from different walks of life and time periods, people who are significant because of their accomplishments, not their beauty quotient. Aside from a small number of performers included in Index I, Famous Faces, few of these famous people could get a job as a photographic model. Many might be considered *plain*. Their celebrity does not come from being a pretty face. And the more obstacles they must overcome, the more the faces show asymmetry, wrinkles, and shifts towards more extreme physical traits.

Dr. Narayan-Singh, one of America's leading physiognomists, chatted with me once about world-class achievers, like Abe Lincoln and Helen Keller. He put it succinctly: "By the time they've accomplished their mission, their faces look like they've been caught in a Waring Blender."

Q. Are you saying that people who look extraordinarily beautiful on the outside, on the inside are better adjusted?

A. Apart from the major adjustment to being a beauty (or handsomeness) symbol for others, yes, people who have "average" features generally have the advantage of flexible styles. They're most likely to fit in socially, assuming that people will let them.

Q. What about auras? Many of the people who are considered "beautiful" don't have those standard features. But they glow, which makes people respond. Even if you can't see auras consciously, you respond to them when you notice someone's stressed out or taking drugs. Something inside you goes yecch, regardless of the pretty features. Are you going to deny the role of auras in how we respond to people attractiveness-wise?

A. No. In fact, I encourage every face reader to develop your aura reading abilities (which, incidentally, don't necessarily involve *seeing* as the main way of gaining information—learn more about this from *Aura Reading Through All Your Senses*). Much of what registers as beauty or ugliness, apart from physical features, does relate to the level of auras. It's fascinating, and you can definitely learn to read it.

The paradox of talent

Imagine that you are setting up your birth contract before a lifetime. It's a little conference, attended by your soul, your guardian angel, and whoever helps you to draw up the Official Agreement, be it St. Peter, the Fates from Greek mythology, whoever you believe is involved in the decision-making process. For this example, let's call that person St. Peter.

You, your angel, and St. Peter fly over to the meeting. St. Peter says, "Let's start off with one of the most important questions. Your decision about this will affect how we shape this lifetime. How do you feel about being talented?"

"Yes, please" you say. "If possible, I'd like to be extremely talented."

Watch out. This was a trick question because of **the paradox of talent**. To understand how the paradox works, ask a simple question: "How many?"

That's right, how many souls choose to have major, unusual talent? Only a relatively small number dare to take the leap into being truly extraordinary.

In theory, yes, it seems lovely to have a distinctive talent for work, an exceptional leadership style, and so forth. But in practice, it means that few people will understand you. Their personal styles will be different—and to such an extent that although they may admire you greatly, they won't have a clue about how you operate.

For instance, let's take the example of nose length, which relates to planning and strategy when working. The more VERY your length, the more astounding your potential achievements. But also, the more VERY your discomfort with most employment opportunities. Unless you have carte blanche to design one major project at a time, you're going to feel stifled. All the positive thinking in the world won't keep you from feeling miserable in any other kind of job, even a job that would, to most people, be a dream come true.

Does this pickiness, as related to face traits, come as a surprise? Statistically, the vast majority of souls choose to, mostly, be average. Maybe six traits out of the entire face are VERYs.

Check this by doing your own experiment. Pick a face category, especially one related to ears, eyebrows, and nose (where career-related talents are most intensely clustered). Read faces of 50 or 100 people you know, emphasizing that one trait. For instance, if you choose nose length, write down how many fall into the category of average nose length. How many are somewhat short or long? How many are VERY in either direction? Graph your results and you'll end up with a bell curve.

Statistically, most people wind up agreeing to a small number of somewhat extreme traits. Only highly courageous souls opt for a face full of major talent. *

Popularity is one reason to choose a face that is relatively average. More people will have your same personal style. They will think and feel like you. They will be able to relate to you.

Beauty is a second consideration. Remember, beauty means looking average. So if you choose traits that are extreme and unusual, the inner talents that go with them may not always seem a fair exchange for the lack of prettiness. Especially during your teenage years, you will sob, "Why me?"

Now you know the answer. Why me? "Me" chose the lifetime, including the face.

Q. You could be talking about me, and the nose I've hated all my life. You really think it's a talent?

A. Yes, and the price you've paid for it is a face that, with all respect, does not look mainstream.

It's unlikely that you'd choose only one VERY, the nose length. To help you carry out your chosen destiny, most facial extremists need their biggest talent to be supported by other, related extreme traits. In your case, along with being VERY long, your nose is VERY arched and narrow; your chin is VERY prominent and VERY short.

What will it mean to wear this particular selection of VERYs?

Physically, your nose and chin will NOT qualify you for a beauty contest.

In terms of your personal style, you will be unusually dedicated to work, creative and independent as a worker; ethically, you'll be dedicated to truth. And when push comes to shove, you'll be highly competitive.

---

* They may be called kooky or brilliant—or first one, then the other. No matter how lavishly they ultimately may be praised, all strong individualists have great need for courage.

"Great," you told St. Peter during your conference. "All those talents should be easy to live with."

"Maybe not," sighed St. Pete "but okay. You'll find out."

Each of these VERY traits goes with equally extreme life lessons to be learned. In our example here, you must to deal with these challenges, representing the flip side of your talents: difficulty with handling routine work, intense dislike of being micro-managed, super-sensitivity to criticism. For your whole life people will be telling you, "Lighten up." And add one more thing: unless your job is defined in a way that allows you to work creatively, you'll be bored to death.

"Sure," you say to St. Pete, all aglow with your vision of great potentials. "I want to do outstanding work. I'm strong enough to handle this."

Zap! You incarnate. And now you get to live the paradox of talent:

- The more extreme your talent, the greater your chance at making a highly distinctive contribution that nobody else can make. And also the more likely that you will be drastically different from others.

Q. That's for sure. I've never fit in. But you're saying it's not just a matter of attractiveness, and that talent is also involved?

A. With your magnificent, highly distinctive face, your personality will not be what most people expect. Your style won't be in their comfort zone. In every area of life where you have talent, you'll struggle with being misunderstood and lonely. But to your soul, at least, the tradeoff is worthwhile. I hope that face reading can help you to reframe the prettiness challenges.

Q. So it's not a coincidence that many top business executives, computer geniuses, or college professors, look like real characters?

A. You've got it. For a new way to reframe your history, go back to your high school yearbook. Look at the faces of those who won honors in popularity, compared to those who were the nerds. Look at the moderate features of those who won points for being attractive vs. the more extreme features of those who didn't. Everyone gets something. Faces *are* fair.

Q. Go to my yearbook? Hey, I want to go to my next high school reunion. Wouldn't that be a great research project?

A. Absolutely. Talk to the former social outcast who's now a multi-millionaire. Extreme talents in her face, that may have caused her to lose pretty points, score big in career. And the popular folk with the even, average features may still look attractive, still be socially influential. But ask about their accomplishments and you'll learn that, for many, careers have depended less on originality and more on social skills. Most of your high school buddies are mixtures, mostly average with a sprinkling of VERY traits.

Accidents

So-called accidents don't seem to add much to a person's beauty or self-esteem. How can face reading explain them?

Simply put, with faces there are no **accidents**. Usually faces change without drama, in response to a person's inner evolution. Gradually inner changes work their way outward. *Accidents* happen when a person's soul says no to how a face physically looks. Sometimes the inner person demands a physical trait that can't be reached through the gene pool or gradually altered. So the soul creates whatever drama is needed to make the needed trait happen.

Wayne broke his nose when he was a boy. Until we talked, he figured what happened was tough luck but otherwise meaningless. But I related the resulting arch in his nose to a highly creative work style. Given the position of his arch, right at the bridge of his nose, I suggested that Wayne's special trick was to find an outrageously creative way to begin work projects. "Without making each project one of a kind," I told him, "I doubt you can even stay interested. You need to do this right at the start. Then the rest of the project just flows."

"That's true!" Wayne admitted. "And the funny thing is, none of my relatives has a nose profile like mine. Everyone else, on both sides of the family, has a pretty straight nose."

"And do they have your creative way of working?"

"Well, no."

Aha! That's the point.

In a similar way, sometimes a soul needs to create accidents that "ruin" changes brought about by cosmetic surgery. Though frustrating, at least it's meaningful.

Consider Christine's story. For years before she studied with me she believed she was the victim of a cruel accident. In her thirties, she had undertaken cosmetic surgery to narrow her nose for aesthetic reasons. But as soon as the surgery healed, she injured herself "because of an accident." Her nose broke and widened back to its original shape.

Through face reading, Christine learned that this much-despised trait was related to one of her most cherished strengths in the workplace: her talent with teamwork. Christine could work with people right from the start of a project. In fact, she delighted in sharing the credit right from the beginning.

This independent work style would have been gone if her surgery had worked as intended. Vanished. Vamoosed. But, inwardly, Christine's new-fangled narrow nose bridge didn't suit her. It would have been such a *major* mistake that her soul had to intervene. Sure this "cute" artificial new nose was much desired and terribly expensive. Nevertheless, under the circumstances, it was more important to sacrifice her fantasy nose than her soul's reality.

Another student of mine, Anthony, expressed anger about a **scar** over his eyebrow. He thought it ruined an otherwise handsome face. I invited him to consider it an adornment. Nobody wants to look flawed. But every scar and wrinkle, every change to a developing face is like a soldier's medals. It's a badge that shows spiritual learning. What could be a higher honor here on The Learning Planet?

To interpret a *scar* takes basic knowledge of the meaning of face parts, the intent to find helpful knowledge, plus becoming the clearest channel possible for intuition. Given that Anthony hated his scar, I offered to look within for an interpretation.

Anthony's scar was located above the right eyebrow, in the position his eyebrow would have had if it were up-angled; his physical eyebrow angle was straight. The color of the scar was white—indicating pure learning (by contrast, red scars show a component of rage).

Here's what I told him: "This scar reflects conflict in your work life related to new ideas you had that others wouldn't accept. Before the accident that caused this scar, I believe you struggled over having patience with others who weren't able to keep up with you. The fact that the scar is white suggests that, although you went through a period of frustration, you came out the other side, into understanding and acceptance.

"What's your version of what happened?" I asked.

Anthony's face lit up. "It was computers," he said. "My company uses an antiquated system. Nobody there could understand why I wanted to change to more modern software. I fought people for months, and it was driving me crazy. I lost that battle, but kept my job, which I could carry out regardless of whether we used the software or not.

"Shortly after this happened, a filing cabinet fell on my head. I got stitches—and this scar."

Q. Are you suggesting that we stand up and cheer on the way to the hospital? Face reading or not, who's going to like scars?

A. Interpretations from face reading won't keep you from suffering when you're in pain. Afterwards, though, you have an opportunity to consider what happened from a spiritual perspective. Could there have been a positive meaning? Interpretation creates a form of empowerment, compared to the widely held view in our culture that major difficulties in life strike as random accidents* where people are helpless victims.

Face reading gives you the opportunity to interpret so-called imperfections in terms of self-esteem. Scars won't win you pretty points, but faces (as you have learned) are about more than prettiness. On The Learning Planet, education counts more than appearances.

Q. With little scars like Anthony's, I can see the point you made earlier about faces being fair. But how about the self-esteem of people with birth defects? How about burn victims or others who have gone through catastrophic accidents? How can face reading deal with an accident of that magnitude?

A. First, let's acknowledges the terrible suffering that shows in **facial deformity**. As a face reader, the fact that you know how to look for something beyond standard beauty can help you to muster up a much-needed kind of courage. Remember, you know how to take a deep breath and see individual traits, one by one. This gives you a way to clear-sightedly probe for the talents that show in an injured person's features.

People without the benefit of what you've learned, sure, they may shudder in horror and avert their eyes. Face reader or not, you may shudder, too. But afterwards you can take a deep breath and find the courage to see the face, and talents, that remain. Help that disabled or deformed person not to be invisible. Dare to see the physical face. Look for the talents still there.

* Most accidents, in my opinion, do have a spiritual level of meaning. Not all—some accidents really are cosmic goof-ups. A balanced approach, therefore, is to ask to learn what you can from the experience. If your contemplation turns up a meaningful answer, more power to you. Otherwise, don't linger in what author Joan Borysenko has termed "New Age guilt." Heal yourself as best you can and move on.

Q. Nobody who has been through such an experience would believe what you imply about faces being fair. How can you say such a thing without being either complacent or cruel?

A. My long-term sense of fairness is tied to a belief in reincarnation—optional for face reading but one way to explain how it could be that, despite appearances, faces are fair.

Reincarnation holds that we have many lifetimes, not just one, and what we do comes back to us over the course of these many lifetimes. So yes, it could be fair, though extreme, that someone would need to endure a lifetime with physical deformity. Maybe that individual was once extremely vain, or caused someone else to be deformed; perhaps that soul has volunteered for a heroic life of service where she will show how to live with courage, despite monumental challenge.

The reasons for ugliness, deformity, and other disabilities are unfathomable. One common denominator, however, is the challenge an ugly face presents to everyone. Will you choose to see the inner person and not just the outer face? In such cases, spiritual understanding can't be a luxury. It becomes a necessity.

Aging

Fairness again! Physical aging seems pretty awful, until we consider the alternative.

Q. You're talking about death, right?

A. No, I'm talking about *The Portrait of Dorian Gray*.

Well, you're right really. Death is the dreaded alternative. But Oscar Wilde's novel about Dorian Gray has such a fascinating premise, it should be required reading for all who are serious about face reading.

Like many who lived in Victorian England, Oscar Wilde knew about physiognomy. The trick to his novel was the premise that, for once, a face *wouldn't* change to reflect the inner person.

Due to a diabolically clever arrangement, the consequences of Dorian Gray's monstrous inner self and outer actions didn't show on his face. Instead, they transferred to a hidden painting—until the end, when the wicked guy got what he deserved.

Gray looked pure and innocent, his awful self notwithstanding, which caused confusion to everyone who came into contact with him. One of the laws of this planet, whether we like it or not, is cause and effect. As kids, the consequences of our actions bring us time outs. As adults, we're stuck with the faces we create.

Wrinkles are God's Makeup explores wrinkles, plus many subtler ways that faces change over time in ways that are meaningful. Until you read it, the most important concept to understand is that **stereotypes about aging** are wrong. Commonly, people fear that every important part of their face will sag, due to gravity, except for the parts that puff out because of fat; meanwhile they live in dread that the only face parts that look perky will be the permanent press wrinkles. If fate doesn't cause them, ultraviolet rays will.

Look, my advice is to keep on wearing your sunscreen, but don't be so sure any facial change is inevitable. You are not doomed to develop wrinkles in a particular place, regardless of how your mother may look. With each passing year, your face becomes more your own. And whatever happens, happens for good reason. When you understand the reasons, you will have more (not less) justification for self-esteem.

■■■

Family resemblance

Forgive your family for being who they are and looking the way they do, if you can. Chances are that you have some things in common.

When it comes to your facial inheritance, though, your deep choices about personal style can separate you a surprising distance from your family of origin. In high school history classes, did you ever read about The Hapsburg Nose and The Hapsburg Chin? They were distinctive face traits found among the royal German family that ruled Austria and Spain for longer than may have been good for them.

Was the predominance of these traits just a matter of in-breeding, as my history teacher used to joke? Maybe these not-terribly-nice people looked alike in those traits because, inwardly, they were alike—including an arrogant refusal to change. When your family has been governing Europe for generations, maybe you don't see much need for personal growth, especially if your populace believes in The Divine Right of Kings.

Moving on to today's faces in general and yours in particular, yes, you can read your own family's faces for nobility. Or scrutinize their visages for shame and pathology. You can visually grope for growth. Hey, it's up to you.

Why not line up your relatives, or at least your pictures of them, and look more carefully than has been your wont. See, really see, which cheek traits "go" with your father's side of the family and which traits are more likely to be ordered *à la carte*.

Look at pictures of how family members have changed over time. Whether you're looking at black-and-white photos or color, you'll gain a renewed respect for the ways your loved ones have aged.

As a face reader, you have the delightful option of playing contrarian, too. Usually people look at family faces for the express purpose of finding resemblance. "Little Ernestine has Wendell's nose and Frederika's lips," Grannie will cluck, as though that explains Ernestine through and through. Identifying people in terms of resemblance goes with a belief in one or more of these ideas:

■ Genes determine your face.
■ Genes determine your life.
■ It is possible for you to be "just like" another family member
■ Even this: Because of your ancestors, your destiny is fixed in all important respects e.g., Hatfields are one way, McCoys another.

I don't think so. If you, too, are a champion of free will, face reading can prove your point. Go ahead. Find five ways your mother's fiftyish face is unique, unlike any of her children or sisters or parents. Find three aspects of Ernestine's nose that have nothing to do with Grandpa Wendell. Liberate all in your family who'll listen.

Q. Even so, won't you find some patterns of resemblance?
A. Sure. And it's fascinating to follow and interpret those patterns, especially if you balance commonality with originality. If genealogy is your thing, write a family history to match, a history of life lessons-in-progress from generation to generation.

Q. What if a person believes, as I do, that your only immortality comes from your children? Couldn't it be threatening to think your blood relations don't resemble you as much as you expected?
A. If you're looking for ways your children carry you forward, what better heritage can you give them than your life learning? Tell them stories, backed up by your pictures, about the ways you have changed. Share what you have endured and how you have grown. Their lessons may not be your lessons, just as their face traits may not be your face traits, but the memory of what you tell them about inner history can inspire them, and their children, forever.

Beauty, who needs it?

What if you're at the opposite generational extreme, more concerned with founding a family in the first place than making sure they remember you? What if you're, frankly, desperate to find a mate? There must be ways that face reading can help you build self-esteem as a single.

You guessed it! There are two ways, actually. One concerns you. The other concerns appropriate date material and how you now define it.

First YOU—for a single today, face reading is as indispensable as an appointment book. You need more than a normal share of self-esteem to fend off the social pressures. The propaganda singles receive today about attractiveness is more overwhelming than at any former time in history. We're whelmed and overwhelmed by ads in the media, the pitches for cosmetics, hair regrowth products, cosmetic surgery. Hair stylists and fingernail artists are dying to make us more marriageable, not to mention the clothing designers and retailers, the color analysts and image consultants, plus the multitudes who are anxious to fix you through health clubs and diets.

Many of these beauty makers for hire will make you feel better about yourself. But sometimes their work carries a subtext that actually makes you feel worse. That kind of beauty you need like a hole in the head.

For instance, ladies, has a makeover artist ever shown you how to give the illusion of making your eyes look closer together or farther apart? How about making your lips look fuller or slimmer? Hey, what's wrong with how your face was put together in the first place?

Gents, more of you every year have been buying facelifts and nose jobs. Please!

Singles, have you pushed yourselves to work out at a health club, on top of all your other pressures... or gone on a guilt trip over the money you've spent for an unused membership? How about the pressure to have the right-looking kind of date on your arm as a status symbol?

Society's standards of attractiveness, for yourself or your dates, make for a status game set up for precious few people to win. How often have you judged other singles to be "losers" based on standards of attractiveness that neither of you set in the first place? Have movies and mags made you believe in a fantasy scenario where all hinges upon your finding the "one" (i.e., the predestined person who has the right number of cuteness points) after which cosmic event the rest of your life will proceed like a fairy tale?

For any man or woman who has been programmed to believe that our date's face or body is an important status symbol, a real-life romance may remain a fantasy. You're a face reader now, so consider this totally counter-culture idea: The behavior traits that would make a fantasy romance worth living simply may not come with the face.

That's right. The face data you've been programmed to judge desirable may go with character qualities inappropriate for your happiness! So if you've been feeling like a loser, maybe it's time to recognize a status game you can't win. Reprogram yourself.

- Reread the chapters on face parts. This time, read with a very specific agenda. Underline the behavioral traits in a mate that would make you feel good, regardless of whether they have anything to do with the facial traits you've been programmed to want.
- On an index card, list three of the face parts that go with the inner qualities you'd like to date: traits like a chunky nose tip, small eyelid thickness, a large Priority Area III, a big, broad chin, enormous ears—whatever, *inwardly*, turns you on.
- Carry that card with you, in pocket or purse. Let it symbolize a new attitude: *So-called beauty, who needs it?*

There is no one standard for what looks right. But if having your spouse be a good listener is vitally important to you, it makes no sense at all to prefer dates who have cute little ears, and so forth. Many guys have been trained to believe that a babe should be what author Tom Wolfe calls "starved to near-perfection." And how about the idea that a woman's value is inversely proportional to the size of her nose and directly proportional to the size of her chest?

Real life has more nuances. For the self-esteem of your dates (and also yourself, on the receiving end) set a face reader's standards. Don't just look at a face. Look into it.

■■■

15. How face reading can help your career

You've done it. You've mastered the facts, the features, the completely new way of looking at people. Undoubtedly this will result in benefits to your career... more confidence, for starters. If you're like my typical student, you're now soaking in **self-esteem** like a freshly watered tomato plant on a hot August day.

Whatever other kinds of knowledge you've gained to help yourself earn a living, now you have a core of knowledge relating your face to personal style. How can you NOT feel better about yourself, both how you physically look and your talents? *Self-esteem* is one name for the justifiable pride that you feel. Even if face reading did no more for your career than to give you this kind of inner glow, it would be worthwhile.

But self-knowledge from face reading can lead to benefits beyond temporarily feeling better—like making more money. We've already considered how face reading can boost a sales career. Beyond this, it's exciting to look at the growing field of professional physiognomy, where you can choose one or more specialties from the 10 different areas we'll discuss in this chapter. Maybe your high school guidance counselor didn't tell you that money could be made in the face reading field, but it can.

First, though, I want to make sure you learn about a technique that will make face reading an even more powerful tool for your confidence on the job... whatever your current employment or underemployment or would-be employment.

Facing up to your strong points

Connecting your talents right to your face can bring you more self-confidence. Partly it's a matter of **Aha! experiences**. How many times, since you've been reading this book, did something inside you go "Wow"?

"I'm really good at this!" you've said to yourself. Be it working with people or working alone, starting new projects or wrapping them up, some of the biggest talents that show in your face have made an inner flash of recognition go off. Those are spiritual "Kodak moments." Later you may forget what caused the particular aha! but, I believe, your soul has collected those photos of who you really are at your best. This photo album is yours to keep forever.

A specific technique related to face reading helps you to draw inner strength from this album. The technique is called **Facing up to Your Strong Points.** If you can manage to do this technique at a time when you have an extreme need to feel better about yourself, that's actually a plus. Considering how rare it is in life for something to work *better* when you're feeling crummy, you've just gotta love this technique. Here's how it works.

1. Focus on your expression for a change.

Scrutinize your face in the mirror. Focus on your expression. When you're in the doldrums, your expression will supply perfect material for this part of the technique. Wallow (for about 30 seconds) in that expression. Is it mopey? Dejected? A face can show a thousand nuances of human misery. Which one did you achieve this time? Observe. Then talk back to it: "Hey, who cares? I've got *my actual face.*"

2. Choose something to stare at

Your "actual face," of course, refers to your physical face parts. Go straight to whichever part of your face attracts you most. In a surly state of mind, you may be drawn to your most detested physical attribute, be it a pimple, a wrinkle, anything on your face that is large or small or unusual in any way. Well, shift to the nearest *wonderful* face trait. Or if you're feeling particularly daring, stay with the detested trait itself.

3. Praise your chosen face part. Lavishly.

Whether you love or hate the face part that has drawn your attention, praise it lavishly. Yes, you *can* do this.

For instance, when I'm feeling vulnerable my attention goes to the Gucci luggage underneath my eyes, a.k.a. the bags. **Bags** and wrinkles have specific meanings, depending upon their location on the face. Learning to interpret them is part of *Wrinkles Are God's Makeup.* (Not to worry, this follow-up book is about *all* the ways that faces change over time, and wrinkles amount to a surprisingly small percentage.)

As you'll read in *Wrinkles*, the meaning of *puffy circles under the eyes* is intense striving to see more deeply. "Thank goodness I care so much about seeing the deepest truth in life. And, lucky me, it even shows in my face!" is the appropriate comment to make. On those mornings when I wake up to see that the bags are especially big, I fine-tune the compliment: "Today I must want to see the truth even more than usual. Isn't that great!"

4. Move on

After you have complimented the "bad" face part, don't linger. Immediately shift your attention directly to a part of your physical face you already love. If it's hard to choose just one, pick whichever face trait is most distinctive.

5. Praise your chosen face part. Sincerely.

Interpret that distinctive face part. Sing it out for all the world to hear (unless you're in public—in which case it may be more prudent to give a modest mumble).

Another personal example: my most distinctive face trait involves my front teeth. Instead of being flat at the bottom, like most of the **front teeth bottoms** you'll encounter, they're VERY **curved**. Earlier in this book I didn't bother to mention the meaning of *curved front teeth bottoms* because it's so rare. But the answer, Ta da!, is that the tooth curves relate to learning life lessons through the heart.

As opposed to what? Most people, in keeping with their *straight front teeth bottoms*, learn major life lessons through the intellect. Don't be jealous of those of us with the tooth curves, however. We use up more hankies than you do.

Here's a sample pep-talk comment I might make to myself and my teeth: "The story of my life is that I learn straight from the heart. Thanks, God. This has made it possible for me to develop my system of face reading!"

6. Go deeper by questioning

Ask yourself, "Of all the talents that show in my face, which do I need to find *most* right now?" Take a deep breath or two to clear the air—and maybe also clear your head.

7. Listen

An answer will pop into your mind. When it does, pay attention. Don't wait for some "ultimate" answer. Work with what you are given.

For instance, say I'm going into a meeting with an executive from a Fortune 500 company to discuss giving trainings. And I feel a bit like David meeting Goliath... except that the proceedings are to be friendly, I hope. The word for what I need most this minute is: "Power."

8. Find what you need... in your face

Figure out which physical face trait of yours most closely corresponds to what you need. (Since you haven't necessarily *memorized* this book so far, just *read* it, you may need some help here. Look in Index III, Behavior, which relates qualities like "Power" and "Leadership" to specific face parts. Keep looking up traits and searching your face until you come up with what you need.)

9. Affirm your talent

Find the relevant trait on your face. Stare at it. And let the pep talk begin. For example: "My VERY angled eyebrows show a managerial mindset. When I go into this meeting, instead of being intimidated by how much money those executives make and their fancy offices, I'll look at their eyebrow shapes. I doubt that any of them has finer eyebrow angles. No wonder I'll have such an advantage over them! I'm going to accomplish great things in our meeting today."

10.   Anchor in the truth

Program yourself for the rest of the day: Look at that part of your face in the mirror, stroke it gently with your right hand. Say your pep talk words. Then repeat: looking, stroking, and affirming—only this time use your left hand.

Now you're set. Any time that day you need a boost, touch that part of your face.

Q. What if the expression you see when you look in the mirror just makes you feel even more depressed, like this beaten puppy dog look that sometimes comes into my eyes?
A. Use your watch, if necessary, to remind yourself to view your initial expression for no longer than 30 seconds. (It sounds like, for you, three seconds is plenty.) Immediately move to Step #3.

Q. I still don't get it. What makes your "Facing up to Your Strong Points" technique different from an ordinary pep talk?
A. The most important difference is that you're **anchoring in** the pep part to a physical face part. *Anchoring* is a term from psychology; I first learned about it in the context of Neurolinguistic Programming (NLP). Imagine a ship that sinks an anchor to secure itself in a desired place. Like a ship, your attention is free to roam. By anchoring, you gain stability. So find a great location, put down your anchor, and enjoy the resulting presence of mind.

What might you wish to anchor? Several systems are available for learning about your anchorable strengths in life—not only NLP but also Myers-Briggs typing, graphoanalysis, the Ennegram, in-depth astrology (as distinct from the quickie newspaper horoscopes, which are more for entertainment than true astrological knowledge). Study any one of these systems in depth and you can access helpful insights. In many cases, the information you learn will be similar to what you've discovered with Face Reading Secrets.

However, face reading has a unique benefit for anchoring because you can connect the good stuff about you directly to a part of your physical face. You can see that vital face part right in the mirror, can touch it, can talk to it. And in the case of this anchoring technique, you can do all three at once, which makes it triply effective.

Now that you've learned how to anchor in qualities that you need to succeed, here are more practical ways that face reading can boost your career, or even help you to start a new part-time business. We'll be considering 10 different specialties and conclude with information about setting up a business and training to read faces at a professional level:

Career opportunities for physiognomists

- Diversity Training
- Human Resource Training
- Conflict Resolution
- Genealogy Readings
- Party Entertainment
- Life *Potential* Readings
- Life *Progress* Readings
- Compatibility Readings
- Cosmetic Surgery Consultations
- Becoming a Social Commentator

Diversity training

Pollsters will tell you. Nobody thinks "I'm prejudiced." It's always the other guy's problem.

But racial tensions in America today are everyone's problem. As a face reader, you can become part of the solution. Inform local companies that do diversity training about how you can supplement their services.

Diversity training means teaching people to see human beings rather than stereotypes. You're going to help folks stop making assumptions and start making friends. And, really, what better place to begin this kind of training than with the way people literally see each other? Teach people to lift their vision from coloring and type casting. Challenge your audience:

"You think that you see each other as individuals, right? I wonder if you really see diversity or if, without realizing it, you see mostly stereotypes. Let's find out. Choose a partner right now, someone out of this group you don't know very well. Take 10 minutes to write down all you can tell about that person. No talking. Make your observations directly from looking at your partner's face. Whatever you write will be kept confidential."

Pitiful little lists will be turned in to you, I can predict, based on times I've asked non-face readers to make such lists. Not knowing systematic ways to gain information, people are at a loss to read anything but expression, then make hopeful, global assessments. "She looks like a good person. She has a nice smile."

Now you can start to teach face reading as a real alternative, a way to access quality information with both depth and detail.

- Begin by teaching the face parts that carry a relatively small emotional charge, like eyebrows or Priority Areas.

- Get the group laughing before you turn to the big item of controversy, Mr. Schnozz. And when you do noses, make sure you help participants see that it's not just a Black nose, a Filipino nose, or a WASP nose. Show how people from seemingly different groups can have exactly the same traits whereas folks who assume they're like cousins can have drastically different ones.
- With each face category you cover, take the group through the same ritual: see the real face, identify what you have along with what others have, and learn to interpret in terms of personal style.

Yes, it's more typical for diversity training to emphasize differences of background and culture. However, the relevant details of this kind will emerge as a byproduct of your group's facial discussions. When they do, acknowledge them. For instance, it's sure to come out that some of the members of a diverse workforce have been raised differently about looking people in the eye. Who has been taught to avoid? Who has been taught to stare?

As a word of caution, professionals at diversity training have to be highly skilled: experienced at handling groups, sensitive, courageous, and very effective as communicators. Team up with a pro. Add to someone else's more conventional training design, rather than attempting to jump into the diversity training field and reinvent it entirely by yourself. Also become familiar with approaches that facilitate emotional healing. Nobody growing up in America has escaped subconscious programming with negative stereotypes, and the healing process can unleash intense emotions that you, as a trainer, will have to be prepared to handle. Don't start off working alone.

But just because this kind of training can be so painfully serious, face reading adds a welcome breath of humor. Your contribution to diversity training can make a big difference. While you train people to recognize and interpret face parts, what else are you teaching? Sneakily, beautifully, your message can take hold....

"See the individual. Communicate with the individual."

Typically, today's diversity training means raising consciousness about *lifestyle*, factors like social inequities, economic problems, ingrained fears, family expectations, language and other cultural differences. However, it may well be that people will be helped even more in the long run by raising their consciousness about *personal style*. Lead your group to discuss the difference between someone who needs self-disclosure versus someone who mistrusts it. Point out the perpetual tensions between people with out-angled ears and those whose ears lie close to the head; between the different cheek styles; between folks who love to follow procedures and folks who feel it stifles them.

And point out the value in *every* style. We all need to feel and show more tolerance towards those who work differently. Companies today know that our increasingly diverse workforce demands deeper human understanding. Money is budgeted for these trainings. If you're qualified to design and follow through with diversity training, this could be one of the most lucrative uses to make of your face reading knowledge.

Human resource consulting

The art of managing **human resources** has, to a large extent, become an exercise in managing fear. Personnel staff fear making mistakes. Applicants fear prejudice. And when stakes are high—as with employment—minds can slam shut extra tight. So you could talk 'till you're blue in the face about how color doesn't matter for physiognomy and still you'd be suspect. Ironically, physiognomy is probably the exact opposite of what anyone fears: It's face reading, not race reading. But an anxious job applicant may not be open to hearing the truth.

So circumvent controversy. Be discreet. Offer a training for human resource staff. Otherwise, work behind the scenes as a consultant.

As a consultant, you can either sit in on interviews or analyze photographs privately, then offer your findings to the executive who hired you. Handwriting experts consult in this manner. Physiognomists can do the same. Here's how to proceed when you're hired to help the company choose among candidates for a particular job:

1. Clarify expectations

Put in writing exactly what services you will provide and for how much. Will you set a fee for each individual you profile or charge by the hour? Will you charge for follow-up questions or consider them part of a fixed-price contract? Not only will a written agreement demonstrate your professionalism, you'll prevent misunderstandings.

A simple Letter of Confirmation may be all you need. Ask your client to adjust it as necessary, sign a copy and return it to you for your files. Over time, you may also wish to develop a form that you routinely use to profile job candidates.

2. Ask what the employer wants to know

Which aspects of personal style would be most relevant to that particular job? Work with human relations staff to develop a checklist. Then prioritize.

3. Probe

What matters most to the immediate supervisor for the position you'll fill? Learn which qualities matter (both officially and unofficially). Add these factors to your list of important aspects of personal style. For instance, what if the boss is a stickler for manners? Although he can't technically fire an assistant for acting like a free spirit, he sure would like to avoid hiring such a person in the first place. Okay, then you're especially interested in applicants whose right ears angle inward.

4. Translate job requirements into face data

Write a wish list. For instance, maybe it's an administrative job with lots of repetitious routine work that requires a close focus. Bingo—you'll be especially interested in medium-to-short nose length, average-to-close-set eyes, even-to-ender eyebrows.

5. Read the applicants

Consider the strengths each applicant brings to that job, as shown in face data.

6. Evaluate

Match up your findings with the wish list for that position.

7. Compare and contrast

Human resource staff will already have screened candidates in the more conventional ways, for skills, employment history and references. How do your findings compare? Is there anything you should flag as suspect? A sad fact of life about human resources today is that legal constraints and other factors may cause official references to omit vital information related to character. Face reading can help you pose questions for getting at the truth.

8. Question

Can you think of any questions it would be helpful to ask in a follow-up interview? Write them down, explaining what they are intended to clarify.

Happy chat in the interview room, like written documentation, won't necessarily reveal what hiring managers need to know. Will this be another case where the company invests heavily in time and training only to have the worker resign in six months? You can't predict deaths in the family, illness, and such. But, as a face reader, you sure can predict who has a flair for routine work (turn back to the section on nose length) and who really *enjoys* following through on details (you've guessed it—read distribution of hair on eyebrows).

As for checking out honesty (a major concern for all employers) this takes skill but it's definitely do-able. You'll want to find a person's most distinctive face traits, then frame questions related to them. For instance, when interviewing a woman with a VERY angled chin, you might ask, "When you have an important business decision to make, how important is it to you to stay in control?"

If her response is "Who me? I couldn't care less about control," beware. Either she's lying through her chin or else she's dismally unaware of her real strengths. In either case, don't trust her. Conversely, be impressed if she responds along these lines: "Your company's goals become my goals. And I do what it takes to get what I want.."

9. Prepare a report

Summarize your observations. Write like a journalist, leading off with the information of greatest importance to your reader. Then fill in details about the pro's and con's for each candidate. Give decision makers plenty of specifics.

Conflict resolution

Sure, you could use face reading for **jury selection**. But, personally, I'm more interested in working with negotiators and others involved in **conflict resolution**. How can people resolve their differences without resorting to expensive, divisive legal battles? Divorce mediation holds special promise as an area where face reading can develop into a valued professional specialty.

If you're already a **mediator**, physiognomy will add to your set of skills. If you're not trained as a mediator, work with one. Your contribution will be a practiced knowledge of face reading... plus patience, forbearance, and plenty of courage.

When practical issues need to be settled, it's easy for discussion to break down at points of difference. You can keep the discussion moving by raising consciousness about personal style.

- Show how seemingly incompatible points of view are related to opposite styles. Describe these styles appreciatively, without judgment.
- Give an overview, whenever possible, showing how different ideas can fit together.
- Startle your clients out of their old habits of relating to each other.
- Physically hold out a mirror to help them see their radically different widths of eye set, life priority areas, ear proportions, and so forth. Relate those differences to solutions you can work out together.

In short, you can promote understanding by spelling out how different personal styles may have caused communication problems in the past. Establish an intent of good will that can create its own momentum. Face readers can be peacemakers.

Genealogy readings

Genealogists can be conservative, so be sure to tell them from the outset that face reading has been practiced professionally for thousands of years. Offer to give a 15-minute reading as a free sample. You'll wow potential clients. Genealogists collect photos and you can make those photos come alive in a new way. And genealogy readings offer a fascinating opportunity to find multi-generation patterns.

Your mission with a **Genealogy Reading** is to communicate the importance of patterns. Concentrate on the VERYs. Who in the family takes after whom, and in what way?

If photos are clear enough, you can break up some assumptions that people look "exactly" alike. It may well turn out that three men who are described as having an "identical nose" actually have just one or two nose traits in common, with many significant differences.

How can you get started in this fascinating field?

- For practice, turn to a well-illustrated biography, like Doris Kearns Goodwin's masterpiece, *The Fitzgeralds and the Kennedys*. Buy a good magnifying glass to help you examine tiny images of faces in photographs. Practice finding patterns.
- Invest in business cards.
- Do a few free readings in exchange for references.
- Book yourself to give talks for genealogy clubs and organizations for seniors. One satisfied customer at a time, you'll build up a client base.

Clients have two reasons to be excited about your work because relatives fall into two categories: those about whom much is known and those about whom very little is known. When you read faces from the *known* category and can point out specifics like "Uncle Dan's jaws show he was unusually loyal. He was also as stubborn as a mule." Wow!

Instantly your clients can verify your accuracy. Then proceed to read faces in the *unknown* category; your clients will be even more intrigued.

Genealogy is, in part, a celebration of how people in a family have endured adversity. When your client relates a story of challenge, discuss together how talents that show in the face have made a difference.

For people who prize their family history, face reading has a lot to offer. Regardless of economic status, every ancestor was born with the spiritual equivalent of a silver spoon in his mouth. What use was made of these gifts?

Party entertainment

Face reading is fun, as you know by now. Face reading's a way of life, once you get good at it. Face reading, it turns out, can also be a good way to make money. **Party entertainment** may be the best market of all because you can earn $500 or more for an honorable night's work, and have fun in the bargain.

- To prepare yourself, make sure you're good, really good, at seeing the traits and telling people about them. Folks will think twice if you bring this reference book along with you to the gig and look up their face data in the index.
- When you have practiced enough to feel confident, check your local *Yellow Pages* for talent agencies under headings like "Entertainment" and "Party Entertainment."
- Make an appointment to meet with the heads of these agencies. Show them what you can do.
- Each time you are offered a gig, you'll be able to decide if you like the hours, the location, and so forth. As a performer, you are free to accept or turn down any job. Enjoy the flexibility.

Amazingly, you don't have to sing or play in a band to count as employable "talent." Event planners always need performers to liven up receptions, conventions, spouse programs, and theme parties. Why shouldn't you be one of them?

Sometimes you will be put in the general category of "fortuneteller." Technically, you're not making predictions. However, it's fair game to say "I'll be telling you about talents to emphasize in your work or relationships over the next six months." Although face data changes, it seldom changes faster than that.

Does it get tiring, doing production work at a party, where you have maybe six minutes to spend on each guest? Sure, the pressure can be high. The lines grow long. Hecklers imagine they're witty. However, for me, even the occasional mean drunk at a party is no deterrent. It is pure joy to tell people about their faces, as you help them appreciate themselves in ways that may be entirely new.

Sometimes hosts get so excited, they extend your bookings for hours. I've read faces for 6 or 9 or 11 hours nonstop and left as fresh as a daisy (but richer). It's energizing to help people raise their consciousness about faces.

When you're hired as an entertainer, please contribute to the good name of our profession. Bathe before you put on your gypsy costume. Don't drink. Check with your host before you start nibbling on party goodies. Most important, resist the impulse to insult the occasional obnoxious partygoer. In 15 years, I don't think I've hurt a single client's feelings when interpreting a face trait, though several partygoers have cried because their hearts were touched in a positive way. It's always a privilege to read faces. Event entertainment can be especially rewarding, and your enjoyment of parties is guaranteed to grow when your attendance is paid by the hour.

Life potential readings

Searching for an unusual present for a birthday or anniversary? Why not offer a hundred-dollar gift that won't cost you a cent? Give an hour-long, in-depth face reading.

Life Potential Readings uplift a person by showing the significance of all the major traits on a face. Here's a step-by-step procedure to do readings for friends or relatives—even, eventually, paying clients.... And, yes, let's call the person on the receiving end your **client**. This will encourage you to develop the experience, confidence, and skill to hang out your shingle some day.

1. Set the stage

Find a place where you and your client will not be interrupted. A clean, well-ventilated room will add to the quality of your reading.

And make sure your client takes the commitment seriously: For the next hour, no TV in the background; no phone calls, please. Commitment is especially important when your client is getting a freebie. Understandably, somebody new to face reading may be skeptical. For your own self-esteem, however, you have every right to demand that your work be treated with respect, regardless of skepticism.

Sitting together at a table works well. Place a mirror within reach, explaining that you'll probably point out things your client never has noticed before about her face. Make a pad and pen available for taking notes. Even better, supply a tape recorder with a new cassette tape.

2. State your intention

Before beginning your reading, formally state an *intention*. Otherwise unconscious habits will take over.

What would be a worthy motivation for this reading? To prove you're "smart enough"? To show you won't fail? Bosh! That's old subconscious habit. You wouldn't choose it consciously, but unless you take the precaution of setting an intention, just that kind of foolishness will be in the back of your mind. Count on your subconscious to be, at a minimum, at least as predictable as the default settings on your computer screen.

Old patterns limit us. By contrast, a simple act of free will can point your mind in a helpful new direction, such as:

"I invoke the wisdom within both of us to guide this face reading session. My goal is to help you understand yourself better and use your talents in life most fully."

Note: If you're feeling really spunky, say your intention aloud, rather than silently. Whoosh! Feel the air in the room turn magical.

3. Choose a face part and go

Start with your client's eyebrows, then proceed to read one feature at a time. Choose a category, then a trait. With each item, begin by pointing out the physical aspect, such as starter eyebrows. Make sure your client sees it.

Then explain the meaning of the trait. Ask your client for feedback.

Which order is best to go in? Design your own facial tour or use the order of the chapters in this book:

- Eyebrows
- Ears
- Eyes
- Noses
- Cheeks

- Mouths
- Jaws
- Chins
- Priority Areas

4. Emphasize the VERYs

As you give your interpretations, remember that VERY = VERY. Extreme features parallel strong characteristics. Moderate features correspond to inner characteristics that are less intense.

5. Use tact

Sometimes your clients' challenges will strike you like a slap across the face. Well, don't forget the strengths that can go with them or you might just deserve a slap yourself. Be kind.

For instance, you may notice the lip proportions for Outspoken Lips and, based on what you know about your client's blabbermouth tendencies, be tempted to say:

"Your lip proportions show you say too many personal things, which gets you in trouble. Bite your tongue, you idiot."

Nope. The kinder, and more helpful, comment would be to describe his talent for perceptive speech, then mention the possible challenge. Any client of yours is no blockhead. A gentle mention will suffice.

6. Trust your timing

What if you miss something along the way and don't notice it until later in your reading? Let's say a vital ear trait has escaped you, only to surface after you've moved on to the eyes. When this sort of thing happened early in my face reading career, I felt embarrassed. It was as if I had made a horrible *faux pas* and any trained physiognomist who was watching would be snickering like crazy.

Well, ditch that critic committee. It's all in your head. Improvise with the order of your comments, just keep your integrity straight. There may even be a wonderful intuitive reason why you noticed that face part when you did. You've set your intention. Now trust that it's going to come true.

The face reader's rule is to *talk about what you notice when you notice it*, whatever the order. In fact, as an experienced face reader, you'll tend to notice related characteristics simultaneously. You may prefer to dispense with lists altogether and let your client's face tell you where to go next.

For example, your first thought might be to wonder, "What do Sally's huge puffy earlobes have to do with her close-set eyes?" Eureka! Her talent for fine-tuned observation goes with an interest in the physical level of life. If Sally were playing Musical Chairs, she'd notice just where each seat was placed (thanks to earlobes), plus she'd probably be the only person playing the game to attempt to equalize the space between the chairs. Why? With her close-set eyes, she'll zero in on every lop-sided inch of distance.

Sally's potential challenges are to be overly critical and frighteningly literal. Yes, she has what it takes to scare people. Still, she'd most likely be a champ at Musical Chairs—and more lucrative projects as well.

7. Welcome puzzles

Stumped by seeming contradictions in a face? Great! You're on the verge of greater depth in your reading. Think of two or more conflicting traits as a puzzle to solve. Your client has had to deal with the conflict for a long time. What a wonderful opportunity for you to bring understanding.

Take a deep breath. Relax into the challenge and patiently explore the mystery. Contradictions are one of the most meaningful parts of face reading.

Clues come from which part of the face has what. For instance, this might be the appropriate interpretation for Zach, a client whose straight chin goes with curved eyebrows:

"Your eyebrow shape shows you have an emotionally engaged, sensitive style of relating to people in social situations. By contrast, your straight chin reveals a much more detached, analytical style when making important decisions."

8. Use concrete examples

If Zach's reaction is, "Huh?" make up a specific example. "Picture yourself on election day," I'd tell him. "You've gone to the polling place with your wife, and you've pleased her by listening to her problems in your usual sensitive fashion. Then you disappear into the booth, where you vote strictly on principle.

"When voting, as opposed to being with your wife, you don't give a hoot if what you're voting for will make some people cry if you win. What matters is that you vote for what's right. Maybe you've wondered why you can seem so sensitive in certain situations, so insensitive in others. Now you have an answer. It's your eyebrows versus your chin."

9. Don't play God, play Friend

At the beginning of your face reading career, it may be tempting to think, "Gee, this stuff makes me a mind reader" and make pronouncements to your client with the subtext, "This is the truth." or "This is your Destiny."

Well, think again.

If infallible insight were common, why would you feel as you do about your most hated talk show host? Heaven forbid, you'd make yourself that obnoxious by playing God!

So let's be kind to everyone concerned and stick to playing it mortal. Even if you'll never see your client again, do your job like an old friend, complete with a friend's desire to be of service. Ultimately your friend will decide what is helpful, not you.

Life progress readings

Have a friend who is turning 40 or 50? Do I have a present for you! Life Progress Readings are the ultimate validation for someone who is entering a new decade or making a major life transition, such as divorce or retirement. And by doing practice readings for free, you can build your skill and confidence to the point where you can charge for your services. Especially as the Baby Boomers age, the market for this kind of reading is bound to grow.

Meanwhile, here you are giving a birthday present to your friend Beth. When you schedule your appointment for her reading, ask that she bring along photographs of herself from childhood onward. Spread them out, arranged chronologically, and let the fun begin.

Your goal with a **Life Progress Reading** is to validate change. From picture A to picture Z, keep looking for every discernible way that your client has physically changed—anywhere from the chin to the hairline. Each time you point out a facial nuance, interpret it. Compare the youngest picture to the next, and so on.

Life Progress Readings even allow you to comment on a person's looks before the age of 18. It's okay because your client is no longer an impressionable youth. Ideally the minimum age for this sort of reading is 35; the older your client, the better.

So often people think of aging in terms of losing youthful attractiveness. Your reading will offer an entirely different perspective, acknowledging the wisdom gained during a soul's journey through many faces.

Compatibility readings

Next time a friend gets engaged or an anniversary rolls around, you can offer the perfect present, the most romantic of readings. Eventually you may be ready to offer **Compatibility Readings** of professional quality, too. Then you can land paying clients galore, especially if you make yourself known at singles groups in your area. Give a free talk, hand out your card, and prepare to start booking appointments.

Reading couples is a bargain, and not only because it's two-for-one, whatever your hourly fee. When you educate a couple about their similarities and differences, you can save them hassles, even heartache.

Make it clear right from the start: "This reading isn't about IF you're compatible. It's about HOW—ways you are similar and ways you can make your differences work for you."

In relationships, the catch is that we expect everyone to be "just like me." Your Compatibility Reading will clarify ways that partners are diametrically different. The happier the couple, the more heartily they'll laugh in recognition of what you show them.

Here's how to proceed:

- Sit your clients down with a mirror and tape recorder
- Taking one facial category at a time, compare and contrast for an hour.
- Praise their similarities, which make it easier for the couple to get along. (Be sure to point out all cases where they may suffer from a lack of tolerance for the rest of humanity.)
- Praise how differences enable them to learn from each other.

■ Above all, notice how they react and, as appropriate, remind them to respect and learn from their differences.

I remember the compatibility reading I gave for some newlyweds I'll call Howard and Kathy. Their personal styles differed in many respects, which isn't unusual. But Howard's reaction was. At each point of dissimilarity he visibly preened. "You see, Kathy? You ought to be more like me in that way. My way is more spiritual."

Within six months, she left him. Coincidence? Unfortunately not.

Another time, at a party, I did a reading for Anna and Victor. Every time I pointed out a trait belonging to Anna, she would simper into the mirror, as if she had nothing to look at beyond admiring her makeup job. Then she would turn to Victor:

"Gee, I don't know. Honey, am I like that?"

Being a trophy wife isn't necessarily bad, but when it goes with so little integrity, there's tragedy in the making. I wish women like Anna could have Compatibility Readings, tape record them, and play them back daily. When Anna decides to value herself as more than a pretty face, her life can only improve.

It isn't a bad idea, actually, for people to invest in a Compatibility Reading *before* they get married. I'd especially recommend this for couples who meet over the Internet. While your words won't tell a pair of love birds they have awful relationship skills, a thoughtful partner will pay close attention to how the other one responds during the reading.

And if you know a couple you really wish would wait before marrying, it might be wise to send them to one of your face reading colleagues as an engagement present. What they learn may lead them to re-evaluate a marriage that obviously is going to fail.

Romantics, rest assured that most people who come for compatibility readings will deepen their mutual respect, not reveal the lack of it. And you may even be lucky enough to be hired to read a couple at their Golden Wedding Anniversary party. Bring along a full box of tissues.

Cosmetic surgery consultations

Don't expect cosmetic surgeons to hire you, but as word of your services gets around, their customers may—and plenty of them. Surgery is big business today, not just the number of clients but also the big bucks it takes to alter a face. As a physiognomist, you can offer a true second opinion. Since your hourly rate costs far less than the proposed operation, and may supply important insights, it's cheap at the price. To do your reading:

- Ask your client what change he or she proposes to make.
- Follow the basic steps given previously for doing a Life Potential Reading—but be sure to save for last the feature your client contemplates changing.
- The highlight of a **Cosmetic Surgery Consultation** comes at the end, when you show the relationship of that problematic part of the face to the whole person. Which life themes does that face trait bring up? For example, if the proposed operation would alter nose length, review all the patterns in the face related to timing and creativity. What natural balances would be destroyed? How could your client reasonably expect to benefit? Which hidden issues might your client wish to consider?

For all its vaunted benefits, cosmetic surgery can't claim to be holistic. It's exactly the opposite. But face reading is holistic. The goal is to acknowledge your client as body-mind-spirit, with full respect for what makes that person distinctive.

We are more than our social selves, the level of life where it's perfectly natural to evaluate people based on status and stereotypes. The clients who will be drawn to you sense that deeper inside they have irreplaceable talents that cry out to be used. Face reading can help reveal them.

Your reading will help your client think through what matters most, including understanding that a human face is not so much Play Doh™. It cannot be rearranged without inner consequences. Because of the reciprocal relationship between the outer face and the inner person, these consequences will go far deeper than the level of vanity. For instance, a nose job will rearrange work talents; chin procedures will change the handling of conflict; facelifts change people the least, merely erasing years of wisdom.

Wise people will get the idea. No surgical procedure to change the face is merely "cosmetic." And the time to become fully informed is *before* going under the knife.

Your job isn't to choose for your client. Raising important questions is enough. Sometimes my clients leave happy, more convinced than ever than surgery is desirable. Other clients leave equally happy, having decided not to operate. They haven't only chosen to save money. In a profound and personal way, they have learned to save face.

Becoming a social commentator

Does the term "Social Commentator" make you think of your drunken Uncle Buddy or obnoxious Mrs. Yenta, the neighborhood gossip? Well, think again. Many consulting specialties require that you have the skills of a sophisticated social commentator: political pundit, futurist, campaign designer for advertising and public relations, radio talk show host (or producer), journalist, sociology professor, student writing papers for a sociology professior. I'm not saying that face reading is the only skill you'd need to qualify for these interesting jobs. But you can do any of them better with well honed face reading skills.

Consider the example of pop culture which, for a variety of reasons, is of interest to people in all of the previously mentioned professions. American culture and media are rife with celebrities, either performers, politicians, or people who have managed to become famous just by being famous. You can't escape pop culture. (As a face reader, you'll have too much fun to want to escape, even if you could.)

Face reading gives you an entirely new way to deconstruct famous faces. Hunt for a favorite celebrity's genuine talents and challenges. This form of hunting is fun because these people have hired press agents to give a desired impression which you, of course, will see right through. For instance, while you stand in line at the supermarket do your eyes ever wander towards large-circulation magazines like *TV Guide, Redbook, People*? Their covers have great head shots, plus enticing captions. When you compare the caption with what the face really says, it's often quite a contrast.

Commonly you'll see a story about a newly "happy" or "successful" celebrity whose photo reveals lower eyelid curve at an all-time low. Another popular item is cover stories about "The Sexiest Man Alive," evidently a fleeting honor since it is often repeated in different magazine articles, featuring a new fellow each time. Look at the guy's face and check off all the qualifying physical face traits:

In America, at the turn of the millennium, Mr. Sexy is sure to have a VERY defined overlip and (if over 30) at least one dimple. Probably, too, he'll wear a Macho Knob, ears that angle inward, and lower eyelids with a maximum curve of 2 (on a scale from 1 to 10). If he wears a mustache, it's likely to frame his upper lip, rather than hide it. What do changing fads in models and movie stars say about us? Think about it, social commentators. Then find ways to use your skills for profit as well as fun:

■ Many an advertising campaign hires models whose faces subtly contradict the message they're supposed to convey. Marketing research dollars would be well spent on hiring you to explain which models' faces strengthen the ad, rather than the reverse. If you're interested in earning some of those dollars, prepare some commentary on models in the company's existing ads.

Request an information interview with senior staff at the biggest advertising agencies in town, then pitch your services as a consultant.

■ Use your skills as social commentator to broaden your client base. Write an article for a local newspaper, reading celebrities' faces. At the end, mention your other services (any of the other specialties mentioned in this chapter). Although a paper won't usually publish your phone number, it can describe you as "a physiognomy consultant based in Sterling, Virginia"—or wherever you happen to live.

■ Have a favorite chat room on the Internet? Again, give away some attention-getting social commentary. Afterwards pitch your services.

■ Or contact professors at local colleges who teach courses on Film or other aspects of pop culture. Offer your services as a guest speaker. Deliver a great, thought-provoking talk. Afterwards, mention your services and hand out your card.

■ Finally, let's mention a specialized but important application of being a social commentator: **fundraising.** If you work for a school or nonprofit organization in order to attract major donors, you already know you need to psych out those potential contributors and present your cause in the best light. Identifying special concerns of your donor, via face reading, can help you to shape the most effective social commentary (i.e., way to describe) the cause or institution you're trying to sell. Learn from the major donors' faces what enthralls them. Angle your pitch towards that and you'll gain a competitive advantage over fundraisers who fumble around treating all donors alike.

You see, there *are* practical advantages to being a social commentator. Used as a form of **public relations**, it can lead to paying work. Of course it's important to avoid saying or publishing libelous things about people. Just frame your words in a Golden Rule way, referring to talents and potential challenges.

Also, unless you're commenting just for the fun of it, have a business objective in mind. Even if it's tempting, don't give away your services, no strings attached. Sometimes you'll agree to give a free sample to show what you can do, but keep your business card available and tell potential clients how they can follow up.

Going into business

Small businesses are easy to start, especially when you begin them part time. Don't let the prospect of creating a business intimidate you the way it did me when I first got started.

At its simplest, you may find all the startup information you need by meeting with an accountant to set up your books. Find out the best business structure for your circumstances, including which expenses are tax deductible. Then, quick as you can say, "Wow, my own business!" you'll be on your way. If your business starts out as a sole proprietorship, you can ask clients to make out checks to your name; you may not even have to start a separate bank account.

As a consultant, you'll be responsible for reporting your income to the IRS and paying your fair share of taxes. You may also need to obtain a business license from the county where you live, which may not be any more complicated than getting a license for your dog or a license to drive. So don't fret over the legal technicalities. Find out what you need to do and, in the words of a larger business than you'll probably ever have to administer, "Just do it."

A great deal of help is available from the U.S. Small Business Administration (SBA). If you're plugged into the Internet, or can find your way to your nearest public library's Internet hook-up, an exciting resource is to visit the home page for the SBA's Online Women's Business Center at http://www.onlinewbc.org. It's a free, interactive site, with online counseling if you want individual help. It's available day or night, from any location in America. And, of course, the Internet can't tell if you're male or female, so it's an equal opportunity advisor.

Other resources are the Office of Women's Business Ownership home page at www.sba.gov/womeninbusiness. And your local SBA chapter may even be able to provide you with free counseling from a volunteer mentor. Why are these fabulous resources available for free? Small business helps the American economy grow, so encouraging people like you to make more money is a good investment. Just think, your success will be helping America. Think of it as your patriotic duty!

Here are the main considerations to get your face reading business up and running:

- Pick a specialty that particularly interests you. Choose any of the applications of face reading in this chapter or develop a new one.
- Target your customers. Who will they be? How can you reach them?
- Decide exactly which services you will offer—how much you can charge. Usually it's a good idea to develop a few different packages, a range of prices. Some people prefer to go for the bargain basement. Surprisingly or not, some customers will always go for your *most* expensive package. That's why it's wise to offer a selection.
- Develop print materials—a business card may be all you need in the beginning. It's an instant source of credibility, proclaiming to all the word that yes, indeed, you do have a business.

One client at a time, show how you can help people solve their problems or lighten their hearts. Politely ask for their business. Build a solid reputation for integrity and genuine helpfulness. Then watch the dollars roll in.

Professional face reading

How can you get good enough at face reading to turn professional? Party entertainment, private readings, trainings, and consultations all require a high degree of skill for you to attempt them at the professional level.

Studying on your own can get you there. Don't discount the value of teachers, however. A simple two-hour class can move your skills forward by six months or more. Personal study with a master physiognomist can also inspire you.

In response to a growing demand for systematic training, I've developed a Correspondence Course in my system of Face Reading Secrets.

It includes a sequence of projects to build your skills and confidence, with personal mentoring to encourage you to develop as a physiognomist. Electives help you to develop specialties, and you also have the opportunity to do original research in the field.

Learn more at my website: www.Rose-Rosetree.com.

This site can also show you how to obtain my face readings by mail or in person. Individual sessions are another option, where you can learn at your own pace. Or you can join others who are taking a class in person, perhaps receiving Continuing Education Units as a psychotherapist, teacher, or health professional. E-mail your follow-up questions about anything on the site.

Internet skills are not required, however, for follow-up. You're also invited to send me a letter any time. If you're writing for information about classes, readings, or the Correspondence Course, please include a stamped, self-addressed envelope. Here's my mailing address:

Rose Rosetree
P.O. Box 1605
Sterling, VA 20167-1605

Also write to this address to share your success stories as part of the growing ranks of Professional Face Readers.

Finally, I hope you'll consider studying with me to open up your perception further with techniques for aura reading and empathy. These layers of perception will make face reading even more fascinating. I'd recommend that you start with my books—*Aura Reading Through ALL Your Senses* and *Empowered by Empathy*. Then go on to take classes or have individual sessions—with me or other intuitives.

In the past, some of you may have tried to read auras but had limited success. That's because most teachers approach this subject by emphasizing one gift, clairvoyance, over all others. Yet the vast majority of people are not set up, in body-mind-spirit, to be primarily clairvoyant. My approach is different. Over 100 techniques help you to appreciate and activate your gifts, whichever ones are strongest. And not to worry, you *do* have gifts for Celestial Perception. Proven to work over the past 15 years, my system is guaranteed to enrich your experience. That holds true whether you're a beginner or an experienced aura reader.

Each of us has a unique contribution to make in service to humanity. Service to others that involves face reading may be part of your mission. Or perhaps discoveries about your own face will be most important, inspiring you to use your talents more fully. Don't underestimate the value of that. Whatever your work, you help people most when you use your talents—and they can shine their brightest only when you acknowledge them *consciously*.

As you do this, aligning with your true strengths, the power of self-knowledge will show in your presence. Your example can spark the light of deeper self-knowledge in others. So may you go forth as boldly as a Jedi knight. Go light up our world. And may the face be with you!

Free Report on Body Language in Relationships

Think you could write the book when it comes to interpreting body language? Just about everyone's an expert these days, but Rose Rosetree adds some new insights plus her usual irreverent humor in *Body Language in Relationships: 75 Little Things That Mean a Lot.*

Non-verbal communication is a field where experts tend to be overly serious—including the college professor Rose Rosetree skewers in a hilarious introduction. Then she goes on to interpret a wild array of gestures and postures, including "The Magnetic Pole," bowing, and cringing.

This thought provoking mini-book focuses on what Body Language can tell you about relationships. It's enough to motivate you to get off the Internet and eyeball some live specimens. But meanwhile, you can order it for free as an e-mail attachment.

Women's Intuition Worldwide also makes it available in hard copy for $4.50, plus .20 sales tax for Virginia residents, plus $3 shipping per total order. At 38 pages, this staple-bound booklet makes a great present. It's especially useful as a stealth gift for people who think face reading is way too far out. Stretch them with this mini-book!

Or if you'd prefer to order the e-mini-book for free, e-mail your request to Rosetree@Starpower.net.

Annotated Bibliography

While many books have been published on face reading, the following titles are the most helpful I've found, listed in order of my favorites first:

Khalsa, Narayan Singh. *What's in a Face?* Boulder: Narayan-Singh Publications, 1997.
Available mail order, prepaid, $35, 708 Mohawk Dr., Ste. 18, Boulder, CO 80303
Narayan's wit enlivens this survey of some 1250 face traits.

Khalsa, Narayan Singh. *Loving Thy Neighbor.* Boulder: Narayan-Singh Publications, 1989.
Available mail order, prepaid, $35, 708 Mohawk Dr., Ste. 18, Boulder, CO 80303
How a metaphysically-minded physiognomist approaches his work, written with contagious enthusiasm.

Young, Lailan. *Secrets of the Face.* Boston: Little, Brown, 1984.
Quite simply, this is the best book I've found on traditional Chinese physiognomy.

Mitchell, M.E. *How to Read the Language of the Face.* New York: Macmillan, 1968.
When I camped out at the Library of Congress, surveying every physiognomy book I could find in the English language, Mitchell's book was by far my favorite.

De Mente, Boye. *Face Reading for Fun and Profit.* Phoenix: Bachelor Books, 1968.
If you can find this gem, it really is fun—insightful, too.

Hilarion, through M.B. Cooke. *Faces.* Queensville, Ontario: Market Books, 1988.
Channeled books are a taste not everyone wishes to acquire. If you like them, you'll relish Hilarion's unabashedly metaphysical view of The Divine Analogy.

Wagner, Carl. *Characterology.* York Beach, Maine: Weiser, 1986.
Carl is a lively teacher who has brought enormous scholarship to his work, and his drawings are terrific.

Young, Lailan. *The Naked Face.* New York: St. Martin's Press, 1993.
Depending on your point of view, you'll find this book either refreshingly objective or chillingly judgmental. In either case, it's admirably well researched, combining face reading with reading of facial expression.

You also may enjoy these books of related interest:

Wilde, Oscar. *Picture of Dorian Gray.* New York: Modern Library, 1992.
What happens when the consequences of a man's actions do NOT show in his physical face traits? Wilde's novel explores one scenario. He wrote it during the Victorian era, when physiognomy was better known than it is in America today. Satirically treated, Wilde's story served as a basis for Ruddigore, a hilarious operetta by Gilbert and Sullivan.

Dychtwald, Ken. *Bodymind.* Los Angeles: Tarcher, 1977.
This fascinating book does for the rest of the body what physiognomy does for the face.

Carter, Mildred. *Helping Yourself with Foot Reflexology.* West Nyack, NY: Parker, 1969.
Here comes one more highly useful book that can deepen your view of physical reality. In this do-it-yourself-healing classic, Carter teaches how to access nerve endings throughout your body by massaging corresponding areas on your feet. For instance, one extremely convenient way to give yourself a backrub is to massage your arches from the heel straight up to the big toe.

Lad, Vasant. *Ayurveda: The Science of Self-Healing.* Santa Fe: Lotus Press, 1984.
For diagnosing the physical body through looking at the face, this book can't be beat. Caveats: (1) facial diagnosis is just two pages out of nearly 200 in this how-to, and (2) my personal preference is for medical diagnosis by other means. However, Lad's treatment is the best I've encountered. More important, the entire book is crammed with holistic healing tips from the ancient tradition that Dr. Lad summarizes in this excellent book.

Hay, Louise L. *Heal Your Body.* Santa Monica, California: Hay House, 1988.
Especially if your purpose in studying face reading is self-healing, you'll value this book's spiritual interpretation of common diseases. Once again, physical reality opens up to show an inner reality where your free will can effect meaningful change.

Eckman, Paul. *Telling Lies.* New York: W.W. Norton, 1985.
It's expression reading, not face reading, but if what you want is literally to look for trouble, nobody's work beats Dr. Eckman's.

■■■

Index I

Famous Faces

People discussed in this book were chosen to represent many different walks of life. Though all are famous in some circles, not all will necessarily be familiar to you. History fans will recognize Napoleon Bonaparte; English majors, Jane Austen, and so forth. I hope there will be plenty of faces of interest for everyone.

I chose to be informal here and not use titles except for certain celebrities who would be unrecognizable without their titles, like Billy the Kid. I did, however, include some mythic faces, like that of Santa Claus.

Index II

Face Data

For thousands of years, face readers have had access to inside information about people by interpreting the physical face. It's not that face traits *determine* behavior. Rather, the evolving individual creates the face parts that correspond to the inner person. Don't read the face of anyone under the age of 18 because that face still needs time to develop enough for physiognomy to be valid. Anyone else is fair game, however. Use this index to interpret the face data of your choice.

Index III

Behavior

Face readers have the advantage of knowing about the reciprocal relationship between the physical face and personal style. Over time, due to a person's choices with aspects of style like *communication*, the physical face evolves appropriately. But change can happen the other way, too, as in the case of cosmetic surgery, which changes the inner person along with the face. Use this Index to refer backwards from behavior characteristics to the corresponding face data. Index III also contains topics you'd normally find in an index, like *sales, self-esteem*, and *relationships*.

Photo: Stacy Duncan

ree

velop Celestial Perception
rets® and Aura Reading
 this book represent the

her have brought Rose's
. In America, she's been
Washington Post, Ladies
clude Long & Foster Real
he Food Marketing Insti-
University. Her education
e lives with her husband

$\mathcal{R}$ose $\mathcal{R}$os[...]

Since 1971, Rose has taught techniques to [...] in everyday life, including Face Reading [...] Through ALL Your Senses. The discoverie[...] leading edge of her work.

Media interviews for this award-winning [...] insights to Europe, Asia, Africa, and Aust[...] featured on ABC's "The View," *USA Today,* *Home Journal, Redbook,* and others. Clie[...] Estate, Law Resources, Startec Corporatio[...] tute, the Ritz-Carlton, and George Washing[...] includes a B.A. from Brandeis University. [...] and son in Sterling, Virginia.